Maulana Azad, Islam and the
Indian National Movement

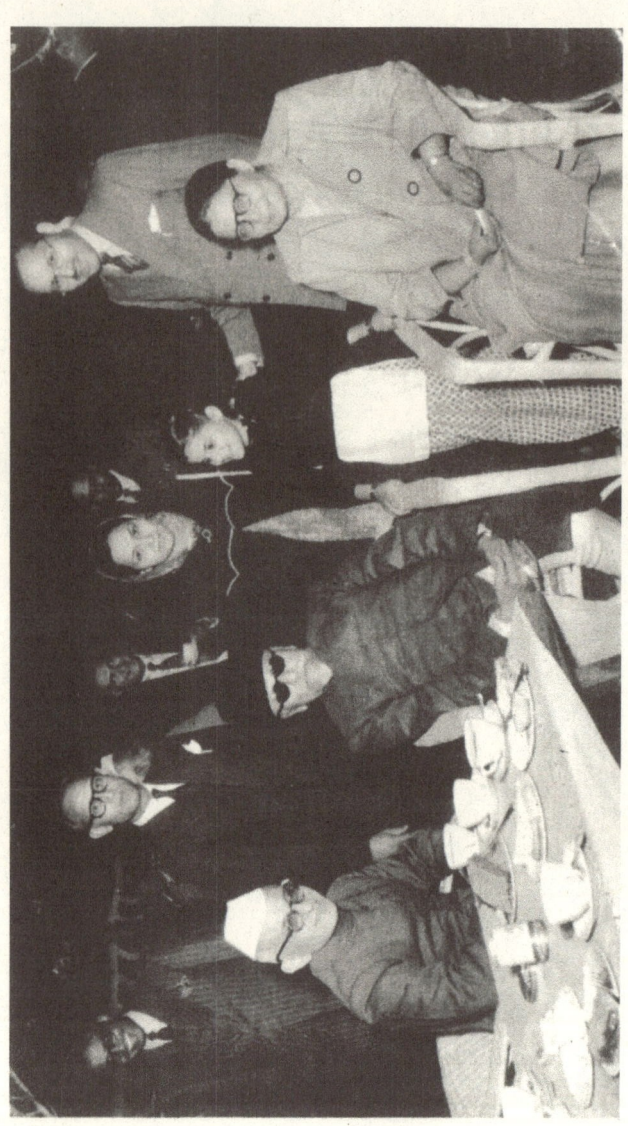

A Link With the Past: Seated in the centre is Abul Kalam Azad. The little girl looking on with great interest is Syeda Saiyidain Hameed, author of the book. The lady seated to the left of Maulana Azad is Aziz Jahan Begum, the author's mother. Standing behind her is K.G. Saiyidain, the author's father, former Secretary, Government of India, Ministry of Education, and a great educationist in his own right.

Maulana Azad, Islam and the Indian National Movement

SYEDA SAIYIDAIN HAMEED

MAULANA ABUL KALAM AZAD INSTITUTE OF ASIAN STUDIES

OXFORD
UNIVERSITY PRESS

OXFORD
UNIVERSITY PRESS

Oxford University Press is a department of the University of Oxford.
It furthers the University's objective of excellence in research, scholarship,
and education by publishing worldwide. Oxford is a registered trademark of
Oxford University Press in the UK and in certain other countries

Published in India by
Oxford University Press
YMCA Library Building, 1 Jai Singh Road, New Delhi 110 001, India

ISBN-13: 978-0-19-945046-6
ISBN-10: 0-19-945046-3

Typeset in 11/13.8 Bell MT Std
by Excellent Laser Typesetters, Pitampura, Delhi 110 034

Every effort has been made to trace the copyright holder of the cover visual.
The publisher would be pleased to hear from the copyright owner so that proper
acknowledgement can be made in future editions.

Nigah buland sukhan dilnawaz jaan pursoz
Yehi hai rakht e safar Mir e Karavan ke liye

(A soaring vision, dulcet speech, and courage in strife
Essential qualities of Leader of Karavan!)

Allama Iqbal

contents

foreword

POLITICAL AFFILIATION, MORE OFTEN THAN NOT, beclouds a public man's eminence. Bias prevents his contemporaries from recognizing his accomplishment in the spheres of knowledge, scholarship, and in literary and artistic fields. Even his political ideals are understood only superficially. That was the case with Abul Kalam Azad. Mohammad Ali Jinnah once called Azad 'show boy' of the Indian National Congress. That was enough for generations of pro-Pakistan Muslims to banish Azad from their minds except as a political adversary to be disliked and opposed. For the Hindus he continued to be understood as nationalist like any other leader in the Indian National Congress.

Many books on Azad have been published in India. For more than four-fifth of a century he has been held in esteem throughout India. His life as an important leader of the independence struggle has been fairly well researched upon and documented. However, Azad's contribution to the freedom struggle of the subcontinent, as a Muslim intellectual and as an independent interpreter of the Koran, as a great man in his own right, and not merely as a leader of the Congress Party, has lain in obscurity both in India and Pakistan.

Who was Azad? He was not an Indian by birth. His mother-tongue was neither Urdu nor any other Indian language. Indeed, no Indian language was spoken in his house. He never went to school—any school. Was he not, indeed, *a foreigner*? What was his path to leadership of India? What was the nature of his genius and beliefs that got him recognition as a front rank *Alim* and *Maulana*—almost an *Imam-ul-Hind*—of Hindustan, when he was still in his twenties? The circulation of his journals *Al Hilal* and *Al Balagh* touched the unheard of number of 26,000 copies in the second decade of the twentieth century. What was the content of the political appeal derived solely from the injunctions of the Koran? This aspect of Azad's life never received the attention it deserved. His political call was staunchly anti-imperialist. In those days, friends, allies and inspirers of Azad, barring a few revolutionaries in Bengal, were found in Egypt, Syria, Iraq and Turkey. Then does it follow that in the first part of this century, the Muslims of India led by Azad and others formed the van-guard of the freedom struggle of the subcontinent and had their allies in West Asia? These were the days, during World War I, when Gandhi, not yet a *Mahatma*, was urging Indians to join the army to fight Germany and its allies. At that time the political demands of the Congress and the Muslim League had not gone beyond Dominion Status for India, similar to Canada, Australia and New Zealand. These questions and many others shall continue to attract the interest of scholars and investigators for a long time to come.

As a scholar of Islam and as a political fighter against imperialists, deriving his inspiration purely from his understanding of the Koran, Azad preceded the great illustrious fathers of the independence struggle by almost two decades. The lifting of the veil from Azad's many faceted eminence was long overdue. Syeda Hameed has done just that.

1997   Dr Mubashir Hasan

Foreword

preface to this edition

THIS IS THE INDIAN EDITION OF A BOOK that has become more relevant with the passage of time. I am grateful to Oxford University Press for offering to publish it in 2014. Turned down in 1997 by this very publishing house, I was saddened because it was a biography of none other than Maulana Abul Kalam Azad. I was convinced then and am convinced today that he holds the key to some of the most vexing problems of our polity and that his writings need to get a wide readership. When I wrote this book, 9/11 had not happened and Islam had not been clubbed with terror, but after the demolition of Babri Masjid something ominous had happened in the hearts and minds of Indian Muslims like me. Babri made us acutely conscious of our identity. The rejection of my manuscript also taught me a lesson in humility and when it was accepted by Oxford University Press, Pakistan, it confirmed my feeling about the need to explore opportunities beyond the customary *lakshman rekhas*.

The relevance of a man who was dismissed by Mohammad Ali Jinnah as the 'Showboy of Indian National Congress' had begun to be realized across the border. It was reflected in several Urdu books which were being published there, in particular books of Abu Salman Shahjahanpuri. The way politics had unraveled in the five provinces of Pakistan (now four since the birth of Bangladesh) vindicated what Azad had been saying all along. In 1947 he spoke to a group of Muslims from the United Provinces who came to him before leaving for the newly created country, the dream homeland of the Muslim League, 'Land of the Pure, Pak-is-tan':

> You are leaving your motherland. Do you know what the consequences will be? Your frequent exoduses such as this will weaken the Muslims of India. A time may come when the various Pakistani regions start asserting their separate identities, Bengali, Punjabi, Sindhi, Baloch may declare themselves separate quoms. Will your position in Pakistan be anything better than uninvited guests? The Hindu can be your religious opponent but not your regional and national opponent. You can deal with this situation. But in Pakistan, at any time you will have to face regional and national opposition. Before this opposition, you will be helpless!

My study of Maulana Azad began in the mid-1980s when the country started preparing for his birth centenary in 1988. Although I read several folio-sized volumes of his *Al Hilal* and *Al Balagh*, along with the rest of his literary corpus, I always felt that I had only touched the visible edge of Azadiyat; there was much more there waiting to be revealed. My objective was to share with the non-Urdu-knowing world his view of Islam, minorities, nationalism, and education. I wanted to display before the world his engagement with aesthetics and philosophy, which formed the exquisite epistolary collection *Ghubar-i-Khatir* (The Soul Unburdened) with its own challenge of translating the best Urdu prose into a language that has very limited scope for such genius. Despite the work done during his centenary year, and all the hype around Azad, we find that his life and works are restricted to our history texts and his face and form is confined in a corner of publicity materials of political parties as the national movement's Muslim face. But now, more than ever, we need to reflect upon his thoughts and works and interpret them not only for Indians but also for global audiences. The question is, why? Why do we need to resurrect his ideas? How are they relevant today? Why should we read him or about him?

There are three essential conjectures drawn from Maulana Azad's works and philosophy that can inform the context of contemporary India's sociopolitical set-up and go beyond the geopolitics of this region to other parts of the globe. First, he rectifies the misinterpretation and misrepresentation of Islam, whether by Muslims or non-Muslims. Second, he captures the true essence of secularism; and third, he places the highest stakes in education and development of the human mind and man's consciousness about himself. The three conjectures flow out of one another and flow into one another, as exemplified in Azad's writings.

Designed and structured on the tripod of secularism, democracy, and social justice, the country has seen systematic onslaughts on all three in the 67 years since independence. We have witnessed the growth of communalism and rampant politicization of religion. Bigotry and xenophobia have found comfort inside the minds of some leaders, institutions, and organizations. Given these imperatives, the book tries to bring Azad's ideas out of the oblivion, on to the centre stage to create not merely tolerance and coexistence (both are passive conditions) but also harmony and understanding across the world.

In his address as the President of the Congress, 1923, Maulana Azad proclaimed:

> Today, if an angel were to descend from the heaven and declare from the top of the Qutab Minar, that India will get Swaraj within twenty-four hours, provided she relinquishes Hindu–Muslim unity, I will relinquish Swaraj rather than give up Hindu–Muslim unity. Delay in the attainment of Swaraj will be a loss to India, but if our unity is lost, it will be a loss for entire mankind.

At the time he spoke these words, Azad was a young man of 35 years—a scholar–politician—giving this call to the nation on behalf of the Indian National Congress. What did he mean by this bold declaration, since as President, he was not speaking for himself but for the party, which was at the vanguard of national movement? It is clear that he saw the danger of a Hindu–Muslim divide as more lethal than delayed *Swaraj*. The book offers a detailed analysis of this declaration.

About two months after August 1947, he addressed the Delhi Muslims from the steps of Jama Masjid. That was the eve of independence when India was caught in the worst Hindu–Muslim communal killings across the country. If not tackled befittingly, this could rip apart the very essence that amalgamated the existing diversities into a union. A nation that had liberated itself from the clutches of colonial power was confronted with a greater adversary. Communalism had seeped into the body politics; *gullies* and *mohallas* were infected as were the public spaces. Azad as the prophet and the witness, the oracle and the outcast, transmitted his ideals and philosophy to the dispirited and disillusioned Delhi Muslims in these words:

> It was not long ago when I warned you that the two-nation theory was death-knell. Leave it! I said. I said that these foundations which you had trusted were breaking up very fast. To all this you turned a deaf ear. You did not realize that fleet-footed time would not change its course to suit your convenience. Time sped past, and now you have discovered that the so called anchors of your faith have set you adrift, to be kicked around by fate.

Then he said almost plaintively, with the pain of a father, whose progeny had gone wrong: 'The partition of India was a fundamental mistake. The manner in which religious differences were incited, inevitably, led to the devastation that we have seen with our own eyes.'

From the day Azad picked up his pen at the age of 24 as editor of *Al Hilal*, the most revolutionary weekly newspaper of Calcutta, his three objectives were Hindu–Muslim unity, an undivided India, and *Purna Swaraj* (total freedom). The message of *Al Hilal* was to bring Muslims into the freedom movement as their religious duty and responsibility. From this beginning until 1947, he did not deviate from this stand. At every platform, whether of the Congress Party, the Khilafat forums, or a religious gathering, he allayed apprehensions of Muslims that in an independent India they would be sidelined as minorities. As the Congress President in 1940, at the Ramgarh Convention, he described the Congress as a national party representing India as a whole and said that every move it makes is in the interest of the entire Indian nation:

> In this regard, Congress has always stood by two basic principles, and every step it has taken has accorded to them, clearly and categorically.
> Any constitution that is framed in future for India, must contain the fullest guarantees for the protection of the rights and interests of the minorities.
> What are the necessary safeguards for the protection of the rights and interests of the minorities? This judgement rests with the minorities and not majority. The safeguards must, therefore, be formulated by their consent, and not by majority vote.

This book is both an account and an analysis of Azad's solutions to the crisis of Muslims of India. Placing Islam at the core, Azad asks Muslims to join Indians in the struggle for freedom. For a Muslim, he avers, there is no choice but *Hurriyat* or freedom. It is the injunction of Quran and essence of Islam. This one theme runs through all his writings and finds the final and strongest expression in his Jama Masjid speech in which he refers to the path of freedom as *Siratul Mustaqeem*, which, literally translated, means 'The Straight Path'. This is the most powerful concept in the first Surah of the Quran, *Surah-e-Fatiha*, the seven-line essence of the entire book. Need one say more?

Young minds, intellectuals, and responsible citizens need to be taught about Maulana Azad, who, more than half a century back, had realized and propounded ideas that are universally applicable and can be used to resolve the most complex issues facing world leaders. His secular tenets and his presentation of Islam in its undiluted form need to be encrypted within the heart and soul of all thinking men and women, transcending borders and particulars. This is the main reason for resurrecting his ideals; hence this book.

2013   Syeda Saiyidain Hameed

acknowledgements

MY GRATEFUL THANKS GO TO THE Nehru Memorial Museum and Library under the auspices of which I was awarded the Fellowship which enabled me to work on Maulana Abul Kalam Azad. In particular I wish to thank Professor Ravider Kumar and Mr P.N. Haksar who gave every moral and intellectual support throughout the Fellowship period. I am also deeply indebted to the Library staff for their gracious help. I pray for Begum Mumtaz Mirza who is no longer with us for her help in understanding Maulana Azad's use of Persian poetry. Finally I thank Oxford University Press, Pakistan, for publishing this work.

I dedicate this work to Aziz Jahan and K.G. Saiyidain.

introduction

amir of the karvan

THE IMAGE OF MAULANA ABUL KALAM AZAD is an integral part of my childhood memories. Azad was Minister of Education from 1947 to 1958. My father, Khwaja Ghulamus Saiyidain, served him for a few years as Secretary, Ministry of Education. Some other members of my family were also close to Maulana Azad. They all used to go to see him in small groups for what seemed to me to be serious consultations. I recall my elders holding Azad in great respect and awe, always reading and quoting his commentary on the Koran and discussing his views on all issues of national importance.

My father's family hailed from Panipat, a town known all over India not only for the battles fought in its fields, for its schools of *quir'at* (the art form of the recitation of the Koran), but also for the independent views of its scholars of Islam. Therefore it was no wonder that Azad's *Tarjumam-ul-Quran* (translation and commentary on the Koran) was always referred to in the discussions that raged in our household. To a child who was brought up to listen quietly to her elders, their discussions in those highly traumatic post-partition days, with occasional references to Azad, seemed most mysterious and incomprehensible. Once on Eid-ul-Fitr I was asked to accompany my father to see the great man at 6, King Edward Road (since then renamed Maulana Abul Kalam Azad Road). The occasion is vivid in my memory. He seemed happy to see us and I was struck by the elegant picture he presented. Immaculately dressed in a cream coloured *achkan* and an *Aligarh pyjama*, he was gracefully reclining on the sofa of the drawing room, smoking a cigarette with a slim silver holder. That image of him, I have carried in my mind throughout my years of research and writing on his life and works.

My father's association with top Congress leaders began in 1937 when Gandhiji started his Basic Education campaign. A committee was appointed by him under the chairmanship of Dr Zakir Husain. It was assigned the task of preparing a scheme which came to be known as the Wardha Scheme of Education. Zakir Husain invited Saiyidain to help him in the task. Guidance from Azad was often sought in the preparation of the Wardha Report. This was the beginning of a relationship which endured through tough times, and was responsible for hard decisions, which affected at least three generations of my family. My father was an unabashed admirer of Azad. In his book *Aandhi mein Chiragh* (Lamp in the Storm) which is a collection of essays on the personalities which had the greatest influence over his life, he uses the epithet *'mir-e-karvan'* (the leader of the caravan) from the couplet by Allama Iqbal to describe Maulana Abul Kalam Azad:

Nigah buland sukhan dilnawaz jaan pursoz
Yehi hai rakht-e-safar mir-e-karvan ke liye.

A soaring vision, dulcet speech, and courage in strife
These are essential attributes of the leader of the caravan.

When I started work on this book, the questions that arose in my mind were: in what sense can Azad be called the *mir* or *amir* of the *karvan?* What *karvan* was he the *amir* of? According to Saiyidain, Azad fulfilled the requirements of great leadership, that is the vision of a statesman (*nigah buland*), speech that is heart warming (*sukhan dilnawaz*), and a compassionate soul (*jaan pursoz*). But being ideally equipped for being a leader does not ensure leadership. Who should one lead? One needs followers.

Therefore the question—who constituted Azad's followers? What was his caravan? Whom did he lead? The people of India? The Muslims of India? The religious leaders of the Muslims? Why did he not become a leader of Muslims in the sense Mohammad Ali Jinnah did? Why did he lose to Jinnah—an individual who stood for everything which generally ran counter to the spirit of Islam and nationalism (as Azad defined it)—the one caravan which he felt was his sole entitlement? He had hoped to lead not only the Muslims but all Indians towards the goal of freedom, right from the time he picked up his pen in 1903 to launch his first journal. From then until the end he never lost sight of his larger constituency—all Indians regardless of religion—although mostly he was circumstantially compelled to view himself as a leader only of the Muslims. Why was one, who aspired and worked for national leadership, always projected in the post-independence period as a 'Muslim Leader' or a 'Leader of the Muslims'.

Furthermore, why is there a feeling among some of Azad's biographers and historians that his meteoric rise as a leader reached its zenith in 1923, when he was thirty-four years old and elected the youngest President of the Indian National Congress? Where does the trajectory of nationalist politics place Azad during the tempestuous decades of the twenties, thirties and forties? Speaking about his post-partition role, Ansar Harvani, Azad's young companion of the Bankura prison, told this writer that after 1947, Azad was a broken man, as if he had lost everything. Does Azad's post-Independence role justify Harvani's assessment?

The conventional wisdom of his era had made Azad ideally suited for leadership. By birth he was *Najib-ut-Tarfain* (of noble lineage on his mother's as well as on his father's side), he was educated under the personal supervision of his disciplinarian father. The future was offered to him on the silver platter of the unquestioning loyalty and devotion of his father's *murids* (followers). In *Ghubar-i-Khatir*, he recalls holding forth before an enthralled gathering of his father's *murids*, delivering to the measure of their unstinting praise lengthy sermons on things which he barely understood himself. Later, as he was to record in *Ghubar-i-Khatir*, he privately recoiled before their adulation.

His revolt against the rigidity of his father's regime, despite his great love for the patriarch, cannot be categorized as 'growing pains'; it was the first sign of his fierce independence. His interest in Urdu literature, which was forbidden in Maulana Khairuddin's domestic regime, his secret subscription to Sir Syed Ahmed Khan's *Tehzib-ul-Akhlaq*, his painstaking study of the *haram* English language, and finally his taking music lessons on the sitar from a professional, all hold testimony to the growing rebellion within him. The penultimate break with tradition occurred the night he stopped offering *Namaz* (prayer). It is another matter that this very rejection was to squarely plant him on the road to enlightened religion. But the revolutionary spirit continued unabated in him as reflected in his writings during the period he launched his journals, *Al Hilal* and *Al Balagh*.

Fortunately, Azad has left behind sizable evidence about his family, childhood, education and upbringing and about his religious, philosophical and political beliefs in the four autobiographical and semi-autobiographical works, *Tazkirah*, *Ghubar-i-Khatir*, *Abul Kalam ki Kahani khud unki Zubani*, and *India Wins Freedom*. During the course of editing and translating his writings in four volumes, *India's Maulana* Parts 1 and 2, *Imam-ul-Hind: Intikhabat-e-Mazamin* and *Imam-ul-Hind: Pramukh Kritian*,[1] and 'Sarmad Shaheed',[2] I could draw several hypotheses about the course India's history would have taken if Azad had had his way.

Firstly, had the Muslims of India heeded the call of Azad, the course of history could have been different. Partition may not have occurred. The terrible migrations and their concomitant massacres would not have taken place. Second, the communal virus which was exacerbated by the politics of partition, may have been contained in the same degree in which it had existed all along. Third, had Azad rather than Nehru or Patel occupied political centre-stage with Gandhi during the years preceding Independence, India's history could have taken a different course. These hypotheses, however, receded from my mind as the research for this work proceeded. I became involved in unravelling for myself the personality of a man who could have been a messiah and latter-day prophet for the Muslims but whose call went unheeded.

I was soon to find out that Azad as a person was made of a clay quite different from that which moulded the other leaders who were his contemporaries, whether Hindus or Muslims. His entire set of beliefs, social, political and cultural, in fact, his very world view was firmly anchored into his understanding of the Word of the Koran. It was an understanding which radically differed from what was expounded by the religious scholars of the day. His interpretation was that of a man of extraordinary intellect and sensitivities whose mother was an Arab, who was born in Mecca, and whose family conversed in the house in Arabic. It was written by one who grew up to become the scholar's scholar, but without any formal or modern schooling—a highly refined and cultured individual synthesizing in himself the best of the Arabic, Iranian and Indian civilizations.

It was, therefore, inevitable that this work began focusing on the above aspects of Azad's personality and development, which most scholars and researchers seemed to have ignored. Of necessity it had to be built upon the foundation of his written and spoken words. But due to the fact that in his writings and speeches he freely used Arabic and Persian words, terms and concepts, and verses from Iranian and Indian poets, it became a daunting task. To do justice to the finer points of the nuances of his prose is a challenge for the best of translators.

What Azad started writing at the age of eight or nine has fortunately been well preserved. His early writings of political and religious significance, *Lisan-us-Sidq* in 1903 to *Al Hilal* and *Al Balagh* in 1912–16, offer a panoramic view of the incredible young genius, from age fifteen to twenty-four. These impassioned writings reveal several ground realities about Azad.

First, the reader is struck by his total commitment to reform and to awaken his *quom* in the light of the teachings of the Koran. A word about *quom*, since it is one of the most often used words in this book. The word *quom* has been subject to extremely varied interpretations in the subcontinent. The Muslim Leaguers used it to assert the right of Muslims as a *quom* to have a separate nation state. Two decades later the East Bengalis were to use it to lay the claim to bring Bangladesh into being. The word is used in the Koran to distinguish the 'transgressors' (*quom-uz-zalimeen*) from the rest, and the 'non-believers' (*Quom-ul-kafireen*) from the believers. In northern India *quom* may be used to distinguish between tribes, castes and sub-castes or to express distinctions based on heredity and professions. Indeed, to establish the identity of a person in revenue records or for registration with the police, an official may insist on entering the individual's *quom* in the sense of caste along with the father's or husband's name and residential address. This is equally applicable to Hindus and Muslims. The latter are subdivided into a profusion of *quoms* such as Syed, Sheikh, Mughal, Pathan, Rajput, etc. However, it is clear from the writings of Azad that he used the word *quom* to mean those who derived their guidance from the Koran, regardless of any other' distinction. In addressing an exclusively Muslim gathering in 1947, he reminded 'the *quom*' of the days when their forefathers had arrived as conquerors and had performed the ablutions for their prayers with waters of the River Jamuna.

Secondly one is struck by his implacable hatred for British rule; his perception of the Raj as unjust and immoral, and his determination to expel them from India a religious duty, a jehad. Such feelings and such a political programme formed a common ground that he shared not only with the Bengal revolutionary groups such as Anushilan and Jugantar but also with the schools of revolutionaries of Egypt, Iraq, Syria and Turkey. In such circumstances, therefore, it was natural for some historians and biographers to speculate about his primary association with the Pan Islamism of Jamaluddin Afghani and his followers.

Thirdly, the genius of Azad as a writer and speaker stands out as extraordinary. His mastery of the written and spoken word in what may best be defined as poetic prose, extremely rich in metaphor, is an unusual combination with politics. Such oration, totally different from the style of Gandhi and Nehru with their use of simple language and common idiom, was immensely popular with the *ashraaf,* the literate Muslim population of India. Even the common people were transported to dizzy heights by the *lehar* (wave) of his speech. Qazi Jalil Abbasi remembers the effect of this *lehar* as mesmerizing, carrying away with its tone and rhythm the entire crowd of literates and illiterates.

Young Azad, disenchanted with many practices of Indian Muslims in the name of religion, appeared on the political scene in 1903 as a social and religious reformer. His first articles were about religious reform and social advancement. He was attempting to create in his fellow Muslims a heightened sense of political awareness and a recognition of the importance of their unified strength in the struggle of the peoples of Islamic countries against imperialism. Indian national leaders had not yet taken up the cause of complete independence, Gandhi was on the side of the British in their war effort and other important leaders, barring a few outstanding sons of Bengal, were thinking only in terms of attaining Dominion status under the benign patronage of the British Crown.

Operating out of Calcutta (the importance of this city in Azad's life must not be underestimated), Azad gained prominence through his writings and speeches. His fame spread among the Muslims of India, and gradually to other parts of the Islamic world. There is evidence of copies of *Al Hilal* being shipped to Indian patriots all over the globe.[3] Outside of Bengal, Azad's leadership, prior to and during World War I, although of a high level, remained confined to the Muslims. Yet the British considered him a revolutionary and much too dangerous to be permitted to operate freely. Therefore, he was extradited from Bengal and placed in detention at a village near Ranchi. In a nutshell, therefore, the genius that manifested itself in action in 1903 with the launching of *Lisan-us-Sidq*, was unstoppable during the decades that followed, no matter how hard an oppressive state clenched its iron jaws. That was his first period of leadership.

The second period of *rahbari* (leadership) began with the completion at Ranchi of what was to become the foundation of all his life's work. It had been a few years since he had started the momentous task he had assigned himself of *Tarjuman-ul-Quran* (literally meaning 'spokesman for the Koran.') In reading Azad's preface one sees that he was not satisfied with the message of the Koran as it was being conveyed to the Muslims of India. For him the Koran was the source of all guidance. His vision of reforming his *quom*, therefore, depended upon the Muslims seeking guidance from the Holy Book—but as *he* understood it. He felt that the existing translations and commentaries of the Holy Book did not fully meet the needs of the time. A new translation and a detailed commentary were required and who would be better equipped to provide it than one who saw his destiny as the *amir* of the caravan?

Azad's decision to work on a new translation of the Koran in Urdu and, more importantly, of providing fresh elaboration and explanation, was an extremely courageous one. For all Muslims, the Koran is the undisputed word of Allah. The conservative have held that the interpretation of the Koran is the preserve of scholars and experts who have been educated and trained at acknowledged schools of Islamic studies. They are quick to point out that it is not for ordinary mortals to claim that they understand the meanings and messages in the Koran which universally recognized religious scholars and interpreters have not been able to fathom during the last fourteen hundred years. Besides, in every era, strong vested interests are involved in guiding the adherents to faith in accordance with the currently established patterns. These patterns are inbuilt in the rituals led by the *mullahs* and acknowledged by the states and governments. Any individual who tries to define a different path runs the risk of inviting the wrath of the established 'authorities'.

Young *Abul Kalam* ('Father of the Word', as he had decided to call himself) possessed in full measure the courage of his convictions. By deciding to write a new commentary he joined the company of hundreds of his illustrious predecessors who had taken upon themselves the interpretation and reinterpretation of the Koran. The history of Islam is replete with the names of the founders of new ideological, philosophical and religious schools who still remained within the fold of this great religion. In Islam, the freedom of an individual to interpret the faith according to his own light is as old as the faith itself. Although the Prophet of Islam combined in his person the spiritual leadership of the faithful and the temporal leadership of the state, he did not nominate any individual nor did he found any institution for the guidance of the Muslims or the administration of the state. Indeed, through the Koran, Allah had revealed that Muhammad (PBUH) was the last of His messengers and there would be none after him. Thus the option for the establishment of an authoritative religious body, as for example that of the Christian Church, was sealed off forever. The right of a Muslim to interpret Islam for himself is also reinforced from other messages in the Koran.

We are nearer to him (man) than his jugular vein (50:16).

There is no compulsion in religion (2:256)

Further, the great orders of Muslim Sufi saints and *Walis* are based on the belief that it is possible for an individual to seek *Ilm-ul-ladunni* (intuitive knowledge), and through 'Inward Light', achieve a personal understanding and knowledge of the Creator in order to chart out for himself the *Siratal Mustaqeem*, the Straight Path in this world. In his celebrated essay, 'Reconstruction of Religious Thought in Islam' (1934, Oxford University Press, London) Mohammad Iqbal has taken a favourable view of this proposition. In addition, belief in the Day of Judgement is an integral part of the faith. On that day, all the dead shall rise and shall be judged for their deeds in this world and punished or rewarded accordingly. None shall be able to offer the excuse that not he but someone else should be held accountable for his deeds and beliefs.

Throughout its history, Islam has produced scholars, saints, *mahdis* (guides), and even warriors who did not agree with conventional wisdom about the faith. The period within a hundred years after the birth of Islam was marked by a highly creative interpretation of the Koran. The great *alims* (scholars), Imam Hanbal, Imam Abu Hanifa, Imam Shafi, Imam Jafar-e-Sadiq, Imam Malik, Imam Hasan al-Basri, Wasil bin Ata, the last a distinguished advocate of rationalism, did not agree with each other's interpretation of the Koran and the Hadith but they respected each other's right of interpretation according to his own light. Above all, they remained aloof from the state, declining requests to use their good offices to legitimize state decrees.

Azad had great reverence for this galaxy of *ulema* and *fuquhas* (jurors) whose interpretations of the Koran and Sunnah (the practice of the Prophet) were strictly independent. They never served the state nor agreed to be party to the imposition of their interpretation through decree or legislation. All of them, without exception, were persecuted, jailed, flogged or martyred by the ruling *Khalifas* or their Governors. Azad's writings reflect his profound admiration for these *salihin* (good men of God). In *Tazkirah* he extols their suffering:

> This has always been the fate of the lovers of truth. They have never known a moment of peace at the hands of the enemies of truth and reform. This happened in the past and will continue to happen in the future. If the adversaries of truth asked them to surrender (what they regarded) the most precious substance, namely their life, these lovers of truth readily gave it away as the world's most insignificant and dispensable commodity.[4]

The third period of Azad's political development begins with his release from Ranchi in 1919. He had come to the conclusion that there was an inherent dichotomy between being a Muslim and tolerating an alien rule. This motivated the anti-British stance of his speeches and writings, which were anathema to the colonial government. Within a year he was arrested and put on trial for sedition. *Quol-e-Faisal* (The Last Word), the statement Azad made from the prisoner's dock before the Magistrate at Calcutta Court, turned out to be a landmark document of national importance. The stay in Alipur Jail produced a semi-autobiographical piece, *Abul Kalam ki Kahani khud unki Zubani*, dictated to a friend and colleague, also a fellow prisoner, Abdul Razzaq Malihabadi. By this time his leadership was well established among Muslims. Among non-Muslims too, he was becoming identified with the national movement. Having heard about Azad's reputation, Gandhi had tried to meet him earlier, during his detention at Ranchi. During this period nationalism becomes a concomitant of religion in Azad's writings and speeches. This should not leave the impression that the writings of the *Al Hilal* and *Al Balagh* period are not imbued with nationalistic fervour; several articles in both journals are passionately nationalistic.

The Khilafat agitation, originally a movement started by the Muslims against the policies pursued by the British in Turkey and Southwest Asia, catapulted Azad to fame. Later, Gandhi was to turn it into a common cause involving Hindus and Muslims. Azad became the secretary of the principal organizing body of the movement, and, in that capacity, made the most impassioned speeches among all involved in the agitation. He reminded the Muslims that thirteen hundred years ago they had embarked upon bringing freedom to all mankind. They owed it to their belief in Allah and His Prophet that India's freedom should be achieved and achieved only through their *vaseela* (intercession), that is through their strength, valour and sacrifice. Statements such as these caused great concern to the government and resulted in prison sentences. But in the process Azad earned an all India reputation and the respect of venerable national leaders. In 1923 he was elected President of the Special Session of the Indian National Congress.

For the next four years, India remained plunged in a frenzy of communal riots. Many attempted to build bridges but given the bitterness between the two communities, there was not much the leaders of Hindus or Muslims could achieve. So far as Azad's writings are concerned, this was the second phase of *Al Hilal* (1927), which contains an eponymous essay, *Islam and Nationalism*—eponymous because its title marks the creation of a new balance between Islam and nationalism, a balance which appears in all his future writings. The evolution of his thought during this period is evident in the speeches made at various religious and political forums, always extempore, recorded for posterity by assiduous scribes, who used to sit up front and fold their hands imploring him to go slowly so that they could keep pace.[5] Those speeches, which are directed at an entirely Muslim audience, are replete with Koranic references around which his arguments are structured. Those which are meant for mixed audiences draw upon references from other faiths as well. Nationalism is the common thread. The writings and speeches of this period establish him as a national leader, along with his emerging position as the *amir* of the Muslim caravan.

That the humanist (rather than merely the secular and the nationalist) Azad has moved centre-stage is reflected in his last piece of writing, the literary masterpiece, *Ghubar-i-Khatir*. This epistolary collection was written in the Ahmednagar Fort prison. When the Congress launched the Quit India movement under his Presidency in 1942, all its leaders were placed under detention. Azad, along with Jawaharlal Nehru and other leaders, was detained until 1945 at Ahmednagar. *Ghubar-i-Khatir* may be called an 'epistolary autobiography'. A careful reading reveals hitherto unknown aspects of his personality, an Azad concealed from most of his biographers. The contours which get flushed with life by this account, are of an individual who was serious, learned and enlightened, with impeccable cultural refinement, narcissistic to a degree, one who preferred solitude and abhorred crowds. Such attributes are rare among the public figures of the subcontinent.

During 1946, Azad played a leadership role in negotiations with the Cabinet Mission. It was a last ditch attempt by the British to maintain a unified India. After the 'blood-dimmed tide' of 1947 burst forth with the massacre of thousands, what was born was a nation which split the Muslims three ways, drastically reducing their effectiveness. Azad saw that while India had gained one type of freedom, she was now a slave of religious dogmatism from whose insidious grip there was no escape. The consequences of this new stranglehold were clearer to him than to any other national leader, except Mahatma Gandhi. To a group of Muslims from Uttar Pradesh who were bound for Pakistan, Azad was to say:

You are leaving your motherland. Do you know what the consequences will be? Your frequent exoduses such as this will weaken the Muslims of India. A time may come when the various Pakistani regions start asserting their separate identities; Bengali, Punjabi, Sindhi, Baloch may declare themselves separate *quoms*. Will your position in Pakistan at that time be anything better than uninvited guests? The Hindu can be your religious opponent but not your regional and national opponent. You can deal with this situation. But in Pakistan, at any time you may have to face regional and national opposition; before this kind of opposition you will be helpless.[6]

'Will your position in Pakistan be anything better than uninvited guests'. Fifty years later these words have been tragically vindicated.

During the last decade of his life, left to steer the course of a ravaged caravan, he tried to nurture, once again, the battered *quom* of the Indian Muslims. His appointment to the portfolio of Education is viewed by some as a downsizing from the position he enjoyed in the forties. Contrary, however, to what is seen by some as 'political sidelining', his political stature actually grew by virtue of his marked disinterest in political office and Nehru's habit of depending on his advice. Gandhi was dead and even in his lifetime his voice had become feeble. His own rather famous words to Mahavir Tyagi, *'meri kaun sunega'* ('Who will listen to me?'), are evidence of his declining influence.

During the post-1947 period until his death in 1958, Azad enjoyed a highly respected status in Nehru's cabinet. But the sadness which had become engrained in him during those very years was due to the fact that he had to adjust to an India which was the *ta'bir* (outcome) of a dream gone wrong. All that he had stood for got swept away by the tide of historic forces. The struggle against imperialism being over, the leaders of the erstwhile freedom movement were eyeing the loaves and fishes of office. Azad had lost the battle for both principles to which he had dedicated his entire life—Muslim advancement and Hindu-Muslim unity. From a distance of thirty-eight years after his death, I would venture to say that Azad's tragedy of an unfulfilled mission was equally the tragedy of the Indian Muslims but more significantly the tragedy of the Indian nation.

notes

1 Indian Council of Cultural Relations 1990, *Selected Speeches and Writings* Vol. 1, *Tributes and Appraisals* Vol. 2.

2 Essay by Azad in *The Rubaiyat of Sarmad*, Indian Council of Cultural Relations, 1991.

3 India Office Library, Blackfriars Street, London. Report of the Director of Intelligence, 1913.

4 *Paigham*, 23 September, 1921, p. 9.

5 Related to the author by Qazi Jalil Abbasi, a young man at the time when Azad's oratory moved gatherings of tens of thousands Muslims to tears and to resounding cries of *Allah-o-Akbar*, 5 April 1993.

6 Quoted in *Aiwan-e-Urdu*, Maulana Abul Kalam Azad number, December 1988.

1

the formative years

ON 20 NOVEMBER 1903, THERE APPEARED IN Calcutta a new monthly magazine, entitled *Lisan-us-Sidq*. In Arabic, *Lisan* means Voice, *us* means of, and *Sidq* means the Truth. Its stated mission was *As Sidq Menji, wal Kazb o Yahlak*, an Arabic adage, meaning 'Truth Redeems and Falsehood Kills'. The editor of the journal explained it in the following words:

> The responsibility and duty of *Lisan-us-Sidq* is to guard against Falsehood and lead the nation on the path of Truth. As it has been assigned the duty of speaking nothing but the truth, the nation should not expect it to trill sweet music... The time is not far when redemption through truth and death through falsehood will prevail.

The aims and objectives of the magazine were stated on page one:

1. Social reform, i.e. reform in Muslim society and customs.
2. Promotion of Urdu, i.e. work for the promotion of Urdu language and literature.

3. Promotion of taste for scholarship, particularly among the people of Bengal.
4. Criticism, i.e. objective reviews of Urdu publications.

Explaining his concept of 'social reform', the editor wrote that the present customs and conventions of the Muslims were a result of their encounter with the Hindus. When the first Muslims arrived in India, they felt the need to familiarize themselves with the modes and practices of the native inhabitants. In the process of learning about them, the customs and conventions of the conquered began to infiltrate those of the conquerors. So much so, that the tolerance exhibited by Emperor Akbar produced among his Muslim subjects an urge to adopt certain customs of the Hindus. Over the years, a weakening of faith among the Muslims gave rise to many superstitions. By the nineteenth century, Islam in India was headed in a different direction; its Arabic simplicity and Iranian sophistication had become tainted with new Indian colours. Among the leaders, there was none to tell the Muslims that they had been cut off from their ancient roots and were now unrecognizable as those very same people who had once conquered this glorious land. This decline also resulted in the loss of their old arts and crafts. In addition to losing what they had brought with them, they had also destroyed the wealth of Hindustan.

The editorial continues in the same vein, condemning the negligence shown by the religious leaders, which resulted in people mistaking fallacy and superstition for religion. When no reforms were introduced and these practices persisted for a long time, they became an integral part of daily life. On the authority of a 'Turkish friend' of the editor, the readers were told that the main cause for the economic deprivation of the *quom* was the customs and usages which prevailed in their society. Due to social pressures, people were obliged to squander money. For example, in Lucknow 'a loan of five thousand rupees is drawn for the marriage of *Babban Mian* or two houses are mortgaged for the circumcision ceremony of *Chhuttan Mian*.' The families are consequently reduced to penury. Simplicity, lack of ceremony, and, above all, observance of only the essentials of religion could have saved them from ruin.

> Adherence to customs has given rise to many evils in India. But alas! No one has paid attention to their reform and the disease has spread in this *quom*. The inertia of the *hakim* (physician) and the neglect of the patient has caused the disease to become almost fatal.

Explaining the next objective, the promotion of Urdu, the editor of the new magazine writes that there are four Eastern languages which may be ranked with Urdu: Turkish, Arabic, Persian and Bengali. While Persian and Urdu have only made minor progress, Arabic and Turkish have surged ahead, producing the best treatises in arts and sciences. Urdu lacks both good translations and good publications, although (like Persian), it has no dearth of romantic prose and verse. *Lisan-us-Sidq* will, therefore, undertake putting into practice all that the literary branch of the Mohammedan Educational Conference, the Anjuman Taraqqi Urdu (Bureau for the Promotion of Urdu), has conceptualized for the promotion of Urdu.

Criticism, the third objective of the magazine is considered important by the editor because he feels that in Urdu there is no concept of adherence to the principles of criticism. All that is done in the name of 'criticism' is to indulge in indiscriminate praise. *Lisan-us-Sidq* would change this and live up to its name. It would express its true opinion, exposing the good and bad aspects of any given work, regardless of who the author is, 'because this is *Lisan-us-Sidq* and truth is its creed.'

Promotion of scholarly taste in Bengal, the fourth objective, is based on the editor's claim that whereas the educated class among the Muslim community was increasing in numbers all over India, the Muslims of Bengal were lagging behind. Comparing them with Bengali Hindus, he writes that if two young men, one Hindu, one Muslim, hailing from the same region and from the same university, graduate at the same time, despite the fact that all else is equal, they have no intellectual parity. The Muslim youth, once he finds a certain occupation, becomes so engrossed in it that no further quest for knowledge is left in him. The young Hindu, despite being immersed in his work, continues day and night his quest for knowledge and his interest in intellectual problems and pursuits. The Hindu's intellectual accomplishment is a consequence of his thirst for knowledge, while the Muslim's ineptitude is due to his lack of interest in learning. *Lisan-us-Sidq*, says the editor, will address this problem. The very fact that so far there was no serious Urdu journal proves that intellectual stimulus was lacking. That gap will now be filled.

The editor of this new magazine from Calcutta was one Mohiuddin Ahmad. In Arabic, Ahmad means the one who is immensely praised, and Mohiuddin means the one who brings to life the 'Din' (the religion, the *Dharma*, the totality of the code of beliefs and life). The editor had prefixed to his name the title of Abul Kalam meaning the Father of the *Kalam*, the great explainer, the great elucidator. The word '*kalam*' originates from the Greek word 'logos', which means Cosmic Reason, the source of world order and intelligibility, which had been interpreted by Christian thinkers as the self-revealing Thought and Will of God. It was understood by early Muslim philosophers as the Word or Speech of God. The editor had also assumed the title of Azad, meaning, the free, the independent. The first issue of *Lisan-us-Sidq* bore the inscription, 'Editor: Abul Kalam Azad, Dehlivi'. On the day this issue appeared, Azad had completed fifteen years and nine days of his life.

Azad was born on 11 November 1888 (1305 AH), seventeen years after his parents' marriage, in a barren part of the holy city of Mecca, known as Qidwah. The house in which he was born was located near the Bab-as-Salam. He had three elder sisters. Zainab was the eldest by several years, born in Constantinople. Then came Fatima and Hanifa—with a gap of two years between them, and one brother, Ghulam Yasin, elder to Azad by two years. Azad was the youngest of the five children. His father named him Mohiuddin Ahmad and his chronogrammatic name was Feroz Bakht:

My father gave me the *tarikhi* (calendar) name Feroz Bakht; and derived my birth date according to the Hijri calendar from the following line of a couplet:

Jawan Bakht o Jawan Talae, Jawan-baad
(Of exalted destiny, brilliant future, strong support).[1]

In the preface to *Tazkirah*, 1916, Azad traces his lineage to three distinguished families of India and Hejaz, his mother's family, his father's paternal ancestors and his maternal ancestors. His Arab mother, Aliya, was the niece of Sheikh Mohammed bin Zahir Watri, the last great *muhaddis* (a scholar on the subject of the sayings of the Prophet) and *alim*[2] of the Harmain, i.e. the holy precincts of Mecca and Medina. His paternal grandfather, Maulana Mohammad Hadi was of a noble *silsila* (a Sufi order) of Delhi, which was distinguished by virtue of having five teachers of *tariqat* (a Sufi tradition for acquisition of knowledge) in one single generation. His father's maternal grandfather, Maulana Munawaruddin, whose Sufi lineage could be traced from Sheikh Sadruddin of Herat, was the last *Rukn-al-Mudarrissin* (member of the distinguished board of teachers) of the Mughal empire.

Several years before the uprising of 1857, a large number of the Muslim elite of India had started to emigrate. The scholars among them, often chose their destination as Hejaz, the Western part of the Arabian peninsula, where the holy cities of Mecca and Medina are located. Every year, emigration would take place in groups and scholars from all over India would join the caravans of émigrés. Azad's father, Khairuddin, under the tutelage of his maternal grandfather Munawaruddin, also set out for Hejaz. The grandfather died at the first stage of the journey in Bombay. Khairuddin continued the journey alone and reached his destination in 1858. In Hejaz, which in those days was a part of the Turkish empire, he continued his higher studies. Later, he became a Turkish national and married Aliya, the niece of Sheikh Mohammed bin Zahir Watri, who was one of his, teachers. After completing his education in Mecca, Khairuddin became a scholar in his own right and was, perhaps the first Indian to give a series of *wa'az* (discourses) inside what are the holiest precincts of Islam. During his stay in Hejaz, he toured Muslim countries and stayed for two years at Constantinople (Istanbul), the *dar-ul-khilafa*, or the seat of the Islamic Khilafat. He had one audience with the Khalifa, the Sultan of Turkey, who was pleased enough to award him a stipend. In 1895, when Azad was seven years old, the family returned to India. In *Tazkirah* Azad gives an account of his maternal habitat:

> My native city is Delhi ... but my mother came from the city built on sacred ground, the city to which the Prophet migrated, the city of his Prophethood, of Revelation (Medina). It is the city to which the worshippers of love turn. It is the Ka'aba for those who live in the ecstasies of prayer.[3]

Azad's formal education got off to an unscheduled start. It was customary among the educated Muslim landed gentry that a ceremony called *Bismillah*, literally, 'In the name of Allah' was held to commence a child's education. It is attended by family members and friends and the four or five year old child is made to recite the first words from the Holy Koran. Prayers are recited and sweets distributed as a mark of celebration. In Azad's case, the ceremony was arranged not for him but for his elder brother. It is widely mentioned in the literature on Azad that for some reason this also became Azad's *Bismillah* ceremony; he was brought in unscheduled at the last moment. The presiding Maulana, Shaikh Abdullah, performed the initiation rites. Azad was made to repeat *Ta Fattah* thrice.[4]

Daily lessons of education in the Koran were then started under the guidance of his aunt, an educated woman from the Arab side of his family. The two brothers also started attending the *quir'at* classes at the Haram Shareef. *Quir'at* is the highly developed technique of recitation of the Koran. It involves long hours of rigorous voice training. For the believer, no music is more soul-stirring than a well seasoned *quir'at* which can transport the listener into a state of ecstasy of tears or trance. Azad's lifelong love for music can be traced back to his tutelage under the greatest *qari* (reciter) of Haram Shareef, Shaikh Hasan.

Maulana Khairuddin returned to India with his wife Aliya Begum, his three daughters, Zainab, who was born in Constantinople and was several years older than her two sisters, Fatima, who took on the *takhallus* (poetic name) 'Arzoo' and Hanifa whose *takhallus* was 'Abroo', and his two sons, Ghulam Yasin who became known to the literary world as Abu Nasr 'Aah' and Mohiuddin Ahmad who renamed himself Abul Kalam Azad. By that time, Azad had completed his reading of the Holy Koran, the indispensable first step in the education of all Muslim children.

In Calcutta, Azad's first and most formidable tutor was his father. It was here that he was first introduced to the Urdu language. Khairuddin adopted the shortest route to its teaching, since he considered his children's background in Arabic as an adequate base for quickly disposing of the learning of Urdu. Azad writes that he always heard his father refer to Urdu as 'Hindi', which was the common practice in those days.[5] He had no real interest in Urdu. Any more than its elementary study was considered a waste of time and therefore forbidden to his children. Azad's mother preferred to converse in Arabic instead of Urdu and initially his sisters could not speak the language at all. Despite these restrictions or perhaps in defiance of them, all Khairuddin's children became Urdu poets and littérateurs.

As soon as Azad was able to read basic Urdu, he was taught texts such as *Khulasa-e-Hindi* (Principles of Prayer and Fasting) and *Masdar-e-Fayuz* (Rules of Persian). In Arabic the first book was *Ajromia*, then *Meezan* and *Mansha'ab*, *Nahv Mir* and *Surf Mir*, and *Kafia*. In Persian, after a study of *Masdar*, Shaikh Saadi's *Gulistan* and *Bostan* were started together. Special portions were assigned for learning by rote. In Fiqah (Islamic jurisprudence), *Kunz*, and in Logic, *Sharah Tehzib* were introduced. All of this curriculum was personally taught by Khairuddin to his two sons and two daughters. The eldest daughter was several years senior and, therefore, not a part of this class. So long as they were tutored by the father, the female and male children were treated alike. When tutors were engaged, the girls' education was curtailed. The first tutor was Maulvi Mohammad Yaqub of Delhi. Then came a teacher described by Azad as possessing extraordinary pedagogical skills, Maulvi Nazir-ul-Hasan Amethvi. He had complete mastery over *Dars-e-Nizamia* but was also aware of the shortcomings of the syllabus. Azad's own assessment of the inadequacy of this course is recorded in *Ghubar-i-Khatir*:

> What was the state of the curriculum in which the first part of my life was spent? The briefest answer to this question would run into several pages. An archaic system which had become obsolete from every angle. Deficient in technique, deficient in subject matter, deficient in prescribed texts, and deficient in linguistic style… Just think what would have happened if this had been the end of my education! If I had not developed the urge for the new paths of knowledge which were acquired later, how miserable would my state have been. My early education would have given me nothing more than an unrealistic and intractable mind.

Azad's other tutors included the second senior-most teacher of Madrasa Aliya, Calcutta, Maulana Sa'adat Husain. But the strictness of Khairuddin's selection of tutors became the overriding factor in Azad's education. Very few tutors could come up to his father's high standards. His standards were not confined only to academic excellence but extended to the individual tutors' beliefs within the rubric of Islam. Those of the Shia sect were generally suspect and rarely allowed access to his children. But it was the Wahabis who were regarded with contempt, and the slightest suspicion of Wahabiyat was enough to disqualify the best and ablest. In *Ghubar-i-Khatir* Azad states that the only likely source of outside influence was shut off by his father's rejection of the well known institution, Madrasa Aliya of Calcutta as being below standard and preferring private education for his children.[6] The teachers who were engaged by him were rigorously questioned to ensure that they agreed with his ideology. No scope was allowed for debate and discussion arising out of intellectual differences.

In *Ghubar-i-Khatir* Azad records his regret that he was never allowed the taste of free opinion. Learning English, he writes, was out of the question; but even had he been allowed access to the traditional Madrasas it would have been better than the 'restrictive four walls of the house.' It may have given him an opportunity to stretch his mind through intellectual debate. Malihabadi, in his biography of Azad, gives a detailed account of his growing resentment of his father's educational methodology and what must have been his respectful altercations with his formidable parent. But given the boy's temperament and the awesome influence of Khairuddin, it seems unlikely that he ever argued with his father to the extent of the *nafirmani* (disobedience) described in the book. Malihabadi records that the only time the brothers were allowed out of the house was for the Friday prayer at the Jama Masjid. While Hafiz Waliullah, the venerable family retainer who accompanied them dozed during the *wa'az* (sermon), the brothers crept downstairs to play in the *masjid* courtyard.

By the time he was twelve years old, Azad had completed the study of the Persian language and acquired the rudiments of Arabic. His father adhered to Shah Waliullah's tradition of learning one chapter of every subject by heart. Azad recalls that he had committed to memory, the monographs *Fiqah Akbar*, *Tehzib*, *Khulasa-e-Kaidaani*, and that by reciting them at opportune moments he sent his teachers into paroxysms of amazement. He attributes the precision of his memory to this early training which disciplined his mind so that at the age of fifty-three, when he was writing *Ghubar-i-Khatir* he claimed that he remembered every word of the lessons learnt forty years ago. In 1922, he was to describe to Malihabadi the way he had organized his phenomenal memory, a factor which is attributable both to his heredity and childhood drill:

I ... have made compartments in my brain, hundreds of compartments. This compartment for law, this for international politics, this for history, this for mathematics, this for military science. I accumulate information in an orderly and systematic fashion, like a discriminating, accomplished storekeeper, in separate compartments. Whenever information is required at any particular time I open the appropriate compartment and keep the others closed.[7]

This prodigious memory he had inherited from his father. In *Kahani*, Malihabadi quotes Azad's recollection that the contents and format of a book his father had read fifty years ago were imprinted on his mind. During lessons he would call for a certain book and ask for a certain page which would invariably contain the required information. Azad had the same facility for recalling the exact location of a book, the page number and whether the page was on the left or right side.[8] He was always several lessons ahead of his classmates, including his elder brother Ghulam Yasin. While there was only a two-year difference between the two brothers, other boys in the class were in their early twenties. His teachers were both irritated and amazed at Azad's speed of learning which necessitated their having to give him separate lessons. 'This young *hazrat* (reverend) recited the text of *Sadra* to me yesterday', one of them is reported to have said, 'And he is under the false impression that he takes lessons from me!'[9]

At the age of fifteen, Azad had completed the formidable curriculum, *Dars-i-Nizamia*. According to the traditional theory of education, learning was not complete unless the student could teach to others what he had learnt. A group of students was, therefore, entrusted to Azad, whose expenses were borne by his father and to whom he taught the texts *Mir Zahid* and *Hidaya*. Meanwhile he studied *Tibb* (Greek medicine), under the tutelage of Hakim Syed Baqar Husain, a Shia teacher to whom Khairuddin allowed his son access as an exception to the rule. The course of study lasted seven or eight months.

The rigidity of Khairuddin's daily routine permitted no deviation. Times for waking, sleeping, eating, praying were strictly set. Lessons in the morning from the father were followed by lessons from tutors. Afternoons were meant for self study and learning by rote. During evenings, the father would have them repeat what they had learnt, and after the *maghrib* (evening) prayer, once again, there were lessons from the father. The habit of rising early for which he was grateful to his father, as recorded in *Ghubar-i-Khatir*, was part of the strict self-discipline of not losing the most productive time of the day. Over the years it became an exhilarating experience to be, as it were, for those few hours, the sole inhabitant of the earth. Azad recalls in *Kahani* that his father's household always seemed to be in a state of preparedness to return to Hejaz. He had heard his father say, 'It is unfortunate that I have had to stay here, otherwise you would have been educated in Arabia and Syria'.

Aliya Begum died in 1899.[10] The motherless household was now more than ever dominated by the father's overpowering presence which engendered seriousness all around. There was no concept of games; all the time was reserved for curriculum study and practice. It was not as if there was any scarcity of entertainment in a city as exciting as Calcutta. A few years later, Azad was to secretly take music lessons, apprehending his father's disapproval. This was possible only in Calcutta, a city which was large enough to conceal such 'waywardness' on the part of a Pirzada (progeny of a respected divine). But at that time his priority was to glean as much knowledge as possible from every available source, permitted and forbidden. His father was pleased at the boy's dedication to intellectual pursuits, but worried about its effect on his physical health.

Urdu books being generally forbidden, the only way to satisfy his appetite for them was to read in bed at the dead of night by candlelight. There is obvious pride in his recalling that he spent his tiffin money on buying books or that his father gave him an expensive Kashmiri shawl as a reward for high achievement. But at the same time he remarks with some wistfulness that due to the total absence of a normal childhood of games and fun he had become old before his time. Malihabadi records Azad's *rivayat* (information attributable to Azad) that it was not until much later that he learnt about the games boys played, and that too in theory, since there was no sports equipment in the house. Azad's own account of a childhood minus games is important because of the insight that it allows into his personality:

> People spend their childhood in fun and games. But from the age of twelve or thirteen, I used to retire in a corner with my book, trying my hardest to hide from the rest of the world. You must have seen the Dalhousie Square in Calcutta, right across from GPO (General Post Office) which is popularly called Lal Duggi. Inside, there was a cluster of trees which hid a fair size clearing and a bench. Whenever I went for a walk, I took a book along and sitting down on the bench became engrossed in reading. Father's special servant Hafiz Waliullah, who always accompanied me, paced around the cluster of trees saying, 'If you had to read a book why did you ever leave the house?'[11]

It was not as if there were no games whatsoever. Sometimes the brothers and sisters played a game devised by Azad. In an interview held, more than half a century after the event, his sister Fatima Begum recalled the game:

> In his childhood *Bhai* (brother, reference to Azad) was not interested in the games most children play. At the age of seven or eight his games were of a different kind. Sometimes he would line up all the boxes in the house and declare them to be a train. Then placing father's *pagri* (turban) on his head he asked us to say, 'Move, give way, the Maulana of Delhi is coming'. When we said, there is no one here, who shall we push to make way, he said, this is just a game. Just make believe that hordes of people have come to receive me at the station. Then he used to get down from the boxes, walking very slowly, as if he was a much older man. Sometimes he used to get on top of something high and ask us to applaud as if there were thousands of people around him listening to his speech and clapping in appreciation.[12]

This particular disclosure by Azad's sister has been used by his biographers as proof of his aspiration to fame from early childhood. Another view of this interview could be that while it has all the attributes of *rivayat* or oral history it does not fit the image of Azad that configures in *Ghubar-i-Khatir*. It is not impossible that Fatima Begum, a loving sister, recollecting events from her childhood days and, relating them to a scholar who is keen to write something about Azad's childhood, may not have recalled the precise words. The memory factor plus a tendency to see the past through the prism of desire may have coloured the narrative. This is, however, a significant piece of evidence but one sets greater store by Azad's own recollection and account.

In the nineteenth century and the early years of the twentieth, it was customary among the families of the educated Muslims, that from an early age young boys and some girls tried their skills at composing verses. Young Azad, coming from a family with a highly developed literary and cultural background, was no exception. With the youthful experimenters of that era, the genre of Ghazal was most popular, since this particular form of versification lent itself to a literary environment where Urdu and Persian held the fort. At that time Calcutta was an important centre for Urdu and Persian and consequently the rallying centre for hundreds of poets and littérateurs. One such poet was Abdul Wahid Khan Sehasrami. His sister, named Amani, whom he visited often, was employed as a *mughlani* (seamstress) in Azad's father's household. Abdul Wahid often recited his poetry before Azad and told him about poets and poetry and about the *mushairas* (poetic gatherings) of Calcutta. It was on his advice and for a most pragmatic reason that Azad adopted the *takhallus* (poetic name) 'Azad'. It was customary for Ghazals to be published in *Guldastas* (poetry magazines) in alphabetical order. The poems of persons with names starting with the letter Alif (the first letter in the Urdu alphabet) appeared at the very beginning, a factor which weighed heavily with Azad.[13]

In his letter dated 3 December 1936 to Ghulam Rasul Mehr he dates his first forays into poetry at the age of twelve or thirteen. A *Guldasta* appeared from Bombay, called *Armaghaan-e-Farrukh* and the poets of Calcutta started holding *mushairas* on its *tarah* (a verse set exemplifying the particular metre in which a poem is to be composed). Once the *tarah* was:

Puchhi zameen ki to kahi aasmaan ki
(When I asked about the earth I was told about the skies.)

Azad wrote a Ghazal of eleven couplets and recited it to Abdul Wahid whose ecstatic appreciation of it was expressed by jumping to his feet in praise of every single couplet. Azad writes that this encouraged him to send it to one of the *Guldastas* for publication. He then writes about the thrill of seeing his name in print for the first time:

'Today, after thirty-six years, I can still feel the joy that I felt when I first saw my name in print in *Armaghan-e-Farrukh*.'

His later assessment of the same Ghazal was quite different, as expressed in the same letter, 'These verses appear so frivolous now but at that time such frivolity used to stun the public'.

This letter, which is an important source of information on Azad's poetic phase, contains the famous encounter of Azad with the poet Nadir Shah Khan 'Shokhi' Rampuri, who was a pupil of Mirza Ghalib, one of the greatest poets of the Urdu language. One day, as he was leaving the mosque, 'Shokhi' caught hold of Azad saying that a student had been pestering him, and could Azad, please, compose a few verses on the *zamin* (ground) '*Yaad na ho, Shaad na ho*' Azad realized at once that he was being tested. Regardless, he composed six couplets on the spot. 'Shokhi' asked for a seventh couplet, Azad obliged with what turned out to be the best:

Wada-e-vasl bhi kuchh turfa tamashe ki hai baat
Main to bhuloon na kabhi un ko kabhi yaad na ho

Promise of union is a strange jest,
I should never forget, and she should never remember!

'You appear no more than a young gentleman of ten or twelve. But, by God, the mind is not ready to believe', 'Shokhi' must have spoken these words shaking his head in appreciation and amazement.[14]

Azad's well developed taste in poetry at that young age is reflected in the carefully selected quotations he was to use in all his prose works, in particular from the greatest Persian and Urdu poets Urfi, Faizi, Naziri, Ghalib and the master of them all, Hafiz Shirazi. His own poetry too has a quality which bears the stamp of his early genius. Although he condemns it in the letter quoted above, his self assessment is, as usual, too severe. At the age of thirteen or fourteen he could write such promising lines as:

Azad bekhudi ke nasheb-o-faraz dekh
Puchhi zamin ki to kahi aasmaan ki

Observe the ups and downs of my transmutation into the other self
When I was asked about the earth, I responded about the skies.

He could also write, copying Ghalib's style, a lesser known but equally accomplished Ghazal:

Ye bhi qaidi ho gaya aakhir kamand-e-zulf ka
Ley asiron mein tere Azad shaamil ho gaya.

He also became a prisoner of the noose of your hair
There! Azad has joined the band of your prisoners.

The careful arrangement of thought and diction in the latter couplet, the perfection of the internal rhyme scheme, given the *misra-e-tarah* (line illustrating the verse-set to be used) in the former, are most promising in a technical sense. The fact that this particular talent was left untapped is probably a loss for Urdu poetry but the muse of prose is the net gainer, as evident in his literary masterpiece *Ghubar-i-Khatir.*

Khadang-e-Nazar, the monthly magazine from Lucknow, published Azad's next Ghazal which is also imbued with the romanticism inspired by early Ghalib. He is said to have sent his poems to the poet Daagh Dehlavi for *islah* (correction). Azad's own *Guldasta* (poetry magazine) was *Nairana-e-Alam,* which he published from Calcutta, in 1899 or 1900. It included his brother Abu Nasr 'Aah's', as well as his own poems but no more than a couple of issues appeared before it closed down.[15] Both brothers wrote poems and articles for the journal *Makhzan* which was published by Sheikh Abdul Qadir.

At that time, Azad launched a weekly journal, *Al-Misbah* which ran for a few months and featured his articles 'Newton', 'Imam Ghazali' and 'Eid'. Although, short lived, both the *Guldasta* and the journal established his reputation among the scholarly and literary circles. The appearance of his articles in support of Nadwa (a madrasa in Lucknow, U.P. established in 1898) in *Ahsan-ul-Akhbar* published by Maulvi Ahmed Husain and his contribution to the lay out and publication of the journal *Tuhfa-e-Ahmediya* further enhanced his popularity and established his credibility. So much so that Munshi Naubat Rai 'Nazar', entrusted to him the arrangement of the prose section of *Khadang-e-Nazar*, published from Lucknow. It is here that Maulana Shibli first saw his article on X-rays. In addition he served as editor of the *Edward Gazette*, Shahjehanabad. It is of interest that all these accomplishments were made when he was between the age often and fourteen. Azad's desire for prominence is reflected in his frank admission to Malihabadi that all he wanted in those days was to be seen at all important conferences in the country and to write articles so his name would appear in newspapers and journals.

Sarojini Naidu's compliment that Azad was fifty years old the day he was born may seem an overstatement, but not quite. What else can be said of a youth of fifteen years, who a few days after his birthday, starts a journal bearing the grand title 'Voice of Truth' which is as stated above, a diminished translation of its Arabic title *Lisan-us-Sidq*, since no word in the English vocabulary can replace the words. The English words Voice and Truth do not adequately capture the depth of feeling and conviction embodied in the Arabic *Lisan* and *Sidq*. What lies behind the supreme confidence of a young man who claims that his is the voice of truth?

The four autobiographies, *Tazkirah*, *Ghubar-i-Khatir*, *Kahani* and *India Wins Freedom*, yield many answers to this question but all point towards his conviction that the world view held by his ancestors in the light of the Koran, was the only right view. They knew, *seena-ba-seena* (knowledge which is passed from person to person), what *Siratul Mustaqeem* (the Straight Path laid down in the Koran) meant, and now it was his duty to give its *hidayat* (guidance) to the Muslim *quom*.

The objectives of *Lisan-us-Sidq* are a clear indication of the direction in which he had charted his course. The 'Voice of Truth' would hold a mirror to the Muslims and show them the image of truth. In the very first issue, after the objectives were stated, the young editor, without further ado, commenced on his mission to reform his community. He began with a poem which was written by a friend to commemorate the launching of *Lisan-us-Sidq*. Of the six couplets, one relates to Azad by name:

Jo haath Hazrat-e-Azad sa editor aaye
Na kyun ho mulk mein shohra tira al Lisan-us-Sidq

If an editor like Azad be obtained somehow
Why shouldn't *Lisan-us-Sidq* gain utmost popularity in the country

Lavish praise at the age of fifteen in the form of panegyric poetry is enough to titillate the most ascetic of temperaments. But its effect on the adolescent Azad, was to impel him to redouble his efforts to realize his vision of reform.

In the first issue, he wrote in praise of Shaikh Mohammad Abduh, Mufti of Egypt, whose fame as a reformer had spread through the length and breadth of the Islamic world. Implicit in his praise of Abduh is his condemnation of the ulema of Egypt who had turned against Abduh for his liberal outlook. He expressed his admiration of Abduh's interpretation of the Koran in the light of the contemporary needs of Muslims, which was being serially published in the monthly journal *Al Manar*.[16] Abduh's influence is seen later on in Azad's own interpretation of the Koran.

Other items in the first issue include a note of appreciation for the proposal by some Calcutta Muslims to launch an English newspaper. In this he echoes the sentiments of his mentor Sir Syed Ahmad Khan who regarded it as a useful means of communicating with the *sarkar*. The fact that this was the view of a boy whose educational milieu was staunchly opposed to English education due to what his elders regarded as its corrupting influence on youth, proves that he had the courage of his convictions, and full realization that this would earn his father's disapproval. Another article concerns the important work of translation undertaken by the Anjuman Taraqqi Urdu of books in English, Arabic and Persian. An editorial note requests his colleagues from other papers to review this journal, but review in the sense of a critical appraisal and not as a eulogy. The first issue has all the ingredients of Azad's journalistic style as it was to evolve later in *Al Hilal* and *Al Balagh*. Single-minded and serious, the paper combines sedateness with boldness which was to become the hallmark of Azad's later writing.

A few samples from the extant issues of *Lisan-us-Sidq*[17] help in understanding the evolution of Azad's thought from 1903–1905. In the January 1904 issue, appeared his article 'Qaumi Aizaz' which was a glowing tribute to the famous reformist poet Khwaja Altaf Husain Hali for his outstanding work for the Muslim community. The qualities he praises in Hali are what he had dreamt of for himself when, as a child, he wore his father's turban and pretended that the masses were lined up on either side to felicitate him. 'Hali', he writes, 'instructed us that we should stop writing *marsias* (dirges) for others and for once write one about our own pathetic condition. Not only did he instruct us, he wrote the first *marsia* for the *quom*, demonstrating that when something is written with a genuine feeling, it leaves a profound impact.' Hali's poem, written to shake the Muslims out of the stupor into which they had fallen and to make them aware of their abject condition, was titled *Ebb and Tide of Islam* but became known to the Islamic and literary world as *Musaddas-e-Hali*. It begins with the *bund* (six line stanza) which describes the most deadly disease in the world as one which the patient does not recognize as terminal illness. This is the disease that has afflicted the Muslim *quom*. He says further that although several writings have appeared to arouse the *quom*, for example Sir Syed Ahmed Khan's journal *Tehzib-ul-Akhlaq*, the real work has been done by the *Musaddas* of Hali:

The *quom* was aroused by the *Musaddas*. It explained their defects, the patient was warned of the causes of his sickness, the methods of cure were also suggested, and this proved efficacious because, whatever arises from the heart, reaches directly the heart to which it is addressed.

Azad deeply regrets the fact that neither the government nor the *quom* had publicly honoured Hali for his service to humanity. He adds that a poet of Hali's stature does not need worldly recognition; it is the *quom* which needs to recognize its *mohsins* (bestowers of favours). He lambasts the contemporary journals *Vakil* and *Watan* which have preferred to remain silent instead of supporting the campaign launched by another journal *Taleef-o-Isha'at*, for Maulana Hali to be honoured that year at a special function. This article which appeared in 1904, shows that Azad had no expectations of the government. He therefore decided to take direction.

Azad's admiration for Hali was reflected in a lengthy article which had appeared earlier, in the February 1904 issue, about Hali's biography of Sir Syed entitled *Hayat-e-Javed*. The importance of the review-article is that it reflects Azad's freedom of expression in literary criticism. Regardless of whether or not he personally agrees with the viewpoint of the author, he must offer an unbiased view to the reader. Four months later, in the June issue, he triumphantly announces that Hali's name has appeared among the persons who have been conferred the title of *Shams-ul-Ulema* (the Sun among the Learned) by the government.

These initial forays in public life are testimony to his self-confidence. Backed by solid scholarship, fine intellect, and faith in the Rightness of his mission he is able to speak out. Where senior editors remain silent or indulge in equivocation, Azad has no hesitation, despite being very young, in grappling with big issues.

One of the regular features of *Lisan-us-Sidq* was an announcement of forthcoming publications. In the August-September issue, under the title 'These books will soon be published in the country', he describes the book on Mutazilites that he is currently engaged in writing. He says that the Mutazila is the most successful sect in Islam because of its contribution to the establishment of *aqliyat* (Rationalism) in Islamic literature and introduction of philosophy and science. He announced that the book was to be divided into three parts. The first part was to have eight sections:

1. Original condition of Islam.
2. Simplicity of Islam.
3. Propagation of Islam among the civilized nations.
4. Fine distinctions in religious beliefs.
5. Rise of differences and the reasons.
6. Rise of different factions and *Aitezal* (Dissent).
7. The first four periods of *Aitezal*.
8. Decline *of Aitezal*.

Having completed this part, he wrote, that he was now working on the next. He then quotes a passage from his introduction to part one, which states that an upheaval has occurred in the sphere of religion during the last half century due to the influence of European *uloom-o-funoon* (arts and sciences). As a result, religion is disintegrating every day, and a time will come when it may not be able to withstand the onslaught of the *uloom-e-jadid* (modern knowledge). The first effort to provide *tajdid-e-kalam* (modern interpretation of the Kalam) as the fitting answer to *jadid uloom* (modern knowledge) was made thirty years ago by Sir Syed. But that was nothing new to Islam. Those who are startled by the sound of Sir Syed's voice are reminded that this same voice was heard a thousand years ago. Then it was the voice of the Mutazilites, which was their response (in a bygone era) to the onslaught by the *uloom-e-qadeem* (old philosophy). Here Azad adds that he is engaged in working on another volume, entitled *Al Uloom Al Jadeed wal Islam* (Modern Knowledge and Islam).

At this time Azad had read extensively specially in the area of Islamic literature. Desperately seeking his own path, as distinct from the path of his forefathers, he was exploring all the alternative paths. The way of the Mutazila offered the greatest appeal to his questioning mind. The school of Mutazilites (Dissenters) was founded at Basra by Abu Huzaifa Wasil bin Ata al Ghazzal (AD 699–700 to AD 748–9). The general rationalism of his school rallied around him the strongest and most liberal minds, which included scholars, physicists, mathematicians and historians. Intellectuals, even Khalifas, belonged to the Mutazilite school.[18] It was among the Mutazilites that scholastic theology, called *Ilm-ul-Kalam* (*Ilm:* science, *Kalam:* Word of God) was born. The Mutazilites hold that there is no eternal law regarding human actions; that the Divine ordinances which regulate the conduct of men are the result of growth and development; that God has commanded and forbidden by a law that has evolved gradually. The Mutazilites also say that all knowledge is attained through reason, and must necessarily be so obtained. Whereas the *Ahl-us-Sunnat*, the great majority of the Muslims of the subcontinent, hold that God does whatever He pleases, for He is the sovereign Lord of His dominions, and whatever He wishes He orders. This, according to their belief is *adl* (justice).

According to *Ahl-ul-Aitezaal* (Mutazilites), what accords with Reason and Wisdom is *adl* (justice) and deeds performed for the well-being of mankind. They believe that the knowledge of God is within the province of reason. The *Ahl-us-Sunnat* believe that only temporal knowledge is attained by reason, and that reason cannot tell us what is good and what is bad or what is obligatory. This is where the great divide between the philosophical beliefs of the Mutazilites and the *Ahl-us-Sunnat* (the sect to which Azad's family subscribed) occurs. And Azad had the temerity to announce in the August-September issue of *Lisan-us-Sidq* that he was writing a book on the doctrines of Mutazilites! That such a book never came from the ink of his pen is not surprising. There were too many conflicting paths and divergent philosophies vying with each other for his adherence. As will be seen later, however, Azad did adopt in many respects, the doctrines of the rationalist thinkers in Islam, but never attributed his views to the Mutazilites. In fact his admiration for Imam Hanbal, the arch-enemy of the Mutazilites, expressed a decade later in the pages of *Tazkirah*, is indicative of his ambivalence.

Another announcement appeared in the April-May issue of *Lisan-us-Sidq*, regarding the launching of a journal, *Review*. Its purpose was stated as being the review of all the Urdu books published in the country and important Arabic books published elsewhere in the world. It would also serve as an agency through which all the latest books from the Islamic countries would be made available to the public. The journal was to start appearing as a supplement to *Lisan-us-Sidq* from June 1905. The promised *Review* never appeared, since the journal itself was discontinued after this announcement. Nevertheless, the very intention shows the seriousness with which Azad approached his work.[19]

An early indication of what Azad was planning for the future is found in the front page editorial of the last issue, entitled 'Mubadla-e-Sanin' (Change of Year). The article begins with philosophizing on the birth of a new year, as he takes stock of the progress of *Lisan-us-Sidq*. He writes that the journal was first launched in 1903 and was now going into its third volume. With profound apologies to his readers that the journal had not lived up to its original intentions and expectations, he confesses that he encountered several troubles and misfortunes during the current year. It is obvious that the 'trouble and misfortune' referred to here, is the great mental and emotional upheaval he had experienced in his rejection of *taqlid*, (rigid adherence) and finding his own path. Regardless, he puts on a brave face and says that his personal life cannot serve as an excuse for unfulfilled promises! The events of the preceding year, he says, have taught him the lesson of *m'arifat-e-Ilahi* (cognition of Allah, a personal and private achievement) and he has finally understood the *quol* of Hazrat Ali ibn-e-Abi Talib, *Arafat Rabbi bi Fasakhal Azaim*, meaning 'I recognized Allah in the shattering of my objectives'. This failure, he writes, has in fact turned out to be a blessing because now a new *Lisan-us-Sidq* will be born which will make up for the former lapses.

He then discloses his new set of objectives which are a reflection of the direction of his current thinking. He writes that his journal will address itself to those matters which are the need of the times, and not pander to the prevailing tastes and popular preferences. It will attempt to mould the taste of the audience, after determining that which would lead to their greatest good. This is the first time he makes this claim, which was to be repeated in his later writings. At the age of sixteen, young Abul Kalam, aspiring to lead the caravan of the Indian Muslims, claims that he will show the path to his flock, because he knows what is in their best interest. The senatorian tone persisted throughout the editorial which ran into several columns, the import of which was that *Lisan-us-Sidq*, being the 'Voice of Truth' should not be expected to speak anything but the truth. The ideas germinated here were to become, eight years later, the baseline of *Al Hilal*.

'Allah Allah!' as Azad would have said, the presumption of a sixteen year old to sit in judgement on venerable contemporary journals like *Asr-e-Jadid* and *Zamana*. Continuing his statement of revised aims and objectives, he praises both journals but at the same time, claims that there is no paper which promotes literary taste. Therefore he must take the responsibility of 'curing the ailment' and developing literary taste among his readers. Given that a single journal cannot appeal to all tastes, which is why Europe produces a variety of journals, he affirms that his journal will have a focus and a clear target. He further states that for the fulfilment of these objectives he will have to carve out his own path.

This revulsion against the *shahraah-e-aam* (common path) is found in all his writings. Here he wants to carve his own way which will lead him to the *manzil-e-maqsud* (final destination). Later in life this was to become his creed. His obsession for striking out on his own is attributed to the suffocation of the *piri-muridi* atmosphere in which he had lived and breathed all his life. It is interesting that he views his desire for exclusivity as stemming from his concern for his *quom*; that his way was the right way which, if followed, would lead them to their *manzil-e-maqsud*.

Furthermore, he declares that the mission to inform and reform the *quom* would tolerate no interference or distraction. He would therefore eschew the *baagh-o-gulzar* (gardens) of literature, and enter the 'barren fields' of the sciences. In future, *Lisan-us-Sidq* was to have the following subject content:

1. Scholarly and learned articles.
2. Articles on the *Mashahir* (famous figures) of the East with their photographs.
3. Scientific articles with illustrations.
4. Serialized articles on the sciences.
5. Articles by famous authors who rarely write for ordinary journals.

Henceforth the articles in *Lisan-us-Sidq* will be on three subjects, science, history and culture. To this is added one more subject which he says would become increasingly important, i.e. religion. He also wants to include *islah-e-khayal* (reform of thoughts). The purpose of this would be to remove all the religious, cultural and historic misunderstandings which have been deeply rooted in the *quom*. With the help of reasoned arguments, an attempt would be made to develop people's capability to think for themselves, and to become accustomed to light instead of the darkness in which they were groping at present, 'so that the future generations are protected from these weaknesses and the new age is not contaminated by the darkness of superstition.'

In 1904, Azad writes, he and his brother left for Iraq. *Lisan-us-Sidq* did not appear after that.[20] The discrepancy in the dates, given the fact that the last issue is dated 1905, may have been due to his having prepared the material before he left on his trip, which was compiled and published in his absence. Soon after Azad's return from Iraq and following the closure of *Lisan-us-Sidq* Maulana Shibli Nu'mani invited him to assume the assistant editorship of *Al Nadwa*, the monthly journal of Nadwatul Ulema.

Shibli had a very important influence on Azad's life. It will be recalled that he had read Azad's article on X-rays even before he had met him. When the two met in Bombay, Azad requested the use of Shibli's library in Azamgarh. Ever gracious and generous, Shibli promised to send Azad a list of his books, which he promptly forgot. But this started a friendship that was to last a lifetime.

Shibli, a towering literary personality of the time, was the principal of Nadwatul Ulema (School for Islamic Studies located in Nadwa) and the author of a study of the Prophet, *Sirat-un-Nabi*. When in 1903, Anjuman Tarraqi Urdu was established as a branch of the Mohammedan Educational Conference, Shibli was appointed as its administrator. The other branch established by the Conference was *Islah-e-Rusum* (Reform of Customs) which was run by the distinguished editor of the journal *Asr-e-Jadid* (The Modern Times), Khwaja Ghulam-us-Saqlain. Shibli chose Azad as a member of the organizing committee of the Anjuman. Since two of *Lisan-us-Sidq's* objectives were in common with the objectives of the Anjuman, Azad's journal was chosen as its official organ.

Azad's letters and biographical accounts contain spontaneous references to Shibli, reflecting their deep friendship in which their age difference was of no consequence. To his friend Habibur Rahman Khan Sherwani he writes about Shibli's habit of rising early in the morning and their mutual savouring of tea.[21] To Malihabadi he relates the incident of Shibli's embarrassment when he was recognized and hailed as the author of the highly respected treatise, *Al Farooq* by a musician. The man was the accompanist of a singing girl, to whose *mehfil* (gathering) he had been invited and where he had gone, hoping for anonymity! Azad must himself have been present at this *mehfil* and must have secretly smiled at Maulana Shibli's awkwardness at the musician's ecstasy at recognizing his distinguished listener.[22]

Shibli's essays and poems often appeared in *Al Hilal*. His death was a personal tragedy for Azad about which he wrote poignant editorials. Shibli had said of Azad, 'Your mind is among the wonders of the world. You should be displayed as a miracle at an *ilmi numaishgaah* (educational exhibition).'[23] Describing to Sherwani the quality of his friendship with Shibli, Azad said that the multifaceted personality of the Maulana is best described in these lines of Hali:

Bahut lagta hai ji suhbat mein unki
Woh apni zaat mein ek anjuman hain

His company is most pleasing to the heart
He is a gathering unto himself.

Azad started work at *Al Nadwa* in July 1905, although his name did not start appearing until October. His tenure in Lucknow lasted eight months, the last issue on which his name appears is dated March 1906. During this period he was avidly reading the Arabic journals that the school subscribed to. The influence of Arabic and Egyptian journalism is evident in the work on hand as well as in his own journal which was to be launched seven years later.

During those days, two important annual conferences were held in which prominent Muslims like Maulana Hali, Maulana Shibli, Nawab Mohsin-ul-Mulk Maulvi Nazir Ahmed participated. The first was Mohammedan Educational Conference held at Aligarh and the second, Anjuman Himayat-e-Islam held in Lahore. Azad attended the conference of the Anjuman in 1903. This he did without his father's knowledge. Here he met these venerable leaders and reformists and impressed them with his seriousness and erudition despite his youthful appearance.[24] We learn from Ajmal Khan's Introduction to *Ghubar-i-Khatir* that by the time he was seventeen or eighteen, Azad had started moving among scholars of the time who were his seniors by many years. Due to his extraordinary intelligence and 'stupefying learning' he had gained the respect of the above named leaders and littérateurs, as well as the regard of Muslims of consequence like Nawab Viqar ul Mulk, Khalifa Mohammad Husain, Munshi Zakaullah and Hakim Ajmal Khan.

Given a bare and brief mention of the facts narrated above, it seems incumbent to take a fresh and objective look at Azad, detaching oneself from the common and stereotype image. What one sees is a boy of an extraordinary intellect, who is brought up under the strict discipline of an authoritarian father and carefully selected teachers. He is well aware of his intellectual superiority to his older brother and much older class fellows. Furthermore, he is never allowed to wander far, and never alone, neither from the house nor from the routine of the established family traditions. He is conscious of belonging to the elite class of Muslim *pirs* which wields a powerful influence over substantial sections of the Muslim population as its *murids*. His family has inherited strong traditions which represent to the best of its convictions, the noblest way of life to be led by a Muslim. He draws his lineage and strength from all the important centres of the world of Islam.

For anyone but an extraordinary young man, so well versed in what the family and its faith stood for, it would have been the most natural thing to follow the trail of glory blazed by such an unusual constellation of illustrious ancestors. But young Azad could not make himself accept it. It is the struggle and conflict in the fourteen year old against what he calls his *nasli virasat*, (the inherited legacy) which is an important key to our understanding of Azad's development. It explains the reason behind what he accepted and what he rejected. He was unable to accept the package of the *weltanschauüng* of the ancestors of whom he was justly proud and for whom he had the highest regard. This struggle and conflict was of a fundamental nature and was going to remain with Azad all his life.

In *Tazkirah*, Azad wrote with considerable pride about his distinguished lineage. The respect that he felt for his ancestors, he says, was due to the fact that they were rich in *Ilm-o-Irshad* (knowledge and teaching) but also because they turned away from worldly riches. In the same account, he writes of many instances from the life of Shaikh Jamaluddin, the ancestor whose life fills 200 pages of his 'autobiography', and which exemplifies this characteristic. Once a nobleman of the Mughal court offered Jamaluddin all the riches of the world. The Shaikh refused and gave the reason:

I am afraid of building a house, lest my heart becomes desolate.[25]

The conflict within him which is reflected in the glowing picture he paints of his ancestors, while, at the same time, turning away from the *taqlid* of their traditions in near revulsion, is evident in all his autobiographies, particularly *Tazkirah* and *Ghubar-i-Khatir*. It translates into the theme of his life which fits under the cliché, 'achievement versus heredity'.

Expressing great distaste for people who promote themselves through cataloguing the achievements of their ancestors, he writes in his short introduction to *Tazkirah*:

Alhamd-o-lillah! I have never felt inclined to arraign a shop of *nasb-faroshi*[26] in quest of a cashing in for respectability. Islam has obliterated all differences and distinctions, leaving for man only the distinction of being a believer. What greater lineage can a man seek? The real distinction for a human being is personal achievement and learning.[27]

A student of Azad's life cannot but be struck by the fact that even as a young boy of fourteen years, when he was under maximum pressure to abide by the traditional practices of his ancestors (such as becoming a *Pir* of a flock of *Murids*), he either refused to act or invoked his own interpretation of Islam.

He illustrates this point by relating an incident from the life of Napoleon. After the conquest of Prussia, Napoleon went to the tomb of Frederick the Great and found his ancient sword hanging over his grave. He handed the sword to an attendant soldier and asked him to deposit it in the Paris Museum. Napoleon's military general who was watching this exchange expressed surprise, 'If I had discovered such a great historic relic, I would never have given it to anyone'. Azad's comment on this incident encapsulates his life's philosophy,

In our scabbard we should keep our own keen edged swords. Even if we get public respect by displaying others' swords, we should remember that the respect is directed at the owner not at us.[28]

Family pride he writes, was one of the idols worshipped during the dark age of *Jahiliyat* (pre-Islamic era). Islam has broken this idol along with many other idols which used to line the walls of the Kaaba (the central place of worship in the Holy city of Mecca). It is possible that tomorrow, a neo-Muslim cobbler may, by his own merit, reach the heights, which the Shaikhs of Islam have never been able to touch. What do we know of Bilal the Habshi or Suhail the Rumi (Bilal and Suhail were slaves freed by the Prophet who acquired eminence for their firm faith), except that they were Muslims? Islam teaches man to rise above *imtiaz-i-batil* (false distinction); the Koran teaches that all ancient religions have indicated the same path. This was the *suhf* (Holy Word) spoken by Abraham and Moses. But the tragedy is that the broken pieces of idols like pride, race and country (*watan*) were once again glued together and new forms of worship were invented. Today there are very few heads which are not filled with the pride of this false intoxication.[29]

Having said all this he then, characteristically, turns the argument upside down by admitting that he too is intoxicated by ancestral pride. But the pride is for the learning and piety of people who have, for centuries, been scholars and teachers. They have passed on this *virasat* (legacy) from generation to generation. Their *amal-e-saleh* (righteous deeds), their truth, sacrifice, and indifference to the owners of *Takht-o-Taj* (crown and throne) and *Maal-o-Jaah* (wealth and riches) is the additional legacy which they have left for their children. For him, Azad says, it has been the richest heritage. He therefore prays that he can preserve for the future generations this treasure-house of *khidmat* (service) of *ilm-o-sidq* (truth and learning) which has been bequeathed to him by the grace of Allah.

Young Azad had chosen his field of endeavour. Since his child-hood days praise was lavished on him for his genius and prowess in learning. So learning it was to be. It was a brilliant synthesis of the conflicts raging within him. He would follow the noble tradition of his ancestors in the acquisition of knowledge and yet blaze a new trail, rejecting what he did not approve of such as the all pervading formula of *taqlid*. Azad would use his own interpretation of religious knowledge to counter the interpretations accepted by his worthy ancestors. He would have radical differences with them and yet he would remain a part of them—the most famous and celebrated *Maulana* of them all.

Admiration runs parallel to disdain; and in Freudian analysis there is nothing unusual about that. We can see concrete evidence of this in Azad's relationship with his father where his intensity of admiration is matched by his intensity of resentment. A child of five or six who is said to have placed his father's turban on his head and pretended to be him, refused *dastaar bandi* (wearing his turban, signifying the acceptance of his vacant chair), when the moment finally arrived. That was Azad's love-hate relationship with Maulana Khairuddin. In *Ghubar-i-Khatir*, the picture he draws of life in his father's home is underlaid with a deep resentment for the rigidity of his early upbringing. Phrases such as 'A hair's breadth of deviation was *kufr* (heresy)', 'My mind was heavy with this adamantine heritage', 'No contrary winds could blow within these four walls', 'Spending my life in the India of a thousand years ago' are noteworthy observations which reflect his resentful, even rebellious state of mind. The added burden on his conscience was the undue deference with which he was treated by the disciples of his father. They sat at a respectful distance from him, hanging on to his every word and not even sparing him the embarrassment of kissing his hands when he was outside his house in the crowded marketplace, in full public view.

I was born into a family which held a very senior status among the teachers and scholars of the age. For that reason the crowds of followers, which are regarded the measure for a political leader's strength, came to me without any effort on my part in the form of *murids* (disciples). I was barely old enough to understand when people started to defer to me as a *pirzada*, kiss my hands and feet, and stand before me with their hands folded.[30]

At the age of fifteen, in tandem with this turmoil relating to his social and cultural environment, he had begun to doubt and question the validity of his basic beliefs. The doubts that had never been articulated before by anyone, became defined in his mind:

> I remember very well that I was no older than 15, when my equanimity was disturbed and the barbs of doubt and suspicion began to pierce my mind… I felt that the universe of knowledge could not be as limited as what stood before me. This rankling increased with age and in a few years the walls of belief and faith which had been built all around me by family and tradition, started to shudder. Finally the time came when these walls had to be demolished by my own hands and new walls built in their place.[31]

Regarding this loss of faith, although Azad writes that he cannot recall exactly when he felt the first sting of doubt it is possible to locate it around the time he became a devotee of Sir Syed Ahmed Khan. In *Kahani* Azad is reported to have said that he used to worship Sir Syed and as he was drawn towards his *maslak* (creed), he moved away from the traditional *Hanafiyat*[32] and *Ashariyat*[33] of his father. Malihabadi records the enthusiasm with which he used to look forward to receiving the issues of Sir Syed's journals, *Gazette* and *Tehzib-ul-Akhlaq*, and the anxiety with which he counted the days until the post brought *Hayat-e-Javed*, Sir Syed's biography by Maulana Hali. He had extolled Sir Syed's rational interpretation of the Koran, and recorded in more than one place, his profound influence in moulding his (Azad's own) religious beliefs. But this total surrender to Sir Syed which became an obsession with Azad during the early years of the century and which propelled him to great heights, did not last long. In *Kahani* is recorded the upheaval of his faith:

> Sir Syed's teachings had elevated me to a new world but I could not be content with it for long, as always happens in such conditions. The

door he had opened led to new thresholds of doubt and consternation until I reached the point of *ilhad* and *inkar*.

It seems that the slow build up of resentment in Azad due to the excessive adulation of the *murids* and the overpowering influence of his father, led to a disavowal of traditional beliefs. His devotion to Sir Syed Ahmed Khan's philosophy and secret subscription to his journal *Tehzib-ul-Akhlaq*, when accidentally discovered by his father earned him what can only be termed the worst possible rebuke in a highly religious family such as his father's—the title *dehri* (atheist) and *nacheri* (naturalist). Considering his reverence for the patriarch this demonstration of extreme annoyance, coupled with the allegation that he was no longer a Muslim must have shocked Azad beyond belief. It must have caused or precipitated a monumental crisis within him so much so that one night he found himself unable to say the *namaz*. Shock, anger, frustration, resentment, sadness felt as a result of what his father said or did was one thing, but his inability to say the prayers to Allah was quite another.

That night when Azad found himself unable to say his prayers the heavens must have fallen! He, like many of his illustrious Sufi saints and scholar predecessors, had now entered the stage of doubt. Was it right that Allah had laid down what his father said about Islam or how he practised it? How could Allah possibly mean what his father said He meant or what he was told by his teachers? The moment of the greatest test of Azad's life—concerning his religious belief—had arrived. It was a test that the entire galaxy of the most brilliant scholars and doctors of Islam have had to pass. Azad was no exception.

The role of the environment in moulding an individual is an established fact. The question Azad asked himself in *Ghubar-i-Khatir* was, that given this fact, what made him turn out the way he did? First, he says that he was fully conscious of his *nusli-virasat* or family heredity. His basic personality was steeped in the conventions of his lineage which, he asserts, had him in their grip. The stamp of the Sufi *silsilas* placed upon him by the maternal and paternal sides of his family was there by reason of birth and in that too he had no choice. But no matter where he looked and how hard he tried, he could not find in what he became, any evidence of his childhood environment. In his own words, now 'nothing matches'.

The subject, however continued to fascinate him. Why did he turn out the way he did? Analyzing the causes, he returns to the theme of *taqlid* (rigorously following the inherited traditions) which is exemplified in the story of Napoleon. The greatest impediment to human progress, he writes, is adherence to the beliefs of ancestors. Nothing can bind and chain man like these can; he cannot question them, nor can he ever violate them. To guard them and protect them becomes his creed. Then what happened in his case which gave him the courage to renounce his *virasat*, to cause in him an antipathy to his traditions? It is clear that his education and environment was exactly according to his *maurusi aqaaid* (ancestral beliefs). Then where did the doubt come from? The first sting of doubt, he suggests, occurred entirely on its own. His mind started questioning and rejecting the fact that his faith was grounded in the foundation of *taqlid* (imitation) and *tavaris* (heredity) rather than in *ilm* (knowledge). When *taqlid*, the foundation of conventional belief, he says, was taken away there was nothing left to prop that crumbling wall:

> Where did this temperament come from? The mould of familial values and beliefs that I wanted to construct, I could not. The direction towards which education should have taken me, it did not. The demands of the circle of influence could not be fulfilled. In life it is possible to trace every effect to a cause. I could not find my cause. Perhaps this was due to the narrowness of my vision. Some other perceptive eye, when it studies my circumstances one day, may discover the cause. I had no choice but to give up.[34]

The fact, however, is that neither did he give up searching for the cause of his renunciation of *taqlid* nor do his present day biographers. The evidence that it never left his mind lies in is his repeated references in *Ghubar-i-Khatir* and other biographies to the incident of his *inkaar* (refusal). At the age of fifteen, he writes, he was filled with new doubts and questions. His first disillusionment was his encounter with the fissures within Islam itself. Later, he became aware of the universal deterioration of the spirit of Islam and the tension between rationality and religion. All these factors aggregated to his loss of faith. This is the path, he writes in *Ghubar-i-Khatir*, which begins with doubt and ends with negation. But he was not willing to stop at negation. Therefore he moved on, and, without explaining the details of this experience, he states that among those gloomy paths of doubts and suspicions there was one clear ribbon of light which was the fountainhead of satisfaction. The symptom of the illness, therefore, became its ultimate cure. But for him the important outcome was that the faith he lost was of heredity and what he gained was the fruit of his own search:

> There is one type of religion—hereditary; believe what your fore-fathers believed in. Another type is geographical, which comprises the well-worn path travelled by many on any given piece of the earth. Then there is religion for the census survey; put down 'Islam' in the appropriate box. There is also the conventional religion-the compendium of rituals and ceremonies, do not tamper with it; allow it to run all over you. Apart from all these there is the *haqiqi* (true) religion and it is the path to this which somehow always gets lost.[35]

The conundrum of Azad is that the more he wanted to be different from his inherited self, the more he remained the same. His life was to become a quest; what was it that he could accept from the past and what was it that he could reject. In finding his own interpretation of Islam, he took upon his young shoulders the greatest burden that a true believer could possibly take. It was the same burden that some of the greatest thinkers in Islam undertook to carry. In the process, they passed the most agonizing stages of *shak o shuba* (doubt), and ultimately emerged purified and cleansed and yet different from the rest of the believers. Little wonder then that Azad assumed the title of Abul Kalam, and believed that he could be the *lisan-us-sidq* (voice of truth). He believed that he could reorientate and reinterpret the religion of his illustrious forefathers and reform the *quom* or the community of Muslims.

notes

1 *Tazkirah*, p. 310. It was a common practice to calculate the numerical value of each alphabet and compose a line or couplet to commemorate special events like births and deaths.

2 *Alim*, interpreter of the Koran, the Hadith and Fiqah.

3 *Tazkirah* translated by Mohammed Mujeeb in The Commemoration Volume, edited by Humayun Kabir.

4 *Abul Kalam ki Kahani khud unki Zubani*, p. 194. Referred henceforth as *Kahani*.

5 This reference is found in Azad's address to the Committee on Hindustani, 1937 in the context of the evolution of Hindvi. See *Khutbat-e-Azad* edited by Malik Ram.

6 Azad agreed with his father's assessment of Madrasa Aliya. See *Kahani*.

7 *Zikr-e-Azad*, pp. 116–18.

8 This was related to the author by Nuruddin Ahmed, Ghulam Yasin's son, with reference to Azad's letters from Ahmednagar, requiring him to provide specific information from the books lining his shelves in the library, 28 April 1992.

9 *Ghubar-i-Khatir*, p. 132.

10 Khairuddin built a mausoleum to her at the Manektala graveyard in Calcutta. It had a marble dome but no walls, just an enclosure made of iron grills. The author visited it in April 1992, and was appalled to see the state of its neglect and encroachment. Azad's father, Maulana Khairuddin, Azad's brother Ghulam Yasin, Azad's wife Zuleikha, their four year old son Haseen, are all buried there.

11 *Ghubar-i-Khatir*, p. 112.

12 Interview by Khwaja Ahmad Faruqui. *Aajkal*, September 1959, pp. 14–15.

13 For an interesting account of Azad as poet see Syeda Shan-e-Meraj's article in *Maulana Abul Kalam Azad: Shakhsiyat aur Karname* edited by Khaliq Anjum, Urdu Academy, 1986.

14 For another interesting discussion on Azad's taste for poetry see Jagan Nath Azad's essay in *Shakhsiyat aur Karname* ed. Khaliq Anjum, Urdu Academy, 1986.

15 Abid Raza Bedar, *Maulana Abul Kalam Azad*, Institute of Oriental Studies, Rampur, 1968. Bedar writes that he has not been able to locate any issue of *Nairang-e-Alam*.

16 Journal published in Egypt by the followers of Abduh. Azad admits to being greatly impressed by its style and rhetoric, an influence evident in *Al Hilal*.

17 'Monthly *Lisan-us-Sidq*, Calcutta', Editor Abul Kalam Mohiuddin Azad Dehlavi. This book is edited by Abdul Qavi Dasnavi, who has collected all the available issues and published them under the auspicies of Maktaba Jamia, 1988.

18 Syed Amir Ali, *The Spirit of Islam*, pp. 414–15.

19 Azad's erudition is reflected in the works he is reported to have written or translated during this period. *Kahani* lists translations of Imam Ghazali's *Minhaj-ul-Abideen* and *Tafahat-ul-Falsafa*, and Jami's *Nafahat-un-Uns*. He was also compiling a Persian dictionary to correct the 'mistakes in the existing *Lughat*.' See *Kahani*, p. 226.

20 See *Kahani*, p. 303.

21 *Karvan-e-Khayal*.

22 *Zikr-e-Azad*, pp. 217–19.

23 *Kahani*, p. 305.

24 Sec Malihabadi's description of this phase in *Kahani*.

25 *Tazkirah*, p. 37.

26 Sale of lineage.

27 *Tazkirah*, p. 26.

28 Ibid.

29 *Ghubar-i-Khatir.*

30 Ibid.

31 *Kahani*, p. 277.

32 Creed of Imam Abu Hanifa, born AD 699.

33 Creed of Abul Hasan Ashari, born AD 874.

34 *Ghubar-i-Khatir.*

35 Ibid.

2

breaking free

AZAD LEFT THE EDITORSHIP OF *Al Nadwa* to join the staff of the journal *Vakil*, in Amritsar where he stayed from April to November 1906. His name, however, does not appear in any article which was published during this period. But his name had appeared earlier in *Vakil* as the translator of the Arabic treatise *Al Miratul Muslima* (Image of a Muslim Woman) which was being copied from its serial appearance in *Al Nadwa*.[1] The literary and journalistic ambience in which Azad lived and breathed is reflected in these lines of a letter written by his friend Habib-ur-Rahman Khan Sherwani:

> I recall the time when two young men Abul Kalam Azad and Abu Nasr Aah emerged on the scene. *Vakil* used to appear with dignity and pride from Amritsar under the editorship of the late Munshi Ghulam Mohammad. Your articles used to appear in it which even at that time were embellished with a rare literary taste and a wealth of meaning.[2]

In December 1906, Azad was back in Calcutta and associated with the weekly journal *Darul Saltanat.* One letter to the owner Mohammad Yusuf, dated 25 December 1906 promises that he will start the *Darul Saltanat* press as soon as he returns from Dhaka. This was the historic meeting of all the prominent Muslims of India under the leadership of the Nawab of Dhaka, when the Muslim League was inaugurated. Malihabadi writes that Azad's association with *Darul Saltanat* did not last long. Once again, he was back in Amritsar editing *Vakil.* This time he found himself in ideological conflict with the owner, Ghulam Mohammad. The pressure of work exhausted him, and he left Amritsar after a period of eight or nine months, first to visit his sister who was living in Bhopal, and then to recuperate in the milder climate of Poona. It was from Poona that he was called to attend to his father's deathbed in August 1908.

The period of four years that intervened between his father's death (1908) and the appearance of *Al Hilal* (1912) gave the final shape to Azad's political and religious goals and beliefs. The most important single event that would leave the greatest impact on him was the death of Maulana Khairuddin. Not unrelated to this event was the death two years earlier in 1906 of his brother Abu Nasr. It appears from various accounts that in 1905 the two brothers went on a tour of Islamic countries. This was done against their father's wishes, a fact that Azad would regret later.[3] On reaching Iraq, Azad fell ill and returned home while his brother went on with a friend to Mousil and Dayar-i-Bakr. He was brought back to India critically ill. His death within a few months shattered Khairuddin since he had pinned his hopes on Abu Nasr taking over his *valayat* (Sufi jurisdiction). But in keeping with the dignity of his position, he gave no evidence of his feelings, a trait Azad inherited and which appears most starkly at the death of his wife in 1944. When Khairuddin was taken ill, Azad was engaged in his second assignment with *Vakil.* He writes that at the exact time he had in fact left Amritsar to recuperate from an illness and the heat of summer. But he was able to reach his father before his death.[4]

Notwithstanding the terrible loss, Azad suddenly found himself free from all the restraining influences of his life. So far he had not been able to extricate himself from his father's overpowering control. His brother, too, although he did not exert much authority, was a restraint on his independence. Abu Nasr represented all that his father would have wanted Azad to be. Although unstated in any of his autobiographies, it is not inconceivable that one reason for his decision to rejoin *Vakil* was his inability to stay in Calcutta and face his father's unspoken plea to fill the void created by Abu Nasr's death.[5] Two important influences were thus removed in a year. Analyzing his state of mind, Douglas writes:

> The passing of this dominant figure of whom he had lived in such awe, gave the young man both a sense of release and a realization of new responsibilities as head of the family and as successor to a *Pir*. Such conflicting feelings often lead to a search for human sympathy, divine guidance, or both.[6]

Several things happened almost simultaneously at this crucial juncture of his life. The storm that had been brewing inside him against all forms of adherence to traditional beliefs, to use his own metaphor—his *ghubar-i-khatir* ('vapour of the self'), burst free breaking with its forceful current all the restraints whether imposed upon him by his family or by himself. The autobiographical portion of *Tazkirah* which consists of twenty pages appended as the last chapter, contains an account of his *Lahw-o-La'ab* (sensual indulgence) or what he calls 'the real season of the madness of youth'. This was the state of mind which produced the most important piece of writing of this period, his essay 'Sarmad Shaheed', about the life of the Sufi saint Shaikh Sarmad. It was the same sense of freedom (with the accompanying sense of the tragic loss) which made him embark on his journey to West Asia right after his father's death. The impact of these years was to shape the entire course of his future.

This journey to Islamic countries was preceded, as stated earlier, by a trip to Iraq which he took at the age of sixteen but it finds no more than a mention in his own writings. It was perhaps too short to have left much of an impression. In *India Wins Freedom* he describes his longer journey to Iraq, Iran, Egypt, Syria and Turkey:

> When I came to Iraq I met some Iranian revolutionaries. In Egypt I came into contact with followers of Mustapha Kamil, and also a group of Turks who had established a centre in Cairo and were publishing a weekly from there. When I went to Turkey I made friends with some of the leaders of the Young Turk movement. I kept up my correspondence with them for many years after I returned to India.[7]

Azad's interest in the Islamic countries was a part of his family background and upbringing, and was augmented by his association with the paper, *Ahsan-ul-Akhbar* whose editor, the indomitable Maulvi Ahmed Husain subscribed to newspapers and journals from all parts of the world of Islam.[8] It is there that he first came across the *Al Hilal* which was published from Egypt, and *Al Manar* which was publishing the writings of the great Islamic scholar Shaikh Mohammad Abduh.[9] Later, he established a reading room (*Darul Akhbar*) in Calcutta which subscribed to newspapers, periodicals and books, largely from the Islamic world.[10]

In Cairo, the followers of Mustapha Kamil were opposed to the *Al Manar* group of Abduh. They believed in pursuing a more intense Egyptian nationalism and uncompromising opposition to the British. Abduh too was a nationalist to the core though not a doctrinaire one. He advocated trying to turn the British presence in Egypt to advantage by educating the Egyptian society. Kamil wanted direct confrontation since he regarded the British as their arch-enemy. In 1907, both men formed their parties, Kamil's Nationalist Party Hizbul Watan and Abduh's People's Party Hizbul Ummah. It was the following year that Azad, then twenty years old, arrived in Cairo. His visit coincided with Kamil's death and its profound impact on the populace. It is natural that at this stage of his life, Azad was drawn not to the thoughtful and guarded aspirations of Abduh's followers but to the vigorous demands of the Kamil enthusiasts whose slogan for the British was 'immediate evacuation without conditions'.[11]

The blueprint for Azad's political strategy was made during this period. He patterned his own doctrine on the Egyptian credo that Egypt's revival would be based on *wataniya* (patriotic spirit). Such patriotism would have no limitations of language, religion or status. It would include all who lived in Egypt, Muslims and Christian-Copts alike so long as their all-consuming passion was eviction of the British. Echoes of this creed were heard throughout Azad's political career which was to evolve later. At this time his revolutionary politics was reflected in the links he had forged with the Bengal revolutionaries who had gathered force following the partition of Bengal in 1903. His links with the militant groups of Bengal like Jugantar and Anushilan, brought him closer to the politics of the Kamilites.

All the Arab and Turk nationalists that he met during his stay in Cairo and Constantinople expressed surprise at the indifference of the Indian Muslims to the nationalist cause. They could not understand how the Muslims allowed the Hindus to handle all issues pertaining to freedom while they were content to be subservient to the British. They felt that Muslims should take a position at the forefront of the struggle and not remain in the shadow of others. The pages of *Al Hilal and Al Balagh*, as will be shown later, resounded with Azad's call to the Indian Muslims, exactly along the lines suggested by nationalist Muslims of the Bilad-e-Islamia (Countries of the Islamic Crescent). This is another evidence of the lasting impact of this journey.

Although he writes that he spent 'a long time' in Egypt, it is unlikely that his entire journey lasted more than a few months. Two references in his letter to his lifelong friend Sherwani, immortalized in *Ghubar-i-Khatir*, further help in locating the time of the visit and the state of his mind. The letter dated 29 September 1940, was written while listening to the radio which happened to play the music of Ahmed Tabrizi which he says he had heard thirty-two years ago in a *bazm-e-uns* (gathering of love and pleasure) in Baghdad. The event was a boating party on the river Tigris:

> I was twenty or twenty-one years old. Every portion of my heart was flushed with the enthusiasm of youth. Whatever I saw was *Jannat* (Paradise) for the eye and *Firdaus* (Paradise) to the ear. A few months sojourn in Iraq now appears no more than a few moments.[12]

He describes the band of musicians who played and sang while they rode the river. The letter is replete with nostalgia for those carefree days. He then recalls meeting Syed Abdur Rahman Naqib, the man in whose father's house his father Maulana Khairuddin stayed during his visit to Baghdad. Naqib showed Azad the precise spot where his father used to sit and write. He also narrated how Khairuddin had sat with Shaikh Alussy, Mufti of Baghdad, and his younger brother Shaikh Nu'man, and criticized the senior Shaikh's book *Tafseer Ruh-ul-Ma'ani*, saying that it smelt of *Aitezaal* and *Wahabiyat*. Naqib introduced Azad to Shaikh Nu'man with the words, 'Do you remember Shaikh Khairuddin-Hindi? This is his son. But I smell in him the same thing that his father objected to in your Shaikh.' These words seemed to have had an electrifying effect. Azad recalls that when he bent low before Shaikh Nu'man to pay his respects, he embraced him with affection and kept repeating, 'We have received this faith from our elders, but you had to find it yourself. This incident is corroborated in the account of the Sufi scholar Louis Massignon who remembered that the first time he met Azad was in 1907–8 in the Mirjan Mosque, Baghdad, 'as pupils of our dear master Hajj Ali Alussy'.[13]

The significance of this record is two-fold. It locates the period of *Lahw-o-La'ab* (indulgence of the senses) and the period of *inkaar* (denial) at around 1907–10. Both conditions prevailed alongside one another during these intervening years. The frame by frame image of Azad sailing with a *taifa* (singing party) on the river Dajla (Tigris) corresponds with the scenes of his sensual pleasures, which are described with great circumspection in *Tazkirah*.

The wise words of Shaikh Nu'man quoted above, 'you have had to find it yourself' testify that by this time he had not only rejected his father's creed but had discovered his own. What was this creed? Luckily for the student of Azad, this creed survives as an essay, a gem of Urdu literature—'Sarmad Shaheed'—which he wrote soon after his return from West Asia. 'Sarmad Shaheed' written just prior to 1910 reveals the state of his mind following his travels. Earlier, in *Lisan-us-Sidq* he had been critical of some aspects of Sufi practice. But the self-righteous reformist zeal which was the driving factor in everything he undertook during that period seemed to have vanished as a consequence of his rejection of Sir Syed's creed and the intensely personal *Ishq-e-Majazi* (profane love) that he experienced. He wrote 'Sarmad Shaheed' at the request of his lifelong friend, the *Pir* of Dargah Nizamuddin, Khwaja Hasan Nizami. What flowed from his pen was entirely different from anything he had written and the end result may have been as much a surprise to the author as it is to the reader.

The question one asks is what did Azad, who saw himself as the *musleh* (reformer), *qaid* (leader), and one who believed in the fundamentals of the faith, find in common with the two men he celebrates in this work, Prince Dara Shikoh, eldest son of Emperor Shahjehan and Shaikh Sarmad, the Sufi saint-poet? One may recall that earlier he had rejected the Sufi rituals of his own household and refused his father's *sajjadah nashini* (successorship). At this juncture of his life, however, he found himself warmly responsive to the creed of love which constitutes the core of Sufism.

In 'Sarmad Shaheed' Azad writes that the story of Sarmad is a prime example of the universal appeal of Islam. Sarmad was born to Jewish-Armenian parents who had settled in Kashan, which at the time was a province of Iran. Originally a student of Christian and Islamic theology, Sarmad studied under the guidance of Mullah Sadra of Shiraz. His Islamic name was Saeed. He entered India to trade Iranian merchandise for Indian spices and gems. But he had not got farther than Thatta, the port of

Sindh, when he fell in love with a Hindu boy, Abhaichand; to quote this very incident from *Miratul Khayal*, an account of the times written in Persian by the contemporary historian Sher Khan Lodhi, '*Dar asna-e-tijarat ba shehr-e-Thatta. Bar Hindu pisar-e-ashiq gasht.*'

Temporal love was the first *maqam* (stage) from which he would move to higher stations. Azad expounds the Sufi philosophy of the journey of the novice which elevates him to higher stations until he is one with the Divine Beloved. Taking it one step further, he describes the Sufi concept of the lifting, one by one, of the veils (*hijab*), until there is nothing left between the lover and the Beloved. He then wonders about the need to remove the *hijab*? 'Why wait for the unveiling? Isn't the beauty of the veil sufficient?' The inference here is that the first stage of temporal love is considered enough to transport the novice to a state of ecstasy. This argument is validated by a reference in the Koran about the prophets, Hazrat Yaqub and Hazrat Yusuf:

> The blind prophet Yaqub's eyes did not need Yusuf to appear before their sightless orbs to regain their light. His vision was restored the moment the perfume from Yusuf s garment wafted towards his nose. The Koran says:
> 'I do indeed scent the presence of Yusuf
> Nay, think me not a dotard.'
> (12:94)

meaning that the slightest hint of the beloved's presence is enough for the true lover.

Sarmad reached the inner circle of Prince Dara Shikoh and remained there in the company of Saints, Sadhus, monks and priests. Emperor Shahjehan's illness and the imminent succession of Dara Shikoh had brought his younger son, Aurangzeb's, designs in stark daylight. Dara had to flee from the court but Sarmad remained behind to face his destiny. Aurangzeb, wary of the growing popularity of the *Pir*, needed an excuse to get rid of Sarmad; so he turned to the ulema for help. Using 'the pen' as an elaborate literary conceit, which serves as a sword as

well, Azad describes the fatwa (verdict) of the ulema as their most
lethal weapon which is always in the service of the state, ready to
descend upon those who dare to pronounce the truth:

> During the 1300 years, since the advent of Islam, the instrument of
> *fatwa* has been a sword without a sheath. The blood of thousands
> of believers in truth is testimony to its cutting edge… Sarmad was
> executed by the same sword.

The mullahs' pens wrote *kufr* against Sarmad's name for three
acts of sacrilege. First, for remaining naked; second, for disputing
their interpretation of *meraj*;[14] third, for refusing to recite the full
first half of the Confession of Faith, *kalima-e-taiyyaba* (*La ilaha
illa'Llah*, 'There is no god but God') always stopping at the first
word '*la*' (no). Thus while the custodians of the Shariah (Islamic
practice) and *fiqah* (Islamic Law) indulged in sophistries and
produced evidence from their lengthy tomes, Azad wrote, they
failed to understand that Sarmad's state was elevated in the eyes
of Allah, far beyond all this.

> These 'god-men' of worldly ways did not realize that Sarmad was
> far above their pedantic discussions of *kufr* and faith. Self-impressed
> with their *fatwas* of execution, they climbed on the pulpits of their
> mosques and *Madrasas* and dreamt about the heights to which they
> could still rise. But Sarmad had reached the pinnacle of love from
> where the walls of the mosque and the temple are seen standing
> face to face.

Azad saw Sarmad as the symbol of *Sidq-o-Wafa* (truth and
love) because he chose the executioner's sword rather than surrender to the mullahs. He ranked Dara Shikoh with Sarmad
because of his capacity to rise above the narrow dogma of state-
oriented religion towards an appreciation of the universal truth
in all faiths. In both prince and saint, Azad saw a reflection of
what he himself wanted to achieve. Azad describes Dara as a
dervish, one who kept company with the philosophers and Sufis.
He was the author of books like *Majma-al-Bahrayn* (Merging
of the Two Oceans) about Islam and Hinduism, *Sirr-i-Akbar*, a

translation into Persian of the Upanishads, and of the Bhagwad Geeta. He compared Hinduism with Islam and boldly proclaimed the similarities that he saw. In every page of the Upanishads he found evidence to support his own belief that this was the 'concealed book' mentioned in the Koran. He was Azad's ideal prince and upholder of the best traditions of Islam.

Azad writes that the pens which wrote the history of the Mughal period were always held by Dara Shikoh's enemies. Therefore, in writing this essay he has very little to go on, but he has reached the following conclusion:

> In pursuing his goal, he (Dara) lost distinction between the temple and the mosque. The humility with which he met the Muslim divines was matched by the devotion with which he bowed his head before the Hindu Sadhus and Saints. Who can deny the purity of this principle? Because in this exalted state of mind, if one can still distinguish between *kufr* and Islam, then what is the difference between blindness and vision? The moth should seek the flame. If it is desirous of the lamp which is lit only in the mosque, its desire for self-immolation is not complete.
> A true lover of God is misled
> Both by religion and lack thereof
> A moth does not choose
> Between the burning candle
> Whether it burns in the mosque or the temple.

In the last chapter of his autobiographical piece, *Tazkirah* Azad recounts the events of his twenty-first and twenty-second year with unusual candour. The events, however, are hidden in poetic language which is regarded in Urdu circles as the perfect rendering of poetic-prose. To those familiar with the literary conventions of the time, the story of his youthful vagaries is clearly visible beneath the intricacies of style. He writes that when he opened his eyes, adolescence had already dawned,

> When I looked at myself, I saw a heart filled with quicksilver instead of blood.[15]

Life was brimming with excitement, 'as if the illusory morning would have no midday sun to dispel it and no shadows of failure or despondency would mark its evening.' Love laid its net of pleasure to ensnare him and he became hopelessly entangled,

> Each temptation shot its arrow, every thief of the senses flung his noose, every enchanter threw his spell of love, each breathtaking vision sought to captivate me entirely to put its own halter of fascination around my neck.

It was then that he fell in love, which he defines as 'love in the narrow, impure, physical sense, not the absolute love which embraces all creation.' He does not doubt that this love was a lapse, 'but what shall we say of the love which casts us at the feet of the Beloved?' So long as one reaches Him what does it matter if lapses and intoxication lead us there?

> All at once the grace of God appeared in the form of profane love, and the meandering paths of pleasure brought me, on their own, to the highway of Love.

Drawing from the Sufi philosophy of the various stages (*maqam*) in the journey to Allah, he says that nearness to the One can be attained only at the cost of parting with all. When all other doors close, only then does the one door open. 'Sacred and profane love have this in common: they attach to one and detach from the rest... That is why the nearest way to sacred love is through profane love.' Thus locating his argument in the Sufi tradition, he says that the counting of beads (*tasbih*) or wearing the patchwork cloak (*khirqa*) is only the halfway house at which one must not tarry long. His 'half-way period' lasted only one year and five months.[16] The fact that his love affair ended in tragedy is seen by him as a defeat in which is hidden the 'joy of victory'.

> The miracle of Allah's mercy was beckoning me for a long time, but my heart was unheeding... Unrequited love struck the last blow at my illusions and all of a sudden my eyes were opened. What I saw

was the breath-taking vision of another world... The world's tavern of oblivion in which the wine of heedlessness had been poured into me, whose visions tempted my eyes, whose melodies charmed my ears—that same world so transformed itself that every little bit of it was a picture of sobriety and wisdom, a lesson for the seeing eye and the knowing mind.

With gentle firmness he then states that in his journey towards faith he has travelled all alone, always setting high standards for himself:

In whatever condition I lived I was always repelled by imperfection and incompetence. I always refrained from treading the path of others... I charted my own course and left my footprints for others to follow.

He has no regrets for the particular path which brought him to the desired goal. He says that he has lived life to the hilt; in a mood of gay abandon he 'drained the cup of pleasure', in this flush of love there was no 'vale of tears' he did not traverse. But if the man of piety can be proud that he has never known anything but the straight path, he affirms that he is equally proud that he squeezed out all that could be drained from life, without leaving behind a single drop.

If there are any who have raced along a straight path, I would call them fortunate, but I do not consider it a misfortune that ... I had to destroy with my own hands the lengthy chronicle of my impulses, my longings, my hopes and my yearnings in order to find rest and peace in the place where I now am.

He says that the easiest path open to him would have been to seek a teacher (*sahib-i-Irshad*) but he did not wish to follow any prescribed path. In fact there is nothing in his beliefs, actions, habits, inclinations, ideas, views and ways which he can 'correlate with (his) natural surroundings'. Whatever he has received has been granted only at the *baargaah* (altar) of *Ishq* (Love). *Ishq* has taught him the profundities of the Shariah, guided him in *Tariqah*

(Sufi path), revealed to him the secrets of the Koran, initiated him in the mysteries of the Sunnah. 'What problems did it not solve, what tangles did it not unravel, what ailment of the head and heart did it not cure.'

Tazkirah is the personal experience of which 'Sarmad Shaheed' is the archetype. When Azad's sympathetic and sensitive approach to the whole episode is studied in tandem with *Tazkirah*, it becomes clear that he has identified himself with Sarmad. He is one with all Sufi poets who have sung of the collapse of theological piety in the face of true love, which they have celebrated as the call to divine love. He sees himself on the one hand as a Mansur Hallaj (the Sufi saint who had spoken the words *An-al-Haq* 'I am Truth') or Sarmad and on the other hand as a Dara; always prepared to ascend the scaffold or place his neck beneath the executioner's sword rather than suffer himself to compromise.

Writing about his state of mind the year after he wrote 'Sarmad' and the year before he started *Al Hilal* he says that at this juncture, he finally got a clear sense of direction. After meandering through a maze of doubt and despair he had arrived at the basic faith contained in the Koran and Sunnah. This was not a simple matter of rejection of one and acceptance of another. 'In Azad conflicting elements were allowed to coexist without any attempt to integrate or reconcile them in a systematic conceptual whole.'[17]

He writes about his future directions in a lengthy article, 'Masla-e-Khilafat wa Jaziratul Arab'. He declares that he would now carefully work towards his goal, and, while entrusting himself in the hands of Allah he would not fritter away his energies. The emphasis he places here on not accepting any worldly offices suggests a distancing from all the organizations he was associated with and about which he had shown such enthusiasm in earlier days:

> In 1911, when my present public life had just begun, I got an opportunity to outline a course of action for the future. There were different courses open to me for the service of *mulk-o-millat* (my

country and people). I wanted my journey to be like that of the wise traveller who had thought about all the problems before embarking on his travels. I did not want to be like the storm-tossed ship which had abandoned itself to the mercy of the winds and waves. One of the basic decisions I had made was to detach myself from presiding over *Majlises* and accepting official positions at *Anjumans;* to eschew such elitism forever.

This decision was the consequence of my basic religious faith. My chosen path was that of *Dawat-o-Tabligh* (invitation to faith and teaching), not of the expedient leadership of today. Before me were examples of those members of the human community who had been called *Rasul* and *Paighamber,* and whose practice has been called in Islam, *Hikmat* and *Sunnat.* I was anxious to place my searching hand in the hand of Prophet Ibrahim and Prophet Muhammad (PBUH) I had no desire to become another Garibaldi, Mazzini, Gladstone or Parnell. I was prepared for the possibility that my existence should become an uninteresting frieze, in an unknown corner of the world, depicting service and toil or even an unheeded voice in a crowd. But it was impossible to see myself as a president or office-bearer of these twentieth century *Majlises* or *Anjumans* which had forgotten the *mazhab* (religion) and the *ahd-e-naboovat* (age of the Prophet). One single life cannot combine the technique of *khidmat-o-da'wat* (service and invitation to faith) of God's prophets with the technique of *riyast-o-hukumat* (power and governance) of men's leaders.[18]

notes

1 Azad translated into Urdu this book by Farid Wajdi Afandi. The author describes the position of women in modern Egypt.

2 In a letter to Azad, Sherwani nostalgically remembered the times. *Karvan-e-Khayal,* pp. 82–3.

3 *Kahani,* p. 156. 'Our trip was against his wishes, but when he saw our keenness he kept quiet'.

4 This is how the event is recorded in *Kahani.* The time sequence is differently recorded in *India Wins Freedom* where he says that he rushed to his father's bedside, cutting short his trip to West Asia. The account given in *Kahani* is more credible due to other circumstantial evidence. See Douglas and Bedar for further details.

5 See *Kahani*, p. 383. When Khairuddin expressed concern at Azad's 'radicalism' he told his father not to worry about him because he had a son who had all the qualities necessary for the natural successor to the *Piri-Muridi* tradition.

6 Douglas, p. 88.

7 *India Wins Freedom*, p. 7.

8 *Kahani*, pp. 272–3. For an account of Ahmed Husain's adventures in Calcutta and their impact on Azad, see *Kahani.*

9 Azad writes that these writings had a profound influence on his style. *Kahani*, p. 273.

10 *Ibid.*, p. 294.

11 See Douglas for this overview of the political conditions prevailing in Egypt, pp. 83–6.

12 *Karvan-e-Khayal* ed. Mohammad Abdul Shahid Khan Sherwani, Aligarh 1946. This is a collection of Azad's and Habib-ur-Rahman Khan Sherwani's correspondence.

13 See Louis Massignon's article in the Commemoration Volume, ed. Humayun Kabir.

14 Prophet Mohammad's (PBUH) ascent to Heaven, where he saw the vision of Allah.

15 '*Tazkirah:* A Biography in Symbols', by Mohammad Mujeeb in the Commemoration Volume contains the translation of a part of the last chapter.

16 One wonders how he calculated the time with such precision.

17 Syed Vahiduddin, 'Religious Philosophy', in *India's Maulana*, ed. Syeda Saiyidain Hameed.

18 Introduction to 'Masla'a-e-Khilafat-wa-Jaziratul Arab', quoted by Abid Raza Bedar, p. 75.

rise of the crescent: *al hilal*

WHILE HE WAS EDITING *Vakil,* Azad realized the importance of having a journal of his own. In *Kahani* he says that during this period he came to the conclusion that the objectives that he had defined for himself could not be fulfilled unless he could, with careful preparation, launch his own newspaper. On 13 July 1912, the first issue of *Al Hilal* (literal meaning, The Crescent) appeared in Calcutta, a royal size, twenty-four page, two column paper, subtitled *Ek Haftawar Mussawir Risala* (A weekly, illustrated newspaper). This opened a new chapter in Urdu journalism in which a political weekly was presented in an artistic format. Although the tradition of typesetting was not new to Urdu journalism, *Al Hilal* used a highly refined type, due to the editor's special interest in the method. The photographs added to its appeal. Starting with a circulation of 2000, it reached 26 000 at the time of its closure, surpassing all other Urdu weeklies in the country.

There was much excitement built up from 1910 onwards for the appearance of Azad's journal.[1] Several names were being suggested for it by friends and patrons including Maulana

Shibli Nu'mani, who fondly suggested 'Azad'. The name finally selected was inspired by the Arabic journal *Al Hilal* published from Egypt by Harji Zaidan which was also the model upon which Azad's paper was patterned. Illustrated journals in type were not uncommon in Egypt. The mark of Arabic literature and journalism had been left on Azad by his early life in Mecca, his upbringing in a primarily Arabic speaking household and his stay at Nadwa. The other impact was created by Azad's two journeys to Islamic countries. During the second trip he had met Arab and Turk revolutionaries and visited Iraq, Egypt, Syria, Turkey and France. Some of these contacts and friendships were to last a lifetime. This journey was undertaken almost four years before the appearance of *Al Hilal*. The Young Turks, followers of Mustafa Kamal, the Iranian Revolutionaries, all expressed the view that Indian Muslims should lead the national struggle for independence instead of remaining 'camp-followers of the British'.[2] That advice further strengthened his desire to build political consciousness among the Muslims. From past experience he knew that the best vehicle for it would be a political journal of very high calibre, outstripping all existing journals in the excellence of its form and content.

Al Hilal's appeal to the Muslims of Calcutta was instant. The combination of style and subject-matter was electrifying. Erudition combined with clarity of thought and mastery of language made a formidable combination for an age that loved rhetoric. Frequent quotations from the Koran to establish the Islamic basis of the subject-matter created a religious fervour in the reader. His initial circle of readership probably included the *murids* of his father, who had always valued the word of their young *Pirzada* (son of the teacher). Although he had refused to don the *khirqa* (cloak) and sit on the *sajjadah* (mat) of their *Pir*, Maulana Khairuddin, many of them could recall the child prodigy, the young 'Hazrat' (reverend) who, at the age of nine or ten, used to hold them in thrall by the amazing discourses he gave in the meeting chamber of his father's house.

Al Hilal's most popular contemporary Urdu journals were Zafar Ali Khan's *Zamindar*, Wahiduddin Salim's *Muslim Gazette*, Hakim Mahboob Alam's *Paisa Akhbar*, Hakim Brahm's *Mashriq*, Ganga Prasad Verma's *Hindustani*, and Mohammad Ali's *Hamdard*. *Zamindar* was the senior paper and a daily. Azad regarded the forfeiture of its deposit on the charge of printing what the government considered seditious literature, a deplorable act and he wrote passionate articles in its condemnation.[3] Although *Zamindar* was the older paper, it did not have the high standard of journalism achieved by *Al Hilal*. Mohammad Ali, the editor of *Hamdard* was Azad's senior in journalism, but his paper too ran second to *Al Hilal*. The reason was that it had appeared later and was a daily newspaper, while *Al Hilal* had the advantage of being a weekly, and of having an excellent editorial staff.[4]

During those times, most of the Muslim press was imbued with the spirit of Pan Islamism, a trend which had appeared as early as 1870.[5] That was around the time that one of the distinguished figures of contemporary Islam, Syed Jamaluddin Afghani first came to India. In 1882, thirty years before the appearance of *Al Hilal* he visited Calcutta, little knowing that a young man from the holy city of the Prophet's birth, was to settle in this very city and become his most illustrious torch-bearer. Two years later, in collaboration with his pupil and close associate, the Egyptian scholar Mohammad Abduh, he started *Al Urwatul Wusqa*, a revolutionary Arabic journal which is considered by some as the herald of Pan Islamism.[6] Azad's reverence for Jamaluddin is reflected in the glowing tributes to him in several writings. No other name occurs with such frequency as that of Afghani in the pages of early *Al Hilal*. Events such as the 1908 constitutional revolution in Turkey, the Balkan war, the war of Tripoli revived the spirit of Pan Islamism in India. On this issue, Azad took his lessons from Jamaluddin Afghani.

In *Al Urwatul Wusqa*, Jamaluddin had projected Iran, Turkey, Egypt, Sudan and India as a single Islamic unit crushed under the colonial heel. He urged these constituents to collectively rise from under its oppression. Similarly, in *Al Hilal* Azad projects the entire Islamic world as a single unit, the centre of which is Turkey, the *Khilafat-e-Uzma* (Great Caliphate). Abid Raza Bedar draws attention to the similarities in the styles of Azad and Afghani, particularly what he calls the linguistic 'exasperation' with which they shake the slumbering *quom* to an awareness of its abject condition and its responsibility for it. The other similarity of their style is frequent quotation of Koranic *Ayat* which they weave into the text as its integral part.[7]

The first appearance of *Al Hilal* lived up to the expectations which had been built among the young and old alike, such as is evident from these lines of the poet Akbar Allahabadi:

Farogh-e-Haq ko na hoga zawaal duniya mein
Hamesha badr baney ga Hilal duniya mein

(Proclamation of Truth will never decline in this world. The crescent will always become the full moon in this world)

Al Hilal's appearance was duly noted by the government. In his weekly report dated 24 September 1912, submitted to the Secretary, Home Affairs, the Director of Criminal Intelligence wrote:

In Calcutta, the newspaper *Al Hilal* replaced the *Comrade* as the leading Pan Islamist organ. It contained on September 8 an article in which passages from the Koran were quoted to show that no government which was not democratic in form, could be acceptable to the followers of Muhammad.

The epigraph placed at the top of the first issue was a line from the Koran, *La tehnu wa la tehzinu wa antumul alon in kuntum mominin*, meaning 'Do not be disheartened, do not lose courage, do not be sad; you will be victorious if you are a *momin'*. The name of the editor was given as Ahmed Al-Makani Bab-al Kalam Dehlavi (Ahmad from Mecca, the portal to *Kalam* with abode at Delhi). The first issue consisted of the editorial, the *aitezar* (an explanatory editorial), a major article on Rashid Raza, and several other pieces.

Azad admired Rashid Raza who was the pupil of Mohammad Abduh and had inherited the reformist zeal of his master. For the first issue of *Al Hilal*, he chose the topic of Raza for a good reason. The article 'Al Muslahul Azeem Wal Murshidul Hakeem Syed Rashid Raza' (The Great Reformer and the Wise Guide, Syed Rashid Raza) is an account of his visit to India and his Islamic mission. It is used by Azad to highlight the abject state of the Indian Muslims:

> Indian soil has been from the beginning, the playground for strangers and travellers... Considering the royalty and nobility which has thronged to these alluring shores, what attention can a dervish-traveller receive? What had Rashid Raza come for in this land of gilded and jewelled *mandirs*?
>
> Perhaps Rashid Raza was the first traveller who had come not to plunder the spring-horn of plenty, but to offer his lamentations at the autumnal desolation of this land. He wandered across the country, but unlike Beruni, hot in search of knowledge and the arts because the Muslims' tradition of love for knowledge lay buried under the dust of history. Unlike Ibn-e-Batuta, he did not witness Islamic grandeur and power, because in place of chambers of valour and virtue are now the nests of crows and vultures.[8]
>
> Rashid Raza came forth and went back. There are probably very few who found out about his visit. But if we cannot see the light of the sun, the fault lies in our vision. Unfortunately, the Indian Muslims are cut off from the Islamic world. Arabic, which was once the language of the *quom* and performed the function of Esperanto for the Islamic world, is no longer a living language. The day is not far when Allah and the Koran will be pronounced in accents dictated by British lexicons.

The opinions expressed in the above passages and other parts of the Rashid Raza article were to develop into major points of debate and discourse in the later issues of *Al Hilal*. First, there is a valorization of men who remain committed, to freedom, e.g. Rashid Raza, Turkish soldiers on the battlefield of Tripoli, Mujahideen in the Balkan wars; second, there is a dirge for the Indian Muslims; and third, a tirade against the ulema, whether at

Al Azhar or at home who serve the state and themselves instead of serving the *Ummah*.

First, valorization of men who had surrendered their lives to Allah (*fi sabil-illah*). Every issue of *Al Hilal* contained eulogies for the martyrs and heroes of Tripoli and accounts of the battlefield at which the Turks valiantly defended their territories against European aggression. Photographs of the leaders appeared in all the issues, interspersed with shots of the battlefield, Turkish soldiers, war camps and scenes of religious persecution. Weekly reports of war, including letters from the field, correspondents' reports, messages, all projected the Islamic world as one entity, centred around the Osmanli Khilafat, fighting a common enemy.

Second, the dirge. Rashid Raza, Azad writes, arrived in India, 'his heart filled with pain and his eyes with tears', at the decline of the Muslims. In the depiction of Raza's despair, Azad reflects his own desperation which is expressed in article after article of *Al Hilal*. The image of Rashid Raza's intense sorrow at the scenes of the emasculation of Muslims slips easily over Azad. He uses different stylistic devices to express his anger and disappointment. Sometimes he feigns indifference:

> For a while, we too have dissociated ourselves from the Muslims. When the government inflicts a new punishment on them, we say in the words of Ghalib, 'Good! Another shoe has been hurled'.[9]

At other times he speaks words of harsh reproof to the errant race, such as this from the article 'Al Jehad fi Sabil Al Hurriyat' (Islamic crusade for the sake of Independence).

> The future historian who will record the chronology of events, will write that ultimately whatever had to happen, happened. In the 20th century, no country could remain in bondage and none remained. The British government was a constitutional entity, not the autocratic rule of Genghis Khan. Therefore it did what was expected of it, and India became free. But the world will always remember that this turn of events owed nothing to the Muslims; whatever happened rebounded to the credit of every other community except the Muslims. The Muslims preferred slavery to freedom, grovelling in

the dust to dignity; Muslims have no share in building this memorial. If amendments were made in the country's laws, if beneficial legislation was introduced, if people were rid of ruinous taxation, if compulsory education was introduced, military expenses were reduced and, lastly, if the country became self governing, it was due only to the Hindus, respectable Hindus, who set an example before the Muslims by starting the political agitation and continuing it. As for the Muslims, they regarded it a sin and remained aloof. And when they tried to start something, Iblis (Satan) exhorted them to prostrate themselves before the government, and, with tear filled eyes, beg for alms. Beg not for a guinea or jewels, but for a rusted copper coin, or a rotten crust of bread.[10]

Third, the question of the state-sponsored ulema. In the very first issue of *Al Hilal*, using Al Azhar as an example, Azad states his views about the so-called custodians of religion:

It is a strange phenomenon that the very same priests, who at the birth of a new faith are agents of uplift and reform, become the instruments of vice and depravity, once the movement has peaked. Rarely has any group caused as much harm to a religion as its own perpetrators and servants. This unscrupulous and dogmatic pack has been a curse of Allah for an orderly, principled and peaceful human race. Since the beginning, the history of Islam has been infested by the superstition and communalism of this group. Whenever the call for truth has been given, the devil has used the ulemas as his agents. Islam's great achievement was to rid the world of the domination of this gang... But much to the world's surprise, in a very short while, Islam played right back into their hands and, today, its controls are firmly held in the dark grasp of their soiled hands.

The first issue of *Al Hilal* also contained articles and despatches on 'Heroes of Tripoli', 'Abdul Qadir Al Jezairi', 'Usmani Mujahid Javed Bak', 'Battleground at Tripoli', 'Letters from Egypt', 'Message of Tripoli', 'Letter from the War by M. Kolyra', 'Shaikh Ahmed Al Sanusi', and other correspondence related to the war. On the front cover was an impressive photograph of Mohammad Rashid Raza, *Alim* (scholar) and *Mujtahid* (one who gives new interpretation), which was reproduced inside the journal along with photographs of Syed Jamaluddin Afghani and Shaikh Mohammad Abduh. Other photographs included ones of Shaikh Sulaiman Haruni with a group of Arab Mujahideen, Javed Bak, a Turkish freedom fighter and an Usmani camp at Azizia. These visual representations of the heroes of Islam were aimed at revitalizing the *quom*. The first three were highly respected individuals with an enduring influence on the entire region of Islam.

Azad admired the reformist spirit of the triumvirate Afghani-Abduh and Raza who preached a return to the original faith, free from the oppressive influence of the Mullahs. Afghani's propagation of Pan-Islamic unity was seen by Azad as the viable solution to twentieth Century Islam under colonial oppression. Abduh, the Mufti of Egypt, had earned Azad's admiration for his effort, albeit futile, to reform the Al Azhar university in Cairo. As an alternative to Al Azhar, Abduh had started another institution, Dar-ul-Uloom. 'He feared not the European suit nor hat', Azad wrote in *Al Hilal*, 'but the twists of the turbans of the ulema'. The greatest proof of Abduh's enlightened mind, according to Azad was that he was opposed by the orthodox *jama'at* of Egypt. He quotes a statement made by the *jama'at* of Arabi Pasha that Abduh's head was more suitable for the European hat than for the ulemas' *a'mama* (religious leader's headgear).

Al Hilal contains Azad's invitation (*Da'wat*) to the Indian Muslims to join the mainstream of life through the trajectory of religion. The article '*Al Hilal* ke maqasid aur political taleem' (Objectives of *Al Hilal* and political education), which appeared on 8 September 1912 is an elaboration of this concept. It was written in response to a letter from a subscriber which stated that in the seven issues published so far, the editor had advised that *mazhab* (religion) and Koran are a panacea for all ailments of the Muslims so long as what they practise is the *original* pristine Islam. Then what about politics? Should religion be kept separate from politics? And if so then what path should the Muslims follow?

Azad uses this opportunity to define the objectives of *Al Hilal*. First he categorically states that his prescription for the community has one, single, unalterable premise:

> We view every branch of human activity from the perspective of religion. If we take any guidance, it is from the Holy Quran; except that one fact we know nothing. Our eyes are closed to the rest of the world, and our ears are deaf to all other sounds. If light were needed, believe me, we have the one and only light bestowed upon us by the *Siraj-e-Munir* (Source of Light). Remove it and we shall be struck blind.[11]

Addressing the reader's question, he then states that religion cannot be separated from politics; Muslims have learnt their politics from religion. Their politics has in fact been an outgrowth of religion. They believe that a concept derived from any source other than religion is *Kufr* (sacrilege), and that includes politics. The greatest tragedy is that present day Muslims, have never seen Islam at its zenith, otherwise they would not need to kneel at the door of the government, nor look towards the Hindus for their political direction. Islam brought to the world the most comprehensive and perfect system for mankind. There is not a single sphere of human activity for which it does not provide guidance. It does not tolerate that anyone who has knelt before it should knock at any other door. Whether it is the ethical, educational, political, economic, religious or temporal life of Muslims, whether it is the life of the ruler or of the ruled, it provides the most perfect system for all. The Koran states:

> From Allah you have received light and a Book which narrates all. Through it Allah instructs you about the ways of *salamati* (peace). Whoever seeks His consent, He brings him from the darkness of instability and places him on the path of *Siratal Mustaqeem*.

The key concepts in the opening passage of this article are 'total dependence on the Koran,' and 'looking at the entire world through the Koran'. Instead of viewing these concepts in the commonly understood sense that there is no truth other than what is contained in the Koran, it will be more in keeping with Azad's growing understanding of Islam if we view them in his light. Azad infers that having closed our eyes to the limitedness of the world, we have opened ourselves to the limitless *Siraj-e-Munir* or source of all knowledge; meaning that while the world is restrictive, the Word of the Koran is boundless.

When the Muslims had the complete code of instruction, he asks in the same article, what caused their *zawaal* (downfall)? The Koran, he emphasizes again and again, is nothing new. It reiterates and verifies the truths that existed before its revelation. It is the *Kaamil Muallim* (perfect teacher) and *quol-e-faisal* (final word) and in all matters its instruction is clear. Therefore, Azad maintains that all miseries of the Muslims are due to their negligence and to their having turned away from this divine source of guidance, except in matters pertaining to *roza* (fasting) and *namaz* (prayer). They do not recognize its relevance to all other aspects of life such as education, culture and politics. The further the Muslims have moved from the essence of the Koran, the faster has the world slipped away from them. Whichever alternative route they took, they ran into blind alleys of missed directions.

Deploring their reduced state, he compares the Muslims to *mushrikeen-i-Makka* (the Quraish who believed in more than one God) whose defiance and vanity was no less. The Quraish of Makka were known to have thrust their fingers into their ears and clapped their hands so that the *quir'at* (recitation) of the Koran would be drowned. This classic image of *kufr* or disbelief is superimposed on the present day Muslims, who have closed their hearts instead of their ears, are silent instead of creating a cacophony, but their souls are emitting the mayhem of their muddle and confusion.

On the question of which path to follow, the three options are: maintain the status quo, follow the moderate Hindus, or close ranks with the anarchist Hindus. Rejecting all three, Azad suggests *Siratal Mustaqeem*, as advocated by the Koran, the well trodden path of prophets Noah, Abraham, Ismael, Joseph, Moses,

Jesus and finally, Prophet Muhammad (PBUH). Six principles on which the Indian Muslims should base their politics are then outlined.

1. *Tawhid* (Oneness of Allah) Belief in Allah and only Allah, as prescribed in Surah 112 of the Koran—*Qui ho w-Allah hu Ahad.*
2. *Ummeed* (Hope) As the recipient of Prophethood and Khilafat, a Muslim is twice blessed; he should expunge his mind of hopelessness.
3. *Aitedaal* (Moderation) The Koran has declared the Muslims a force of justice. They should act with restraint and moderation.
4. *Aman* (Peace) Muslims should raise their swords for peace; if *fitna* is merely forbidden to others, for the Muslims it is regarded a sin.
5. *Amr bi'l Maruf wa nahy an il Mun-kar* (Enjoin the good and forbid the evil). This is their responsibility to Allah.
6. *Jama'at* (Community) The Koran is opposed to the concept of individual power. Its judgement is *mukhfi* (hidden) in the will of the *millat* or *jama'at*. The Koranic injunction is *Yad Allah il al jama'at* meaning, the hand of Allah is placed on the *jama'at*. The only J government sanctioned in the Koran is that of the *quoni* or *millat*. Hence the Koran enjoins *mashwara* or *shura* (consultation).

The above principles are tagged with the advice that *Muslims should strive for legitimate freedom,* and until they form a representative government, they should, in accordance with Islam, continue to struggle. If Muslims base their politics on these six principles, he writes, fearlessness would be written on their faces. The Koran is clear in its injunction, *La tufsadu fi'l arz ba'ad aslaha,* meaning, 'Do not spread *fasad* (unrest) after the earth has been made peaceful' (7:56). Therefore, while stating that it is unIslamic to create *fasad* where peace prevails, he advises distance from the anarchists. But at the same time, freedom is the basis of Islam, and whenever it is curtailed different principles apply. Normally the hand that holds the Koran cannot be used to pull the trigger or hurl the bomb. But the fact is that Islam has taught two lessons, giving freedom and getting freedom. As rulers, Muslims are known to have given freedom to the ruled, as the ruled they demand the same. If that is denied different rules apply. It is the will of Allah that people should have freedom for self-rule. This is the political path of Islam:

> With this political path ... before us, we will be a powerful group, fearless and uninhibited in declaring the truth, because we would fear none but Allah... We may get aroused but our passion and agitation would stay within the limits of good behaviour. So far, our leaders have tried to keep us silent and ignorant; allowed our sores to bleed internally, concealed our embers beneath a pile of ashes. On the new political path, however, our lacerations will not be concealed inside our hearts, instead they would be displayed on our faces.[12]

Al Hilal wrote about the burning issues as they affected the *quom*. Apart from topical issues, there were ongoing matters such as relationship with the Hindus and the question of leadership. Azad spoke his mind without mincing words, and his basic position on both subjects remained substantially unchanged throughout his life. As early as 1912, he started allaying the Muslim fear about being a minority by stating that numerical superiority should not be allowed to become an issue; they should remember that in Mecca they were a small and weak *Jama'at*, but armed with the power of truth, they became the world's most potent force. He said that the Muslims should join with the Hindus to launch a common initiative. With the Hindus already in the thick of the struggle for independence, Muslims should no longer permit themselves to watch from a distance. Freedom is enjoined upon them by Islam. No longer in the national and international forums should freedom for India be discussed as a

'Hindu problem'. This message was hammered into the minds of the readers of *Al Hilal* by using several voices, from mild rebuke, to paternal admonition, to a Swiftian rage; the latter is reflected in articles like 'Al Jehad fi Sabil al Hurriyat':

> The Hindus rose in revolt and dedicated all their energies to the crusade against oppression. Precisely at that time, the Muslims not only broke their own hands but set out to cripple anyone who was possessed of sound limbs. At the time when the Hindus were lighting the torch of the country's independence, Muslims were contentedly sitting around the corpse of education. Someone had uttered the magic words 'time has not come' and they were completely taken in. A genie from the Arabian Nights had, by his magic incantations, turned them into immobile masses of rock.[13]

He asks the Muslims to stop allowing the British to use them as 'sacrificial lambs'. When the British were looking for a set of puppets, 'the ideal dupe presented itself before them in the form of a community which, dissociating itself from the rest of the country, was prepared to toe their line'.

> This community irrigated the plant of British imperialism with the blood of its hopes and aspirations. By placing themselves on the sacrificial slab, the Muslims took upon themselves the burden which all other communities had declined to bear.[14]

And what constituted the leadership of this herd? Referring to the leadership of Sir Syed and later of the Muslim League, he describes them as 'old high priests' leading a herd of pitiable and bewitched people who were transformed into animals by their magic. 'They were led by the nose by their masters, who made them dance to their tunes'. Their (Muslims) fatal error was to empower those who were themselves bound in a thousand chains, and imposed the same bondage on their followers. Their advice to their flock was to beg the government for maximum concessions. Diverting the *quom* towards a secondary issue like education was their ploy to divert it from the primary issue, which was then dismissed as 'someone else's business':

'You have not yet made progress in education', they explain to their circus animals, 'therefore, you must acquire education and recover your share from the Hindus.'

The strength that should have been pitted against the 'government was thereby used against the Hindus.

Summarizing the present Muslim politics in an article about Aligarh entitled 'Muslim University' published in the 1 September 1912 issue, Azad writes that the prevailing conditions which threw up leaders among the Hindus, existed equally for the Muslims, had there been in them any ingredient for real leadership. 'But our so-called leaders always threw a toy in our lap, which diverted us to the extent that we never found time for the real work. First we spent forty years pursuing "higher education" and when that wore off and we became restless, they created the fantasy of the Muslim League.'[15]

Crusade for independence, Azad wrote, is a Jehad for Allah. His *da'wat* (invitation) to engage in this Jehad was open to all the Muslims. Every effort for truth and justice was Jehad, every attempt to break the shackles of oppression and bondage was Jehad. Therefore he asked his fellow Muslims, 'Awake because Allah wants you to rise. It is His will that Muslims, wheresoever they are should rededicate themselves to the duty of this Jehad'.

Secret reports about Azad were prepared by the Intelligence Department and sent every fortnight to the Home Office. An article such as 'Boycott' written in the 10 January 1913 issue, was highly offensive to the government. It displays with impunity Azad's hatred for the government. Its popularity is attested by the fact that it was published as a separate booklet and was in its fourth edition in 1921.[16] The publisher's prefatory note states:

The ability to foresee the future is essential for a reformer, a *quaid-e-azam*, a *musleh*. This quality is present in Hazrat Maulana Sahib. Addressing the future he writes, 'Today if our present *ghaflat* (oblivion) and empty lamentations continue, then that day is not far when their canons will open fire at the last bastion of our pride—the Mausoleum of the Prophet and the sacred House of Ibrahim. And on the ports of Jaddah and Yanboh their iron-clad dreadnoughts will be seen anchored'. We have seen with our own eyes that whatever he had predicted has come to pass.

The essay begins with a quotation from the Koran forbidding the Muslims to befriend those Jews and Christians who are ranged against Islam. The opening lines of the first paragraph have become famous examples of Azad's hortatory prose, which is almost untranslatable but needs to be sampled in both languages:

Mein woh sur kahan se laoon jiski awaaz chaalis karor dilon ko khwaab-e-ghaflat se bedar kar dey? Mein apne haathon mein woh quwwat kaise paida karoon jinki seena kobi ke shor se sargushtgan-e-khwab-maut hoshiyar ho jaaen?

First there is the lament for the *behoshi* (state of forgetfulness) of the *quom*. Quoting from the forty-fourth Surah of the Koran, he recalls that civilizations were wiped off the globe because of their obliviousness and the 'blindness of their hearts'. He says that if Europe wanted to take its ultimate revenge on the Muslims it was better that the bullet was aimed straight at the chest than the noose was placed around their necks. He reminds his readers that Islam saved Christianity from the ignominy that was heaped upon it by the Jews; it protected their churches from destruction but today none of the sacred places of Islam are safe from desecration initiated by Christian soldiers. Then he reminds the Indian Muslims that they constitute the largest numbers even among the Islamic nations. They cannot abdicate the responsibility placed upon them by the Koran. The European nations have arrived at their final understanding with each other about the annihilation of Islam. The Muslims should realize that nothing has ever been achieved by petitions and resolutions. Therefore it is incumbent upon them to take group action by immediately rejecting all European goods. As a matter of fact any Muslim who buys and uses them, disobeys the word of Allah.

When the first issue of *Al Hilal* appeared, the partition of Bengal order had been rescinded and the terrorist movements had declined. Tilak was in prison, Gandhi was fighting for the Indians in South Africa. Gokhale was in India working for South Africa. Among the galaxy of leaders, only Azad's voice could be heard, clearly and unequivocally, condemning the British. He was far ahead of the people who claimed peerage with him after the Independence. His anti-imperialist initiative was taken as early as 1912. Even Gandhi had advocated support for the British during the First World War. Only Azad's stand was consistent from start to finish. More than forty years later he was to stand in his place in parliament and recall the time when he was the sole spokesman for India's freedom:

> Forty years ago, when some of my friends sitting here were un-
> knowns, I decided to dedicate my life to the service of my country. I
> am talking of 1907, when I was eighteen or nineteen years old and
> joined the revolutionary parties of Bengal. Since then my whole life
> has been an open book before the world.[17]

After the Minto-Morley reforms of 1909 the national move-
ment had slowed down because of the lack of a short term goal. The new awakening among the Muslims due to the Aligarh movement, had thrown up an educated middle class partly drawn from the landed gentry and partly also from the liberal profes-
sions. It laid the foundation of the Muslim League, and was now demanding the Muslim University. Under the leadership of the Muslim League and Mohammadan Educational Conference, the movement was gaining ground every day. Tangentially to the Aligarh movement, two other vital social movements were gathering force among the Muslims. There were the enlightened Ulema, led by Shibli, who were opposed to the pro-English orientation of Aligarh, and who coalesced around Nadwat-ul Ulema; and there were a few who had attached themselves to the national movement which had so far been primarily identified with the Hindus.

The Aligarh movement was most popular among the edu-
cated class of Muslims. While they were agitating for a Muslim university regardless of the conditions under which it would

be granted, *Al Hilal* demanded as a pre-condition that government interference should be kept at a minimum. Azad's journal remained consistently critical of the Aligarh movement and its founder. It will be recalled that this was the same Azad who, a few years ago, hero-worshipped Sir Syed. In the 28 January 1914, issue Azad wrote, 'Today in India there are two movements, the first which arose in the majority community the pivot of which is Bengal, and the second, the awakening of the Indian Muslims'. He firmly identified himself with the latter. Although the former is not directly reflected in his writings in *Al Hilal*, but Azad's open antagonism to British rule is more advanced in time and of longer standing than any movement in the majority community. At the time he was, doubtlessly, the staunchest anti-imperialist in the country.

British Intelligence had been keeping its eye on Azad for several years. First it was his association with the Bengal Revolutionaries and tribes of North West Frontier that they watched. Malihabadi writes about his ties with Obaidullah Sindhi and Maulana Mahmudul Hasan, the prisoner of Malta.[18] There is evidence of his involvement with the *reshmi rumaal* (Silk Handkerchief) conspiracy, and the Intelligence Bureau's records indicate that he was active in Punjab with Sufi Ajit Singh and Amba Prasad.[19] Finally, the stakes became too high for allowing *Al Hilal* to remain in circulation. In 1914, an article appeared in the *Pioneer*, a pro-government paper, published from Allahabad, which gave public airing to the secret evidence mounting against Azad in government records:

Al Hilal is a weekly illustrated newspaper published in the Urdu language in Calcutta, and edited by a Delhi Mussalman named Abul Kalam. It has a large circulation among the Mussalmans in these provinces and probably in other parts of India. Ever since the war broke out its attitude has been so strikingly pro-German that it must be a matter of amazement to all those who read the paper that the government has managed to tolerate its writings. Probably this may be accounted for by the fact...' that the style of the most mischievous articles is very allusive and full of veiled sneers and sarcasms and innuendos, most of which either disappear or lose their effect when translated into English, and it is not likely that many European officials read the paper in the original.[20]

This article had the requisite effect. Orders for *Al Hilal's* closure were issued and on 18 November 1914, the last issue appeared. Akbar Allahabadi, the illustrious satirist-poet, wrote to Azad's friend and colleague, Ghulam Rasul Mehr:

> Your friend's security of *Al Hilal* has been confiscated:
> *Maghrib ki barq tut pari us gharib par*
> *Daur-e-Falak Hilal ko laya saleeb par*
> Lightning from the West has fallen on the innocent one
> The cycle of time has brought Hilal to the Cross.

On 1 December 1914 the Intelligence report stated that the vernacular press of Punjab had made sympathetic references to the forfeiture of *Al Hilal's* security:

> *The Hindu* of Lahore which has recently been preaching Hindu-Muslim unity, praises the editor of *Al Hilal* and refers to the forfeiture as 'the most sorrowful event'.

A year later, *Al Hilal* appeared in the garb of *Al Balagh* on 12 November 1915. This time the security had been raised to Rs. 10,000, which was duly furnished. The British had no illusions about this 'new' paper. A close watch was kept on the activities of the editor. In his weekly report to the Home Department, dated 14 September 1915, the Director of Criminal Intelligence stated:

> Attempt to revive the *Al Hilal* newspaper under a new name: Qutubuddin (sic) Ahmed, the manager of Abul Kalam Azad's *Al Hilal* applied in February last to start a new press and was ordered to furnish Rs. 2000 security. He has now deposited the money and notified his intention of starting a press and a newspaper both called *Al Balagh*. Abul Kalam Azad pretends to have no connection with the enterprise but there is no doubt that the *Al Hilal* press is identical with the *Al Balagh* press.[21]

Al Balagh ran for five months, its last issue was dated 3
April 1916. In March 1916, the Government of Bengal passed
an order under the Defence of India Act forbidding Azad to
remain in Bengal. Similar orders had already been passed by the
governments of, Punjab and U.P. against one who was described
in the records as 'Abul Kalam Azad who was the editor of the
defunct *Al Hilal* of Calcutta, is one of the most mischievous
agitators of India'.[22]

The case against Azad was quietly being built up in the
Intelligence reports submitted to the Home Department. All his
activities were suspected. The announcement in *Al Hilal* about
the formation of Hizbullah (Party of God)[23] was made in the 23
April 1913 issue. The intelligence report refers to it a year later
as a 'vaguely worded proposal put forward by Abul Kalam Azad
in his paper *Al Hilal* ... which is generally believed to be nothing
but a scheme for a secret society'. The moot point in the report
was that the society was announced when the 'Mohammedan
feeling was running high owing to the phases of the Balkan war'.

In addition to his writings, Azad's speaking tours were a
cause of great concern among government circles. On 12 January
1915 it was reported that Azad delivered two lectures at a
special meeting of the Inter-College Muslim Association. The
first one had an audience of 1000, and the second which was
delivered outside Mochi Gate Lahore had 4000–6000 students.
The report states:

> The latter lecture is reported to have been an attempt in subtle and
> guarded language, interspersed with quotations from the Quran,
> to appeal to Pan-Islamic feeling. Mohammedans, said the lecturer,
> owed their duty to God alone, and should have nothing to do with
> the allegiance which any earthly power may claim from them. The
> lecture is said to be above the heads of many of his audience, but the
> impact made upon the understanding ones was that the lecturer was
> conveying a veiled incitement to sedition. Abul Kalam is stated to be
> a powerful and fluent speaker. A report received by this department
> states that he intends to complete his mission by touring through

India delivering lectures, directed towards the excitement of Muslim feeling in the guise of religion.[24]

The establishment of Darul Irshad (House of Learning) was another thorn in the flesh for the British. Darul Irshad was conceived as a training centre for Hizbullah teachers, as announced in *Al Hilal* of July 1914. But the actual work did not start until October 1915. The Intelligence report of 24 August 1915 states on the authority of an announcement in *Zamindar*, that Azad intends to start an institution for the training of Muslim theologians at 45 Ripon Lane (his house). The more detailed report appears on 14 March 1916, which, no doubt, was an important factor in his externment orders. It says that Azad, 'one of the most persistent Pan Islamic agitators' opened a school of 'Mohammedan Theology called Darul Irshad'. The Calcutta police, it says, obtained notes of a lecture on slavery.

> The lecturer said that the Koran forbade Mohammedans to remain in subjection. A country like India which had once been under Mohammedan rule must never be given up and it was incumbent on them to strive to regain their lost control. Ten crores of Musalmans were living in slavery; it was a disgrace that so large a number could not make themselves independent. There were two ways of working for freedom; one was for young men to form secret societies and prepare themselves to act with courage, and the other was to create a desire for liberty among the masses, for example, by delivering lectures on self-government. It is possible that the lecture was more guarded than the notes suggest but there is little doubt that pernicious doctrines are being taught at Darul Irshad.

The very next report, submitted after a fortnight, stated that Azad had been externed from Bengal. On the night prior to his departure, Ripon Lane was blocked with the carriages of visitors who came to pay their respects to the 'great leader'.[25] His departure from Calcutta, drew large crowds at the station who came to say farewell, 'Cries and lamentations were raised as the train left the station.'[26]

Thus on 4 April 1916, Azad left Calcutta for Ranchi, accompanied by the District Magistrate, Nazimuddin Ahmed. Having been forbidden entry into Punjab and U.P., Ranchi seemed the ideal place, close enough to continue *Al Balagh*, and other projects such as Hizbullah and Darul Irshad. In his report to the Home Department several months later, the Director of Criminal Intelligence was to write:

> The notorious Abul Kalam Azad, now restricted under the Defence of India Act Rules at Ranchi, has asked that the govt, should prosecute him in a criminal court... I think the latter himself asks for prosecution in order to become a martyr.

After he had been in Ranchi a few months, the Government of Bihar and Orissa passed orders under Defence of India, restricting Azad to Ranchi. Cases against him started piling up. The enquiry into the *Reshmi Rumaal* case had shown that he was partly responsible for the flight of Lahore students across the Frontier in February 1915. Evidence was produced that he was more than once invited to join Obaidullah Sindhi in Kabul. He had sent Maulvi Saifur Rahman across the border in 1915, 'where he and Haji Sahib of Turangzai raised the Mohmands against us (British).'[27] It was reported that Azad had 'professed to his intimates' that he had incurred a good deal of expenditure on these conspiracies.

Ranchi has the unique distinction of being the place where Azad completed his work on *Tarjuman-ul-Quran*. Azad had already started this work in 1914. The announcement was made on the front cover of the first issue of *Al Balagh* which appeared on Friday, 12 November 1915. It stated that first of all Hazrat Shah Waliullah, divinely inspired, felt the need for translating the Koran; hence his magnificent Persian translation. Then his sons, Shah Rafiuddin and Shah Abdul Qadir prepared the ground for the first Urdu translation:

> A century has passed since. It will be no exaggeration to say that ... Almighty God had specially kept the opportunity to complete the task for the editor of *Al Hilal*.[28]

The notice solicited subscriptions of four rupees for every volume of *Tarjuman-ul-Quran* which would be published in instalments. The sentence, 'Almighty God had specially kept the task for the editor of *Al Hilal*', could have been written only by one who had extreme self-confidence. For a young Muslim *Alim* (scholar), there can be nothing more daunting than attempting to explain the word of Allah. The slightest hint of error can lead to a death sentence. It is evident that Azad was fully conscious of the rigorous criterion of a *mufassir* (commentator on the Holy Koran); in his prefatory chapter 'Principles of *tarjuma* (translation) and *tafsir* (commentary)', he writes:

> An author is the product of the mental climate of his age. By this rule only those minds are *mustasna* (exceptional) who are endowed by nature with the taste and *nazar* (insight) of a *mujtahid* (acknowledged scholar who is authorized to issue a fatwa [edict]), and by virtue of this quality, they stand apart from the common row.[29]

Azad's early journalistic experiences had solidified his natural genius and prepared him for undertaking projects which people twice his age and learning would not dare to have attempted.

A historical context underpins every significant *tarjuma* and *tafsir*. It reflects both the age in which the work is done and the individual who accomplishes it. One who undertakes the exegesis of a revealed book of any religion, invests the sum total of his wisdom, experience and learning into his work. Depending on the individual scholar, he may try to find in it the solutions to the political, social and cultural problems of his times. A *tarjuma* and *tafseer*, therefore become their own time-reflecting mirrors. The viewpoint of *Tarjuman-ul-Quran* is not that of an *alim* of the Abbasid dynasty or a *mufti* of the Mughal sultanate, whose interpretation was tainted by his loyalty to the state, but that of a young, fearless and outspoken *mujahid* of Indian independence, and an enlightened Muslim of the twentieth century.

What exactly was the sequence of events that lead Azad to undertake the work of translating the Koran afresh? Several years before, while his father was alive, Azad emerged from his phase of doubt, but rejected the traditional teachings of the mullah. He must have arrived at the conclusion that Allah could not possibly mean what the conventional wisdom of the age was saying about Islam. He would, therefore, cut through the wall of contemporary interpreters which stands between him and his Allah. He will go directly to the word of Allah to discover what He means. He will read the entire Koran on his own strength, and interpret it for the guidance of his *quom*. Explaining the reason for Azad's decision, Douglas says:

> He saw the need for the ordinary Indian Muslim to be inspired afresh by the Koran in ordering all aspects of his life. None of the existing Urdu translations, in Azad's opinion, met this basic need for popular understanding.[30]

His decision also establishes the fact that Azad considered himself capable of making the word of Allah intelligible to the average Muslim. It is important to remember that by his own confession, in writing the *Tarjuman*, Azad's main concern was the average reader, not the erudite scholar. He was not satisfied with his own writing until he had read out portions of it to an eleven year old boy and an adult learner. Only after he had made sure that they understood his meaning did he proceed further. One never tires of reading or repeating the famous dedication of the *Tarjuman* which further testifies to the author's pride in its universal intelligibility.

Azad began the work on *Tarjuman-ul-Quran* at the age of twenty-three. At the start, he had divided his task into three parts; *Tarjuma* (translation), *Tafseer* (commentary), and *Muqqadama-e-Tafsir* (the full case for a commentary). He had targeted special categories of readers; for the general reader—translation, for deeper study—commentary, and for the scholar—the prolegomena to the commentary. It was obvious that his approach to an understanding of the Koran was quite different from the translations and commentaries available at that time. The work on *Tarjuman-ul-Quran* and *Tazkirah* went on simultaneously in Ranchi. The latter was a source of *tafrih-e-dimagh* (mental diversion), a respite from the formidable challenge of translating and interpreting the Koran.

notes

1 Review of *Al Hilal* in *Muslim Gazette*, 24 July 1912, and letters of Shibli. These sources have been identified by Abid Raza Bedar in *Maulana Abul Kalam Azad.*

2 *India Wins Freedom*, p. 8.

3 Reference in Home Dept. Records, India Office Library.

4 Known literary figures like Abdullah Imadi, Sulaiman Nadvi, Abdus Salam Nadvi, Hamid Ali Siddiqui featured on the editorial staff.

5 Aziz Ahmad, *Journal of the American Oriental Society*, July–September 1969, p. 476, quoted by K.K. Aziz, *History of Partition of India*, Volume 1.

6 For a different view on Afghani see K.K. Aziz, op. cit. He holds the view that seeing Afghani as a pan Islamist is an outmoded concept. He quotes Afghani's Paris journal in which he wrote 'In countries like Egypt and India, Muslims should cooperate with non-Muslims, and there ought to be good relations and harmony in affairs of national interest between the Muslims and their compatriots and neighbours of different religions.'

7 Abid Raza Bedar's knowledge about original manuscripts is undisputable. I have not seen any issue of *Al Urwatul Wusqa*, but Bedar's assessment is always careful.

8 The Rashid Raza article is in three parts, featured in 13 July, 20 July, and 27 July issues of *Al Hilal.*

9 *Al Hilal* 4 August 1912. The tide of the article is 'Muslim University'. Azad writes

> Mirza Ghalib faced a few years of hardship after the 1857 *ghadar*. In a letter to Mirza Qurban Ali he wrote, I have become my own spectator. Insult and sorrow pleases me. I regard myself a stranger to myself. Whenever I am hurt, I say, "Another shoe has been hurled at Ghalib".

10 *Al Hilal*, 18 December 1912. The article is subtitled 'Loyalty and Revolt-time has come for both.' The Koranic Ayat in the title is 'Do not be afraid of anyone except Allah, if you are a *Momin*.'

11 The Koran's words are, 'The Koran is a book that has been revealed to bring you from darkness into light.'

12 '*Al Hilal* ke maqasid aur political taleem', 3 September 1912.

13 *Al Hilal,* 18 December 1912. Azad lays the blame for Muslim detachment at the doorstep of Sir Syed Ahmed Khan and his insistence on education as the only goal worth striving for.

14 Ibid.

15 *Al Hilal,* 1 September 1912. 'Muslim League is a counterfeit coin given to amuse the infantile. The new awakening among Muslims was wasted on this futile exercise in politics'.

16 This edition is available in the India Office Library, Blackfriars Street, London. All the quotations from 'Boycott' are taken from there.

17 *India's Maulana* Vol. 2. ed. Hameed, p. 221.

18 Obaidullah Sindhi Mahmudul Hasan, see *Malihabadi, Zikr-e-Azad,* p. 272.

19 Rajat Ray, in *Communal and Pan Islamic trends in Colonial India,* ed. Mushirul Hasan.

20 Quoted by Mahadeo Desai, p. 35.

21 Record available at the India Office Library, Blackfriars Street London. The writer of the report must have mistakenly written Qutubuddin instead of Fazluddin. Fazluddin Ahmed was the Manager of the Press.

22 Report of the Director, Criminal Intelligence, 4 April 1916.

23 The article in which the announcement was made was 'Al Balagh' (The Trumpet Call). He poses a question in bold type: *Man Ansari Ala Allah* (Who are my helpers on the way to God?) He invites readers to send postcards so that he can prepare a list of *Mujahideen-i-Haq* and *Jan-nisaran-i-Millat.*

24 Report, 12 January 1915.

25 'Abul Kalam Azad was in touch in Calcutta with the rich Mohammedan community to whom he appeared a great leader.' Report of the Director of Criminal Intelligence, 20 January 1917.

26 Report, 11 April 1916.

27 Report of the Director of Criminal Intelligence.

28 *Al Balagh,* Volume 1, No 1. The notice is entitled '*Tarjuman-ul-Quran* from the pen of the editor *Al Hilal*'.

29 See Preface to Azad's *Tarjuman-ul-Quran.*

30 Ian Henderson Douglas, *Abul Kalam Azad: An Intellectual and Religious Biography,* p. 197.

guiding the *quom*: *tazkirah*

AZAD'S FIRST AUTOBIOGRAPHY, *Tazkirah*, was written during his Ranchi days, at the insistence of his friend and admirer Fazluddin Ahmed. A native of Gurdaspur in Punjab and an engineer by profession, Fazluddin claims in the preface to have known Azad since 1902, when having completed his education in Japan, he came to live with his brother in Calcutta.[1] Being a close friend and admirer of Azad, he saw how his early journalistic phase matured into the spectacular period of *Al Hilal* and *Al Balagh*. Later as the manager of the *Al Hilal* press during the trying days of its closure by the government, he came closer to Azad. His preface to *Tazkirah* is a glowing tribute to what Azad's 'flaming writings' (*sholabar tehriren*) meant to the Muslims plunged as they were in the 'deepest caverns of *jihalat* (ignorance)'.

The growing fame of the twenty-four year old editor of *Al Hilal* made Fazluddin realize the importance of recording his *sarguzisht* (story). This was the beginning of a pattern which would repeat itself several times during Azad's life—a friend using every persuasive device to overcome Azad's reticence in revealing anything about himself.[2] In 1914, when Fazluddin first broached the subject of an autobiography, Azad laughed it off with the words, 'How many great and glorious lives of our times have gone unrecorded. Recording my life instead of theirs would be ludicrous'. Fazluddin Ahmed did not give up so easily. Persisting in his mission, he finally cornered Azad in May 1916, while he was under detention at Morabadi near Ranchi. 'I knew', he writes in his preface, 'that his twenty-five years of rich experiences far surpassed what most people can gather during their entire lifetime. Thousands would benefit from a study of his life.'

Fazluddin made Azad promise to send him whatever he wrote during the course of one week. On his part Azad extracted a promise from Fazluddin that under no circumstance would he publish anything he had written without his prior consent. Fazluddin writes that he received the first instalment of sixteen pages, two weeks after leaving Ranchi. Reading the contents, he realized that before saying anything about himself, Azad wanted to write about his ancestors. As other pieces trickled through the post, it became evident that there was no foreseeable end to this account of ancestors. Fazluddin expressed his honest concern to Azad in a letter, that the background seemed to be taking over from the real subject, but Azad wrote back, 'Don't create an impediment in the flow of my thought. Whatever the pen writes spontaneously, I pass on. Keep on gathering it. You won't be the loser.'[3]

This process continued for four months. 'But I was really interested in his (Azad's) life; … therefore continuously suggested brevity. I was afraid that the flow of his thoughts in this direction would never allow the book to end'.[4] The ancestral account ended with the life of his father, Maulana Khairuddin. Once again Fazluddin's requests started pouring in. When no excuse worked, Azad, to end the subject, sent a twenty-page chapter with the remark, 'I can't write any more about myself.' Fazluddin records his own reaction to this in the Preface, 'The truth is that he never really wanted to accede to my request. He used my persuasion as an excuse to write about his ancestors—knowing that when it came to writing about himself he could always come up with one excuse or another.'[5]

What further pains Fazluddin took to record the autobiography are not relevant because, in fact, nothing survives except the first part, which was essentially an account of his ancestor Hazrat Shaikh Jamaluddin Dehlivi. One important insight one gets from this 'autobiography' is Azad's attitude towards recording his life. First, one is struck by the fact that he gives the highest priority to writing about his ancestors and the lowest to saying anything about himself. Second, the seriousness with which he approached his autobiography can be ascertioned from the fact that he referred to it as *Tafrih-i-Dimagh* (mental diversion), undertaken whenever he wanted to rest his mind from the monumental task of *Tafsir-i-Quran*. He says that he gave no importance to writing about his life, considering it nothing more than a piece of trivia, hence his indifference to its revision or publication. On the other hand, Fazluddin writes that he had hoped to have given the world a magnificent autobiography of Azad because of what he foresaw would be its importance for future generations:

> Like thousands of others, I believe that his literary and academic accomplishments, achieved in these few years, are just preliminary indications of great things to follow. God will preserve him for the *quom* for years to come, and who knows what future glories are written against his name! Time is not far when great scholars would devote themselves to writing about his life... It may be no surprise, therefore, even if my humble effort is of great usefulness.

Time has vindicated Fazluddin's hope and prophecy.

Azad's role in the eventual publication of *Tazkirah* reveals another interesting aspect of his personality which has a recurring pattern. First, he forbids Fazluddin to publish it unless he has had a chance to revise. When Fazluddin arrives in Ranchi armed with the manuscript, to fulfil the condition of revision, Azad first tries to postpone the issue. When Fazluddin persists, he says, 'I wrote these pages entirely due to your insistence. I did not really intend to have them published', adding that he would look at them as soon as time permitted. Fazluddin was only too aware of the implication of '*Ba-waqt-fursat*' (when time permits), so he quietly packs up the manuscript and slips away to Raipur. He reappears in February 1917, at which time, according to his own statement he stays for six months and presents Azad with a list of fifteen questions which he has prepared as introduction to Azad's life. He knows that once Azad's 'pen starts moving' nothing can stem the flow. Azad, although he starts writing with great indifference and reluctance, ultimately performs miracles with his pen. Fazluddin writes that once his mind was activated, 'thoughts gushed on paper.'

What does this sequence of events reveal? Does it reveal Azad's modesty compared to most people in his position, who would have welcomed an opportunity to write about themselves? Or does the account of his ancestors reveal a pride in his glorious antecedents which distinguishes him above the rest of the populace? A further question may be posed to probe the consistency of this attitude with the leadership role in which he was beginning to see himself? Does an individual who considers himself somehow 'chosen' to lead his people to the Straight Path (*Siratal Mustaqeem*) from which they have gone astray, reject the opportunity of public attention that such an autobiography would bring about? The answer may lie in how he viewed his leadership. One recalls that he deliberately eschewed the *piri-muridi* tradition which would automatically have given him sway over thousands of human beings. Not only that, he sought employment outside Calcutta, putting distance between himself and his father's area of influence. He says enough in his writings to leave no doubt about his intense desire to 'fight with his own *jauhardaar talwar* (well-sharpened sword) rather than rattle borrowed sabres'. This desire led him to reject his father's ready-made fiefdom. But why then the ancestor-adoration in *Tazkirah*? What he rejects he also exults in. The matter of shying away from any attempt at autobiography is traced to the personality of Azad which is revealed in his own writings, particularly *Ghubar-i-Khatir*.

Returning to Tazkirah, Fazluddin's justification for his decision to publish the book without Azad's authorization is based on his awareness of Azad's habits. He writes that Azad never revised what he wrote.[6] 'During the *Al-Hilal* days he often made changes only when the article was at the proof stage. But even these, says Fazluddin, were not substantive. It was Azad's practice to produce overnight finished articles for the entire journal. Fazluddin's announcement of the book came to Azad as a surprise and annoyance. As expected, he immediately stopped the press. Fazluddin rushed to Ranchi and pleaded for permission. Finally, Azad relented. The intended three volume autobiography was thus reduced to one volume, the subject of which was his ancestor Sheikh Jamaluddin Dehlivi. Appended to it was a twenty page poetic essay about himself. The other two volumes were about family history, and his own life—in the form of answers to fifteen questions. The whereabouts of volumes two and three which are described in *India Wins Freedom*, will for ever remain a mystery.

In October 1919, Azad wrote the *aitezar* (apologetical foreword) to *Tazkirah*. Beginning with a discussion about spelling and printing, it moves on to a subject of great importance for any student of Azadiyat. In an extremely lucid paragraph, Azad lays down his standards for scholarship and intellectual labour. In so doing he sets out the criteria for what he calls the 'normal' and the 'super' scholars. The latter, he says, are elevated to the level of saints, a status which entitles them to invite common people to follow the path that they prescribe and the lead they give. In a variety of ways, this foreword outlines the role Azad had demarcated for himself. His comments on the difference between the role of a scholar and the *daiyee* (a guide, a reformer, a creative interpreter of truth, a proselytizer), are a transparent veil for describing himself as the *daiyee* of the *quom*.

A scholar, Azad writes, confines himself to learning in order to discover the truth through external as well as internal methods. A *daiyee* is not content only with the search for truth. He is equally concerned with the external and the practical impact of his scholastic pursuits. The duty of a scholar is to analyze, in the most objective manner, the strength, weakness, beauty and ugliness he observes in whatever he is examining. He needs to express his views boldly and courageously without sentiment or bias. He will be judged by the degree of objectivity he can muster in his scholarly work. In other words, the work of a scholar, is to discover truth, uncover falsehood and expose beauty and ugliness. He is not expected to be emotionally involved with his subject. He neither loves truth nor hates falsehood. On the other hand a *daiyee* or *musleh* (reformer, guide) is one who loves truth and hates falsehood. And because that state of knowledge or achievement cannot be reached without *imtiaz* (spiritual distinction) or *kashf* (illumination), therefore a *daiyee* has first to undergo the grind and travails of scholarship and then reach beyond. Having experienced the *kashf,* the *daiyee* then feels the desire for suffusing the entire world with the same splendour. That is why, while, emotional identification in rigorous scholarship is erroneous, proselytization and invitation to receive the message (*da'awat*) is through and through a matter of emotion.

Clearly, Azad's mission in *Tazkirah* was to instruct. He perceived himself as the *daiyee* or *musleh* for his *quom.* Consequently, when he writes about the *zulm* (oppression) inflicted on the men of piety, his ink is somewhat darker and his words full of passion.

> No matter how horrible evil appears, this is exactly according to what I intended. Similarly, however beautiful is the depiction of goodness this is exactly as it should be. Here unlike the rationalists, I have no *meezan-o-meeqas* (scale or measure) in hand. Only a discerning heart throbs within.

He sees himself as part of the constellation of great and pious men whose 'comet-like appearances' are rare. Not only that, when they appear, they receive the first signs of guidance from the *alam-e-ghaib* (the World of the Unseen).

> Springtime comes with the longing to lavish its verdant green on every little corner of the earth. But the first signs of its beneficence

are seen in the bowers and gardens. The day's dawn though it brings the message of radiance to every nook and cranny of the world, the earliest rays of the sun first touch the high walls and tall minarets... This condition is identical with the dawn of the age of guidance and inspiration, the first signs of which appear before the people of piety and determination, the flowers of humanity, the repositories of the Spirit of the Age.

Azad uses the lives of great teachers and scholars as examples. First there is a detailed account of his venerable ancestor, Shaikh Jamaluddin who refused to sign the fatwa required by Shahenshah Akbar from all the ulemas of the kingdom, which would declare him the *Khalifa* of the age, worthy of *ata'at* (homage) and empower him with *Imamat* and *Ijtehad*. There are other examples of men of God like Shaikh Talai, Shaikh Abdullah Noori on whom untold suffering was inflicted by the state, but who considered their lives as the most dispensable commodity which they could easily offer in exchange for upholding their truth.

The perpetrators of oppression, Azad says, have always availed of the services of the ulema who are more than willing to serve the state. He uses this occasion to lash out against the time-serving ulema. They are described as worse than snakes and scorpions; while the reptiles may occupy the same hole in the ground these men of God can never occupy the same space. Azad's antipathy to this ilk is reflected in his use of lowly animal metaphors to draw parallels. Like dogs whose claws and fangs, the moment the butcher flings them the bone, become sharp, these men cannot keep control of their faculties the moment they reach the spot 'where the bone of the world lies rotting.' Then making the classic comparison between the masjid and the tavern, he says in that one may find 'songs of love' in the tavern but right underneath the arch of the masjid, if the reward is *imamat* or *peshwai*, their hands reach for the throat and their bloodthirsty eyes are fixed on the blood of their brother.

Man's ultimate guidance is therefore to be derived not from these *ulema-e-duniya parast* (world-devoted ulema) but from the word of the Koran and the *Sunnat* of the Prophet. The fact that Azad was at that time deeply engrossed in writing the *Tarjuman-ul-Quran* (which undoubtedly gave him the fortitude to bear his prison sentence with grace), is evident throughout *Tazkirah*. He states that if all the books on Islam were to disappear from the world, and only the Koran were to remain, it would be enough proof of the *seerat* (character) of its Messenger. He then extols the clarity with which the Koran transmits its message, a point he was to make again and again, to warn against the danger of reading more meaning into the Koran than originally intended. The Koran made certain predictions, he writes, all of which have been vindicated by time. The *quom* has experienced the degradation and debasement which is predicted in the Koran. The Koran states that,

> Together, all the *quoms* will descend on you and will call out to each other to destroy you just as the hungry call others to the table. (*Tazkirah*, p. 289)

At that time, he says, though the Muslims will not be few in number, but due to the *wahan* created in their hearts, they will be swept away like trash. *Wahan* means love of the world and hatred of death with dignity. Therefore, he states with undisguised contempt, that for the Muslims it would be better to be buried in the bowels of the earth than remain on its surface. Comparing the lowly creatures favourably with the Muslims, a metaphor he was to use again and again in his writings, he says:

> Insects have comfort inside the earth, the animals of the jungle have pleasure in the forest, but the Muslim has no happiness left on the surface of the world; carrying the burden of his shame, he can only go underneath (to his grave).

Condemning the practice of deviating from the worship of Allah, One and Alone, he writes that like the pre-Islamic tribes, the Muslims in every corner of the world are worshipping Lat and Uzza.[7] Except Allah, there is no deity or entity before which they have not prostrated themselves. He reminds his readers

that the laws of Allah are immutable. To proclaim this, there appears, from time to time, a man of God whose faith in the writ of Allah exceeds his faith in the light of day and the darkness of night. Taking one look at the present he prophesizes about the future; and the world is witness that what happens is exactly in accordance with his prediction. What is so surprising, Azad then asks, about Shaikh Daud predicting the calamitous outcome of the martyrdom of the *musleheen*?[8] The Koran has said time and again that the execution of *musleheen-e-haq* (Upholders of Truth) and *aamireen-e-bi'l maruf* (Enjoiners of the Good) will be the last deed of a *jama'at* before it meets its destruction. If only the Muslims adhere to their faith in the *quawanaeen-e-Ilahi* (Laws of Allah), then they too can read future events in their immutability.

Tazkirah contains Azad's definition of *momin-e-kamil* (the perfect believer). The Sufis and Salehs which feature in the account are exemplary *momins*. They bear untold suffering in the way of Allah; they are flogged, beaten and even executed by the coercive state. But their *imam* (faith) remains unshaken. The very fact of their presence gives glory, even to the humblest surroundings in which they happen to be Azad's description of this phenomenon is among the finest pieces of Urdu prose:

> Wherever the lamp is placed, it will create its pool of light. The bouquet of flowers even if thrown in the trash, still spreads its fragrance. The peacock said, my garden is in me; wherever I spread my feathers a flower-bed will unroll. This is exactly the case with a *momin-e-kamil* (perfect believer) and *sahib-e-ilm-o-haq* (master of knowledge and truth). He is not dependent on time and space. His presence will brighten space and the scented breeze will be proof that he has just passed by:

> *Abhi is raah sey koi gaya hai Kahe*
> *deti hai shokhi naqsh-e-pa ki*

> Someone has just gone by this way
> The playfulness of the footfall says (*Tazkirah* p. 262)

The autobiographical account, *Tazkirah*, was obviously intended as an instrument of instruction. The author not only acknowledges this intention but considers it part of his life's mission. It also speaks volumes about Azad himself. He considered himself responsible for carrying forward the torch of *sidq-o-wafa* (truth and faith) lit by his ancestors. He aspires to become the *Momin-e-Kaamil*, he will, following in footsteps of the prophets of yore, inform the Muslims about their impending doom, he will guide them to the Straight Path, he will above all, become the *fatehe waqt*, the conqueror of time:

> The best among us present the excuse that time is against us and we do not have the wherewithal for the journey. But the conqueror of time rises up and says, 'I will carry time with me and prepare my baggage with my own hands. If the earth is not favourably inclined, the heavens should lend a hand. If men are not available, angels should become travelling companions. If tongues have become mute, stones should cry out.'... It is he who is truly the creator of time and the nurturer of his age. He does not follow the dictates of society. It is society which awaits the movement of his lips. He does not survey the world with an eye for what he can swiftly gather into his cloak; his eye takes in the entire universe to discover what is missing so that he can fill the gap. (*Tazkirah*, p. 272)

Despite the modesty and self-effacement, expressed at the beginning to the irrepressible Fazluddin, the fact that he was now starting to see himself as the *Fateh* of time, with the wherewithal to become the *amir* of the *karvan* of Indian Muslims becomes evident from his first attempt at autobiography.

notes

1 *Zikr-i-Azad*, pp. 109–10.
2 First Fazluddin, then Malihabadi, then Kabir had the same experience.
3 Fazluddin, *Muqaddama* (preface) p. 18.
4 Ibid.
5 Ibid.

6 This assertion of Fazluddin holds true notwithstanding revisions of minor nature here and there in the manuscript of *Tarjuman* preserved in the *Gosha-e-Azad*, Indian Council of Cultural Relations, New Delhi.

7 Lat, Manat and Uzza were among the 300 idols that lined the walls of the Ka'aba during pre-Islamic days.

8 Tazkirah, p. 306.

5

muslim politics: khilafat

AZAD SPENT FOUR YEARS UNDER HOUSE arrest in Ranchi. During this period, he had completed work on *Tarjuman-ul-Quran*. He had also written a lengthy article, 'Jama-ash-shawahid fi dukhul ghair Muslim fil Masajid', (Collection of evidences of non-Muslims entering mosques) in which he gave evidence that from the days of the Prophet non-Muslims were allowed to enter mosques and they could be included in the *majaalis* (gatherings) of the *masjids*. He went on to state that in this age of *fitna* (strife or mischief)/ and *bidat* (religious innovations), if Muslims have made one excellent decision it is to establish *maqasid-e-saliha* (virtuous objectives) in the *masjids*. They have allowed Hindus in their *masjids*, just as the Prophet used to call peaceful and friendly non-Muslims to stay at the mosques.[1] The other important work he produced during these days has been discussed in the previous chapter, the account of his ancestors which Fazluddin Ahmed published as *Tazkirah*.

Azad had not yet met Gandhi, although he had written an article in *Al Hilal* entitled 'Mr Gandhi Rais-ul-Ahrar' (Mr Gandhi, the leader of freedom) about his activities in South Africa. On his part Gandhi, having heard about this outstanding intellectual and anti-imperialist from Bengal, had tried to meet him while he was interned in Ranchi but the state government had not given permission. It is significant that Azad's association was to develop with leaders much senior to him like Mahatma Gandhi, Pandit Motilal Nehru, Lala Lajpat Rai, Hakim Ajmal Khan and Dr M.A. Ansari, rather than with those closer to his age. The reason was that none of the ones who became his colleagues in the first government of a free India had even entered the political arena while he was almost regarded a veteran. 'He was listened to with great interest, even by the leaders who were much older than him'.[2]

Azad had decided that after leaving Ranchi, he would retire with a group of like-minded individuals to a peaceful spot from where he would continue his struggle but on an intellectual level.[3] For a short time he tried to follow this course, but given the contemporary state of affairs, this *gosha nashini* (seclusion) could not last. Eighteen months later he wrote a piece for the first issue of *Paigham*[4] in which he expressed his regret that because of the crisis facing the country, he had to plunge himself into active politics. As a consequence, he was neither able to restart *Al Balagh*, nor engage in any other writing. Political activism had taken precedence over intellectual pursuits, and he found himself doing the very things he had decided to avoid. The growing awareness of the limitedness of days and nights and the boundlessness of his aspirations find expression here:

> It is the same life which has been given to everyone, the same span of day and night which has always existed. The sun cannot tarry longer for me, the night cannot alter its course for my sake. I have one life, but the enthusiasm of a thousand lives is hidden in my heart. How can I upturn the world? And where shall I get the strength which will add the power of a thousand hands to the power of one mind and heart?

This is the present condition and it is difficult to say how long it will last:

Rau mein hai rakhsh-e-umr kahan dekhiye thamey
Nai haath baag par hai na pa hai rakab mein.

Life's horseman is moving, let's see where he stops
Neither is the hand at the rein nor the foot in the stirrup[5]

During his confinement years in Ranchi, several events had occurred for which he had tried to prepare Muslims through the pages of *Al Hilal*. The anti-Rowlatt agitation, Satyagraha movement, Jallianwala Bagh massacre, and Martial Law atrocities had resulted in forging a unity among the Hindus and Muslims as never before.[6] The capitulation of Turkey on 31 October 1918 was a blow to the *quom*. The Indian Muslims led by Dr Ansari demanded that all armed forces be withdrawn from the holy places, Hejaz, Damascus, Baghdad, Najaf and Karbala. A medical team to Turkey called the Red Crescent was organized by Dr. Ansari. The stage was thus set during the Ranchi years for Azad to appear and plunge himself in the political struggle. In the preface to the second edition of *Tarjuman-ul-Quran*, Azad was to write that it was not he who sought politics but politics sought him. The political tide was swirling all around him and he could not keep his 'garment dry' despite the inner urge for a life of seclusion and intellectual pursuits.

The moment Azad returned to Calcutta from Ranchi, he addressed a large gathering of Muslims at the Nakhuda Masjid on the Khilafat agitation. Soon after, he went to Delhi to attend the Khilafat Conference where, in January 1920, he met Gandhi for the first time. Gandhi had always supported Khilafat and had warned the government in November 1919, that if the Muslim demands were not met he would launch his Non-Cooperation movement. Azad agreed with Gandhi in principle. He supported Gandhi's moves throughout the Khilafat agitation. The year 1920 was spent with the Khilafat leaders Mohammad Ali, Shaukat Ali, Abdul Bari and Mahatma Gandhi, on speaking tours of the country, in raising funds and in enlisting support of the Hindus.

The Bengal Khilafat Conference was held in February 1920, under the Presidentship of Azad. Enthused by the fiery speeches of Azad and Maulana Abdul Bari of Firangi Mahal, the delegates resolved that 'Muslims should abandon their loyalty to the British and support the Khilafat agitation, if the pre-war sovereignty and dominion of the Khalifa was not kept intact.'[7] In Delhi, Gandhi announced his Non-Cooperation programme. This happened two days after the Hindu-Muslim meeting held on 22 March 1920, which included Azad along with much senior leaders like Tilak, Malaviya, Lajpat Rai, Ansari, Ajmal Khan, Shaukat Ali and Abdul Bari. Whereas all the others expressed one reservation or another, Azad enthusiastically supported Gandhi's announcement.

In May of the same year, Azad was appointed to the implementation committee of the Central Khilafat Committee for Non-Cooperation. Throughout this period, Azad participated in the Khilafat as well as the Congress meetings which were often held consecutively, such as the June 1920 meetings at Allahabad. By this time the ulema too had become active in the Khilafat agitation and Fatwas had been issued, making Non-Cooperation a religious duty. Co-operation with the Hindus was encouraged and the leadership of Gandhi was endorsed by all.

At the end of that year, while the Khilafat movement was at its peak, Gandhi arrived in Calcutta to inaugurate the Madrasa Islamia. As part of Non-Cooperation, Gandhi had suggested that national institutions be established to replace British run institutions. In Calcutta, Madrasa Aliya was very influential among the Muslims. Azad took it upon himself to provide an alternative education for the Calcutta Muslims, just as he had done on a smaller scale for the Muslims of Ranchi. In his letter to his friend Abdul Razzaq Malihabadi in which he invited him to join the staff of the new Madrasa Islamia, Azad wrote:

Except Bengal, nowhere else is Arabic education in the hand of government. At least two thousand students are enrolled. If such a large *jama'at* takes this step, it will have a profound impact on the country. The long-standing hopes which we have nurtured about educational reforms will be fulfilled.[8]

Azad spoke at the inauguration, outlining his philosophy of education. This was the same philosophy which he was to give twenty-seven years later, to independent India in his capacity as the first Education Minister. He said that the establishment of this institution was in response to Gandhi's call for Non-Cooperation. First he praised the students for leaving the comforts of the Madrasa Aliya and opting for the hardships of their new Madrasa. This he stated was their duty in accordance with *ahkam-e-Ilahi* (Directives of Allah) and their responsibility as loyal Indians. He said further that by their determination to acquire a classical education, the students have restored education to its original dignity, which is learning for the sake of learning and not just as a means for employment:

> Those grand structures which are colonies of English education, who are they filled with? Lovers of learning and seekers of truth? No. They are filled by lovers of a fistful of wheat and a bowl of rice; who have been convinced that without that education they cannot obtain their *ghiza* (food).

Comparing them to the students of Aligarh, he said that not one of them was prepared to leave Aligarh for a nationalist institution, until he had argued with Azad for two hours whether he would still be able to earn his bread if he gave up English education. The Aligarh students wanted to extract a guarantee from him. But these students (of the Madrasa Islamia) have dedicated their entire life to Arabic education, knowing full well that an English education could have got them anything, from the post of a clerk to the status of Lord Sinha. He then turned to Gandhi and said:

> It is only a jeweller who can recognize a genuine gem; and you are indeed that—the finest connoisseur of the jewels of 'sacrifice' and 'genuineness'.

The Meerut Khilafat Conference was held in April or May 1920, at which Gandhi preached Non-Cooperation for the first time from a public platform. Azad gave him full support. The Special Congress at Calcutta held in September 1920, passed the Non-Cooperation resolution, and launched a campaign of intense preparation for the Non-Cooperation programme. Azad and Gandhi toured various regions mobilizing public opinion. Among the Congress leaders Azad's support for the cause was the strongest. By the time the Indian National Congress met in Nagpur in December 1920, most of the leadership had been converted to Gandhi's stand. It was at this time that, as part of the Non-Cooperation, Azad started the Madrasa Islamia and invited Gandhi for its inauguration, as described above.

In March 1921, he undertook a tour of Punjab with Mahatma Gandhi and made the famous speech at the Shahi Masjid, Lahore, which was reported in the *Civil and Military Gazette*. The *Gazette* carried a report about another fiery speech he made a couple of days later in Amritsar. That year, Azad remained busy with Khilafat matters, with Madrasa Islamia, and with preparations for the launch of *Paigham*. In September 1921, the government arrested Khilafat leaders, Mohammad Ali, Shaukat Ali, Shankaracharya, Dr Kitchlew and Husain Ahmed Madani. The responsibility, therefore, for propagating the joint cause of Khilafat and Non-Cooperation fell on Azad. He wrote about the significance of these arrests in the first issue of *Paigham*:

This was their duty, and they have fulfilled it. Is the country ready to fulfil hers? ... All they want from you is that you sacrifice a little wealth, some physical comfort, some real and imaginary *aaraish* (adornment) and every bit of indifference and selfishness. Take a pledge for Swadeshi, Boycott and Non-cooperation. Help the *mujahideen* of Angora, purify your own hearts and surrender yourselves to Allah and His Shariat. This is the real price of the sacrifice of these *giriftaran-e-Haq* (prisoners for truth) which the country owes them.[9]

The Khilafat Conference of 1921, held in Agra in October 1921,[10] was presided over by Azad. In his address to a mixed audience of Hindus and Muslims, he laid down all the basic principles of his political creed. These were to remain the underlying themes of all his speeches on this subject. First, he explained what had been achieved so far by the movement; second, he outlined what needed to be done; third, he gave to his countrymen, particularly to the Muslims, his prescription of success. It is a unique feature of Azad's *khitabat* (oratory) that although the specific Islamic references are meant for the Muslims, he often refers to the universality of the Islamic principles which appeal to all people regardless of the faith they profess.

Emphasizing that Khilafat was a national issue which concerned all the people of India and not just Muslims, he said that Khilafat provided for the Indians a cause, through the means of which they could address the larger problem. In the last forty years they had not been able to find such a powerful cause. Hindu-Muslim *Ittehad* (unity), he said, was the prerequisite for the success of any national movement. Ten years ago he had decided that if the Indian Muslims wanted to fulfil their duty to their country in accordance with the Shariah, they should become one with their Hindu brothers. Giving greater impetus to his contention, he stated that it was his firm belief that Muslims cannot perform their *faraiz* (indispensable obligations) unless, in accordance with the tenets of Islam, they reach a complete accord with their Hindu compatriots.

He then explains the Shariah in the light of the *Surah-e-Mumtahina* from the Koran, which classifies two types of non-Muslims, those who do not declare war on the Muslims and those who massacre the Muslims. The Koran enjoins the Muslims to enter into treaties with the former, and sever all connection with the latter. Whereas the Hindus fall in the former category, the British are undoubtedly in the latter. In the light of the events of the last five years, the British have become for the Muslims according to the Shariah, *fareeq-e-maharib* (the enemy that fights). It is *kufr* (sacrilege) for the Muslims to have anything to do with the British. In view of the rumours of an impending treaty, he declares it unlawful for any Muslim to extend a hand to the British unless they vacate the holy land, take their hands off Asia Minor, lift all conditions which have been imposed on Constantinople and last but not least, give India her freedom. Freedom in the sense of Purna Swaraj (complete self-rule), not a new progressive scheme masquerading as Swaraj. Until such time that this agreement is reached, it is permissible for a Muslim to 'take a snake or a scorpion in his hand and feed it with milk but (he is) forbidden to make peace with the British'.

He reminds his Muslim audience of what he had said in the pages of *Al Hilal* in 1912, that the British government is bent upon wiping out their existence from the globe. Then using the example of the Prophet's covenant with the non-Muslim Medinites, he gives the Indian Muslims the ultimate precedent for uniting with the Hindus against a common enemy. The Prophet's *ahad nama* (written treaty) stated that he hereby makes peace with the Jewish tribes who lived around Medina and declared that they have now joined together to become *ummat-e-wahida*, *ummat* meaning *quom* or nation, *wahida* meaning one. Similarly, Azad says, in accordance with that, the holiest of traditions, the seven crore Muslims should join with the twenty-two crore Hindus and become one nation or *quom*.

He warns the Muslims that the friendship with Hindus should not be regarded by either party as a political expedient. It should come from the depth of their conviction and bear the stamp of sincerity.

> They (Hindus) should have no doubt that the Muslims have embraced them on their own. Their embrace has been extended to them by the Will of Allah and His Shariat.

He then reminds his listeners of the lesson that he had taught in *Al Hilal*, that their duty as Muslims was to work with the Hindus and not to remain separate from them as taught by the followers of Sir Syed. Regarding Non-Cooperation he again refers to the Koranic injunction What Gandhi was saying was nothing new for the followers of Islam. This has been a part of the teaching of Islam for 1300 years and it is thereby the duty of Muslims to endorse it.

This address outlined two goals before the Muslims, Khilafat and Independence. At the core of both goals lay Hindu-Muslim unity. In a fine display of oratory he reminds his listeners of *freedom* as their final goal:

> The ultimate end of all these victories (of the Khilafat) is gliding over your oblivious heads. It is the duty of every Indian, every Hindu, Muslim, Parsi, Christian, everyone who has seen the clear flow of the rivers Ganga and Jamna and has lifted on his head, the star-filled sky of India, to achieve this goal.

He asks the Muslims to follow the Koranic injunction as specified in the *Surat-ul-Asr, Wal asr inal insaana...*, to attain the goal of India's Independence. The *surah* has specified four conditions for success. First, *Iman* (faith); second, *amal-e-saleh* (rightful deeds); third, *tausih-e-haq* (widening the circle of Truth); fourth, *tausih-e-sabr* (exhorting upon endurance). It is important that in the performance of duty there be no concern for rewards; to work without eyeing the prize is the key. He ends the speech on a passionate plea for boycotting imported materials from Manchester and Lancashire.

Azad concluded his address at the Khilafat Conference on the following day. The address is, therefore, recorded in two parts. In the second part he makes two important statements. First, that it is not only against the tenets of Islam, it is blatant *kufr* to accept anything from the British government; and second, it is the religious duty of every Muslim to court imprisonment by the British. Referring to the arrests of Khilafat leaders he says that their 'crimes' are shared not only by all the believers in *La Ilaha illa'llah* ('There is no deity save God') but by all thirty-two crore Indians. Regarding the above *fatwa* against the British, he says that as far back as 1916, when the government ordered his externment for 'conspiring with the terrorists' he wrote a detailed letter stating that even a single moment spent underneath the British flag is *haram* (forbidden) for the Muslim. He then spells out the anti-British *fatwa*, declaring any interaction with the British unlawful. To this he adds his prophecy that the sun is about to set on this empire:

> In my mind is the vision that I used to see in ancient history. I see Rome sinking, I see the end of the Caledonians, before my eyes is the throne of Jamshed being overturned, and now History is making us witness this tableau of *inqilab* (revolution).

He quotes a Hadith of the Prophet which he uttered during his last Haj. When asked, what is the biggest Jihad, the Prophet thought for a moment, then said, 'Proclaiming the truth in the face of a cruel monarch'. This Hadith, Azad said, entitles every Muslim and every Hindu who loves truth to declare that serving the British is *kufr*, it enjoins every soldier to throw away his commission. Reminding his audience of the bitter truth about the hand that fired the first shot at unarmed civilians at Jallianwala Bagh, he says that since the days of the East India Company, the British have insidiously used Indian soldiers to destroy their own motherland. The Hindus, he says, are equally guilty for having sold their *dharam* (faith) and *atma* (soul) and having thrown away the wealth of India at the feet of the British.

To the Muslims he says that Islam has forbidden *qattal* (killing) of any human being unless he is one of those whose existence creates *fitna* (evil) for the freedom of the human race. The Koran states *Walakum fil qasasi*... (Al Nisa 93:4) 'The judge who orders execution does not commit murder. In *qasas*, life is hidden'. The clear implication here is that since Islam does not forbid the killing of a race which has become the cause of *fitna* on earth, therefore the killing of the British is *qasas* (law of retaliation). It is killing of *fitna* to save the world from becoming a living hell.

Finally, addressing those ulema who still entertain doubts about Gandhi's programme of Non-Cooperation he relates the Hadith of Hazrat Usama who killed an enemy in battle. The man had embraced Islam for fear of death and had recited the *kalima* even as Usama's sword was lifted over his head. When the Prophet learnt of this he was deeply hurt. He asked Usama what would be his reply on the day of Judgement when the slain man confronted him in his blood soaked shroud? The Prophet's example is before us, Azad warned. When he was so generous to one who had converted to Islam only because he feared death, how would he regard the true believers? What would he say to 'those wretched Muslims who by continuing to serve the imperial army, were forced to train their guns on the very people who had been the custodians of Islam for a hundred years'.

Azad's address to the Khilafat Conference articulates the tenets of his political philosophy and his prescription for the attainment of independence. It continues the arguments for Koranic injunctions for freedom which were introduced in *Al Hilal*. The anti-Imperialist stand is reinforced. But there is a new emphasis on Hindu-Muslim cooperation, not found in the earlier writings. Arguments from the Prophet's tradition are used to support the contention. The *khutba* seems the outcome of the finest liberal thought. To see it as an expedient of his affiliation with Congress, as some right wing critics have tended to, seems to be a politically motivated view, not worthy of serious discussion.

In November 1921, Azad delivered the presidential address at the conference of Jamiat-ul-Ulema-e-Hind (Council of the Ulema of India) held in Lahore. Malihabadi reports that the speech was written during the train journey from Calcutta to Lahore.[11] This was the third conference of the Jamiat over which he had presided. The Jamiat selected him year after year, in preference to all the senior ulema, but despite being most eligible for it, he could not secure the position of the Imamul Hind (religious head of Indian Muslims). The issue of Imamaul Hind continued to bother him during this period. It is again brought up before the Jamiat in this address. He begins as usual by lamenting the miserable condition of the Muslims. He compares their present to their past, i.e. the pre-Islamic times, during which time, the Ashab-e-Kahf[12] were forced to leave the world and take refuge in the mountains. Since the Ashab-e-Kahf were only a few, they could find refuge in a mountain cave. But the lakhs of Muslims today, where are they going to find asylum, he asks?

There are pits for the snakes and caves for the beasts in which they can spend their nights in peace. But alas! On the face of the entire earth there is not even a space of four-hand spans on which the followers of Islam can live without fear.

The Koran, he says, has used the past to project the future. It uses history to demonstrate the unchanging nature of human behaviour. Events from the days of Prophet Noah to the Prophet Moses are narrated to strengthen the faith of the *momins*. But despite the lessons contained in history, man refuses to learn. The Koran laments at the wretchedness of man, who has ears but cannot hear, has eyes but cannot see. There is, however, a concurrent logic of the Koran-e-Hakim, he says, which expounds a *Qanoon-e-Ilahi* (Law of Allah) according to which *fasad* (unrest) will prevail for a period of time, which is necessary for *zuhoor-e-nataij* (revelation of consequences). After that, the last judgement upon *haq* (truth) and *batil* (falsehood) will be brought down; and the *mazloomi* (humility) of *haq* will gain victory. The Koranic word for this is *qaza bil haq* (judgement of truth).

The ulema, he says, should review the current situation in view of this injunction. He describes the British oppression of the human race, as an aggregate of the *zulm* (oppression) of all the tyrants, the accounts of whom are given in the Koran; Pharaohs of Egypt, Nimrod of Caledonia, the A'ads and the Midians; Egypt, Iran, Babel, Nineveh, Greece and Rome. Pitted against these forces of evil, the ulemas have to understand the crucial role that their leadership will play during these anarchical times. He gives poignant accounts of *Imams* and *alims* who suffered torture and privation in the cause of truth. It is easy to visualize the power of his oratory when he describes the tortures inflicted on Imam Hambal, Imam Abu Hanifa, Imam Shafei, Shaikh-ul-Islam Ibn Taimiyya and closer to home, Shaikh Ahmed Sirhindi.[13]

Implicit in this account is his regret that the *alims* of the present day have lost this quality of *faqr-o-faaqa* (self-deprivation). The Islamic countries have, fortunately, witnessed many *alims* entering the field of reform. Shaikh Mohammad Abduh spent his last days creating an intellectual awakening in Al Azhar. Shaikh Mohammed Jezairi tried to create a *jama'at* for the reform of Jamia Zaitunia in Tunis. In India, first Nadwatul Ulema (School for Islamic studies at Nadwa), then the Jamiatul Ansar Deoband (School at Deoband), was established. But unfortunately none of these measures could achieve the desired objective.

The purpose for which the Jamiat came into existence, was *ahiya-o-tajdid-i-millat*, meaning how to lift the *quom* from its present state of degradation and restore it to its previous eminence. For this, three types of reforms were carried out; reforms against *taqlid* (imitation) of Europe (Sir Syed in India, Sultan Mahmud and Fuad Pasha in Turkey, Mohammad Ali Pasha, in Egypt), political reforms (Syed Jamaluddin Asadabadi Afghani in Egypt, Midhat Pasha in Turkey) and religious reforms. It was for this last category of reform that *Al Hilal* was started. Its baseline was Islam:

> In the Shariat of Islam there is no distinction between *Din* and *Duniya* (spiritual and temporal). Islam has declared Allah's Shariat as the fountainhead for the salvation of all mankind. The foundation of a Muslim's political, educational, cultural, and community life is the Shariat-i-Islamia, the Koran and the Sunnah.

This was the *da'wat* (invitation) of *Al Hilal.* Since 1911, Azad writes, he had spent his days and nights, whether at home or elsewhere, dreaming of this *Yusuf-e-maqsud* (desired beloved).

He asks whether this reform needed *tajdid* (renewal) or *tasis* (foundation)? Answering his own question he asserts that for the *islah* (reform) of *millat-e-Islamia*, what is needed is adherence to the teachings of the Koran and the Shariah. If Islam is the *din-i-kamil* (complete code of life), it is imperative that it also be the complete educator, if it is the *din-i-akhiri* (final revealed religion) the practice of its Shariah should be applicable to all times. There is no reason for us to run after the ways of Europe to organize the *jama'at* (Muslim community). Islam has given the prescription for organization. It has provided a forum for meetings in the injunction to pray five times a day in the *jama'at* (gathering). It has provided a means for fund collection in the Zakat (compulsory surrender of a percentage of income), a method of public education in the *Juma Khutba* (address to the congregation on Friday), and a focus for leadership in the office of the Imam.

Azad finally approaches the subject of leadership. He says that this was an issue about which he had thought for twelve years and reached the conclusion that it is the key to the problem of the Indian Muslims. Muslims have to eschew individualism for collectivism, meaning, that in accordance with the Shariah, accept guidance from one single *amir* or *quaid*. After stating the importance of *nazm-e-jama'at* (*espirit de corps*) in Islam he upbraids the Muslims in these words:

> Ten crore Muslims, who constitute the largest *jama'at* of Muslims in the world are spending their lives in India in a manner that they have no mutual love for one another, no unity, no *millat* (nationhood), no leader, no prescribed Shariah. They are a herd, a crowd spread over various regions.

He asks how can a *jama'at* maintain its existence without a leader? Giving examples from Islamic history he asserts that when a similar *fitna* arose from China and Tartary in the sixth century AH. Imam Ibn Taimiyya gave the *fatwa* that the Muslims should either perform Hijrat from Tartary or immediately appoint an Imam and perform their duties in accordance with the Shariah. This choice is once again posed before the Muslims who are facing the British *fitna*; they should either perform the Hijrat or establish the *nizam-e-jama'at*.

He recalls that in 1914 when he realized the importance of this issue he approached Maulana Mahmudul Hasan[14] to accept the leadership of the Muslims. But he was persuaded by some people to undertake a journey to Hejaz; meanwhile Azad himself was placed under detention in Ranchi. What Azad does not refer to are the efforts he made to get the leadership of the Muslims. Its sequence is recorded by Malihabadi in his book

Zikr-e-Azad. At the Khilafat Conference held in Calcutta in February 1920, Azad had discussed the importance of an Imam with Malihabadi.

> The Muslims of India should be organized on the basis prescribed by Islam. An Imam should be elected, obedience to whom should be considered a religious duty. The Muslims will be willing to accept this *da'wat* if they were told that without an Imam their life and death was unIslamic.
>
> *When the majority of them surrender themselves to the authority of the Imam, he should enter into an agreement with the Hindus and declare Jehad on the British.*[15] By the joint effort of the Hindus and Muslims, the British would thus be defeated. But who should be the Imam? He should be a person with the highest credibility and integrity, and one who cannot be bought at any price. He must have full knowledge of contemporary conditions.[16]

At the end, Malihabadi comments that it was obvious that Azad considered himself suitable for the office, 'and I also believed that he should get the position'.

Meanwhile Maulana Mahmudul Hasan, Azad's original choice for Imam, had been released from Malta and had arrived in Lucknow. Malihabadi records that he waited on him in private and discussed the question of Imamat, requesting him to accept it. Maulana Mahmudul Hasan declined politely but heartily endorsed the name of Azad and gave permission that his endorsement be made public. The next person before whom Malihabadi appeared was Maulana Abdul Bari of Firangi Mahal, Lucknow.[17] His word was important because of his political profile as well as his patronage of the two 'Big Brothers' of Indian Muslim politics—Mohammad Ali and Shaukat Ali.[18] 'These two brothers were not on very good political terms with Azad. It was, therefore, by no means easy for Azad to get himself recognized as Imam by Maulana Mohammad Bari'.[19] His reply, in the form of a letter to Malihabadi was very guarded and non-committal, saying that he would agree to anything , the *jamhur* (public) wanted provided it did not create any schism in the Muslim community.

Azad's reaction was to advise Malihabadi to postpone the issue for the moment.

It was not easy for Azad to give up what he considered essential for the *falah* (progress) of the community. In his address to the Bengal Khilafat Conference, February 1920, he defines the role of the Imam:

> According to the Shariah, we need an Imam who has eyes to probe the depth of matters, a mind to unravel intricate problems, and a heart full of secret knowledge of the Koran and Sunnah. The Imam will apply the principles of the Shariah to the present condition of the Indian Muslims, and will also apply them to the new situation after India becomes independent. He will also apply those principles in the ever changing circumstances of war and peace. He will have the authority to issue *fatwas* whenever he considers necessary. Not every *alim* is qualified to perform this duty, not every madrasa teacher has an idea of the important function of the Imam.[20]

Two of Azad's biographers have written that Azad was elected Imamul Hind at this conference. Although election of an Imam was assigned to this conference by a special *majlis-i-shoora* held at Delhi, it is evident that no one was selected. The conference passed a resolution to elect an Imam-ul-Hind and struck a sub-committee for the purpose. The matter was never concluded, says Mushirul Haq, and the biographers mistook the motion for the enactment.

At the end of the Jamiat *Khutba*, Azad refers to a few burning issues of the time, the Mapila revolt, conversion to Islam and Swaraj. With reference to the Mapila revolt, he condemns the Muslims because what they did was against the decision given by the Jamiat, i.e., to fight for Khilafat using non-violent methods. No Muslim whether from Malabar or any other part of India, he asserts, has the right to contravene the word of the Jamiat. He then makes an important statement about violence and non-violence in Islam. A misunderstanding about violence being an article of faith in Islam, he says, needs to be cleared. In Islam there is no sanction for violence. There is sanction for the organized act of war only if it is waged to establish justice. Azad uses this forum to refute the criticism being targeted at him that he had prevailed upon the Jamiat to adopt the policy of non-violence for political expediency. The foundations of non-violence, he said, were firmly grounded in the Islamic Shariat. Similarly Swaraj (self-government, freedom), the new word which is now entering the vocabulary of the nation, has been engrained in every race, *quom*, individual by his God and his prophet.

A few weeks after delivering this address, on 10 December 1921, Azad was arrested at his residence by Inspector Goldie. Abdul Razzaq Malihabadi had been arrested a few days earlier, and Deshbandhu C.R. Das on the very same day. All of them met at the Presidency Jail where Azad appeared before the Magistrate, a man called M.D. Swinner. Two months later, on 9 February 1922, he was sentenced to a year's rigorous imprisonment under Section 124A of the Indian Penal Code. Azad smiled and said, 'This is much less than what I expected'.

During the prison-term there is evidence of a deepening under-standing of the current issues facing the country. The Congress Address 1923, delivered to the Special Session at Delhi contains substantive evidence of this understanding. For a variety of reasons which have been discussed in previous chapters, Azad saw a natural bond between India and the Islamic nations. In *Al Hilal* he continually refers to their shared heritage and traditions. A strong current of this deeply felt affinity continues to pervade all of his subsequent writings and speeches.

notes

1 The event behind the writing of this article was the furore following Munshi Ram (Swami Shraddhanand) being invited to make a speech at die Jama *Masjid,* along with a large number of Arya Samajists. Azad asks, 'What is wrong with Swami Shraddhnand standing on the *chabutra* of the *masjid* for his speech?'

2 Ansar Harvani, 'As I knew him' in *India's Maulana* ed., Syeda Saiyidain Hameed. Harvani records his impressions of Azad who he first met in 1928.

3 See *Paigham*, Calcutta, 1921.

4 Weekly journal started by Azad in September 1921 from Calcutta, which was different from *Al Hilal* in the sense of simple language and cheaper production. Azad's name appears as the Supervisor and Abdul Razzaq Malihabadi's as editor. It ran for three months.

5 Ibid.

6 See V.N. Datta, *Maulana Azad*, Chapter 4, pp. 104–40.

7 V.N. Datta.

8 Azad's letter is quoted by Malihabadi in *Zikr-e-Azad*, p. 47.

9 *Zikr-e-Azad* contains two of his articles from *Paigham*.

10 Malik Ram has given the date as August 1921. I have used the date given by Abdul Razzaq Malihabadi because Malik Ram has taken the text of the address from *Zikr-e-Azad*.

11 *Zikr-e-Azad*, p. 175.

12 *Suratul Kahf* 11:18. This parable about an ancient people is narrated in the Koran. This band of pious and god-fearing people lived in an oppressive and blasphemous society which did not allow them their faith in Allah. When all doors closed before them, they found refuge in tile cave of a mountain.

13 Khutbat-e-Azad, p. 121.

14 See Marihabadi, pp. 34–9.

15 Italicized for emphasis.

16 Malihabadi, p. 24. Also see Mushirul Haq, 'A Revolutionary Nationalist' in *India's Maulana* ed. Hameed.

17 Abdul Bari said. 'I will be the first man to offer *bayat* to Azad'.

18 Mushirul Haq in *India's Maulana*, p. 175.

19 Ibid., Malihabadi writes that Azad gave no importance to Shaukat Ali because he was neither intelligent nor quick witted. But it was a different matter vis-à-vis Mohammad Ali, with whom he always indulged in *noak jhok*. (reparteé)

20 Mushirul Haq, 'A Revolutionary Nationalist' in *India's Maulana*, Vol. I. Haq has quoted this excerpt from *Khutbat-i-Azad*, 1959.

6

fatwa against the british:
quol-e-faisal

THE NEWS OF THE ARREST OF THE ALI BROTHERS had reached Azad in
Calcutta on 18 August 1921. Immediately, Azad arranged a meeting in Holland Park, and before a crowd of over twenty thousand
he owned with pride the authorship of the Karachi Resolution.[1]
He further challenged the intelligence officers present, to record
his statement word for word, while claiming that this protest
would now be unending.[2] Prior to this, as discussed earlier, he
had made similar speeches at the Central Jamiat-ul-Ulema and
Khilafat Committee meetings in Delhi. The same theme had been
repeated at various public meetings at Karachi, Bombay, Lahore,
Bareilly and Agra. In Calcutta he had made two speeches at
Mirzapur Square on 1 July and 15 July which were most provocative. His open challenge to the government during each of these
meetings led to a wide speculation that he would be arrested
before the dawn of the next morning. But the government still
held back.

In November 1921, Azad was in Bombay with Gandhi, when the news of fresh repressions in Bengal reached him. His return to Calcutta now became imperative because of the fear that the government's new atrocities may unleash the fury of the public. When he reached Calcutta he witnessed scenes of 'extreme forbearance and extreme oppression'. The government had gone berserk under the Criminal Law Amendment Act 1908. The people had, however, decided neither to move an inch from their stand nor to retaliate against the violence. He therefore decided that he would not stir from Calcutta until either the government would repeal its communique and order, or place him under arrest.

The Calcutta arrests of Azad and C.R. Das were to give a much needed boost to the sagging spirit of the national movement. In November 1921, when Gandhi had announced the suspension of the movement, a pall seemed to have descended over the country. But in Calcutta a new hope was born when, while the Government of Bengal declared a ban on the Razakars, the people collected a thousand signatures for a new *jama'at*. Each day, while several hundred Razakars were thrown in prison, new ones were enlisted.

Azad's pride in the role played by the Muslims in placing Calcutta at the vanguard of freedom, finds expression in this description in *Paigham*.

> I have been working in Calcutta for 15 years. It is has been the locus of my family for a half century... The most important work for Khilafat was accomplished by Calcutta Muslims during the last three years. He (the Muslim) will now take the first step in the last stage of this journey. He has learnt the secret of peaceful sacrifice. He will neither flare up nor will he let himself be smothered. To his share has fallen the privilege of reaching the goal of peaceful civil disobedience. He has richly deserved it.[3]

Both Azad and C.R. Das realized that Calcutta would be the new battleground where the government's repressive policies would be equally matched by mass resistance. Azad wrote about this in *Paigham* in the form of a message to the readers, two days before his arrest.

> By deciding to arrest me, the government has taken a great load off my head. Only God knows how difficult it had become for me to stay out of prison. Those who are first in line, how little do they realize the pain of those who are left behind. Mohammad Ali, Shaukat Ali, Lala Lajpat Rai, Pandit Motilal Nehru—their journey has ended, while I still wait for mine to begin. But today my destination has appeared right in front of my eyes. My heart overflows with happiness that I am leaving behind me the last stretch, but a victory stretch. I have called Calcutta the 'last' as well as the 'victory' stretch. This is my firm conviction. Soon the country will see that what could not be accomplished in the entire nation in two years, will be done in Calcutta within a few days.

This message gave hope to the people in a moment of despondency by stating that these arrests will accomplish in a short time what the movement may not accomplish in several years, and that Calcutta will become a shining example for the rest of the country. Then referring to the political awakening among Muslims he writes:

> I see the Muslims of India turning in a new direction as a consequence of my arrest. I have faith in the provinces of Punjab, Bihar and the Frontier. The Muslims living in these areas have heard me with love, trust and acquiescence. For the last ten years they have been the pivot of my hopes. What I could not explain in my speeches and writings in three years, will now be explained by the silence of my arrest. The Government of Bengal is thus doing a service not only to Bengal but to the whole of India.

In the tradition of the leader, the *amir*, the *imam*, he leaves his parting advice. He first addresses his own people, the Muslims, then his organization, Central Khilafat Committee and Jamiat-ul-Ulema-e-Hind, then Mahatma Gandhi, then his successor, Hakim Ajmal Khan and finally his prosecutor, the Government of Bengal. For the Muslims his *paigham* (message) is the same which underpins the writings of *Al Hilal*, i.e. Hindu-Muslim unity, peace, organized resistance and sacrifice. Further, he implores the Muslims, in keeping with the Islamic tradition, to take upon themselves, at this critical time, the leadership role. It is significant that all his messages are consistently optimistic. His overriding concern is to ensure that the differences between Hindus and Muslims are resolved for the common good.

The specific events surrounding Azad's arrest start with his speeches at two meetings held in Mirzapur Square. The speeches were transcribed by the Special Branch of the police department, on the order of Deputy Commissioner, J.A.M. Goldie, and placed before the court as evidence of sedition! That was the ostensible reason for Azad's arrest on 10 December 1921. The events of the arrest were as follows. At 4:30 in the evening Goldie arrived with a 'European' inspector and asked Azad if he would accompany him. Azad asked if he had a warrant for his arrest? Goldie said 'No'. Azad said he was prepared to go without a warrant. The Calcutta correspondent, who wrote a preface for the English version of *Quol-e-Faisal*, states that the whole event was so unobtrusively executed, that no one felt that anything was remiss.[*] When Azad, accompanied by Goldie and the inspector reached the cars which were parked at a short distance from the house, a few wayfarers and shopkeepers gathered to offer their *salaams* (salutations), as per usual practice, but did not notice anything unusual because Azad sat in another car. They too only found out about his arrest when it was officially announced the same night.

Azad was first brought to the police commissioner's office, where he was joined by C.R. Das and both were detained for twenty minutes. From there they were moved to the Presidency jail, Alipur, and locked up in the 'European' ward which was meant for European under-trials. Azad records that by that time it was 7 pm he said his *Isha* prayers, drank a few sips of water and fell into a deep sleep which was not even disturbed by the sounds of the sentry's boots marching up and down on the cement floor. Interestingly, he always remembers sleeping well in prisons, whether it was Calcutta or Ahmednagar. The reason he gives here is that he firmly believed that this imprisonment was a prelude for the successful completion of his work and that now that he was on the right track he could sleep.

A general air of apology was evident in the attitudes of all his prosecutors. Colonel Hamilton, the superintendent and jailor, kept repeating that he was just obeying the orders of his superiors. A.Z. Khan, fourth Presidency Magistrate, who was sent to the prison with a warrant under Section 2-17 of the Criminal Law Amendment Act, was obviously nervous about his assignment, and, making a summary dismissal said that he was only doing what he had been told to do. For two weeks Azad was held under the above Act. But when the minimum evidence necessary for proving the crime could not be obtained, the section under which the case was registered was withdrawn and replaced by section 124A.

In total, Azad appeared eight times before the court, the first *paishi* (court hearing) was held on 13 December 1921. On his sixth appearance he presented his written statement, *Quol-e-Faisal*. This statement, the tide of which may be translated to mean 'The Last Word' was made before the Chief Presidency Magistrate, Calcutta Court on 24 January 1922 by the accused, Mohiuddin Ahmed also called Abul Kalam Azad. He was sentenced on 9 February 1922, to a one year imprisonment with hard labour. In *Young India*, Gandhi hailed this as 'an eloquent thesis, giving Maulana's views on Khilafat and Nationalism ... an oration deserving penal servitude for life'. Azad is reported to have smiled and said, 'This is a much lighter sentence than I had expected!'

Azad's presentation before the court has to be read against the background of a series of repressive measures which had shocked the people into taking a united stand against the common enemy. The Hindu-Muslim-Sikh unity which had been forged in 1919, following Gandhi's call for Non-cooperation, had led to instances of British frenzy such as the massacre at Jallianwala Bagh. This was proof that the British attitude of maintaining a stiff upper lip was starting to crack. Gandhi's successful launch of Satyagraha proved a further setback for the government.

As stated in the last chapter, Azad was released from Ranchi on the first of January 1920. On 28 and 29 February, the Khilafat Conference was held in the Calcutta Town Hall where Azad was President. He once again used the public platform to incite the Muslims against the government. In March 1921, while the Seditious Meetings Act was in force in districts Lahore and Amritsar, Azad, accompanying Gandhiji toured Punjab. At the Friday prayers, he gave the *khutba* in the Shahi Masjid at Lahore. Following the prayers, in the quadrangle of the mosque he spoke passionately about Non-cooperation. The speech was recorded in the *Civil and Military Gazette*, published from Lahore under the title 'Revolutionary speech in the quadrangle of the Mosque'. In Amritsar he did precisely the same thing at the Jama Masjid. Despite its political content, the Punjab government somehow swallowed the provocation. All this has been discussed earlier in the context of Khilafat politics.

In accordance with the tenets of Non-cooperation, Azad pleads 'guilty' of the charges levied against him by the government. Then he verbally parries with the prosecution until he reduces all its arguments to shambles. He starts by blaming them for not presenting better evidence when he had provided stronger proofs of his 'guilt'. In fact it is the weakness of the prosecution's arguments which has impelled him to offer additional evidence to bolster their case. He says he had never intended to make a statement because he wanted to let the government carry the day. But when he realized that the two speeches on the basis of which the case was filed, were not even a faint echo of the provocation that he had offered in most of his earlier speeches, he felt constrained to bring them to the attention of the court.

I confess that not only on those two occasions but in numerous speeches made over the last two years I have used these and even stronger phrases. To say so is my imperative duty and I cannot hesitate from performing it, on pain of being regarded a crime under

Section 124A. I want to repeat this even now and will go on repeating it so long as I have the power of speech.

Since the age of eighteen, he says, he has been preaching *azadi* (freedom) and *haq talabi* (demand for rights). Even during his detention he spent his days and nights in the pursuit of this *tabligh* (preaching) and education. The walls of Ranchi can bear witness. He says that he cannot plead 'not guilty' of this crime because he is the *Daiyee* (guide) of this movement, which created a revolution in the political ideology of the Indian Muslims and elevated them to the position which they are taking today. Meaning, that today every Muslim in India has become a partner in his 'crime'. The reference here is to the lesson of *Al Hilal*:

> In 1912, I started an Urdu Journal, *Al Hilal*, which was the organ of this movement. Its purpose was the same… It is a fact that within three years, it had created a new spirit in the religious and the political life of the Muslims of India.

Before *Al Hilal* appeared on the scene, he writes, the Muslims were detached from the political activities of their Hindu brothers and had become a potent weapon in the hands of the bureaucracy. The divisive policy of the British had convinced them that their existence was in a danger using the argument that since the Hindus were a vast majority, if India was freed a Hindu government would be formed at the expense of the Muslims. But *Al Hilal* appeared and gave them faith to reject the fear of numbers and become one with their Hindu brothers. This wrought the change which is reflected today in the unification of Khilafat and Swaraj.

He then gives a detailed account of all his activities since he was released from the Ranchi detention in January 1920. In February, in his Presidential Address at the Khilafat Conference in Calcutta, he told the Muslims that it was their Islamic duty to withdraw their cooperation from government; later Mahatma Gandhi introduced this as Non-Cooperation and launched the movement. This Presidential Address delivered at the Khilafat

Conference was enlarged and published as a book, which was reprinted several times with its English translation. This he says is the documentary proof of his 'crimes'. Other meetings and conferences were held during the two years since Ranchi. In each one of them he propagated the same ideas as at the Mirzapur Square meetings, except that they were much more explicitly stated. In essence then, he says, 'In the last few years I have done nothing except violating Section 124A.'

That he saw himself doing for the Muslims what Gandhi was doing for the Hindus, in fact preceding him in his work, is reflected in the next few lines:

> I want to say here that *Al Hilal* was a clear invitation to freedom or death... *The spirit of religion that Mahatma Gandhi is creating among the Hindus today, Al Hilal had completed the work (for the Muslims) in 1914.*[5] It is strange that among the Muslims and Hindus the new effervescence started only when their Westernization was firmly replaced by religious education.

Quol-e-Faisal was addressed to the Muslims as if Azad was speaking to them from the *mimber* (pulpit). There is no message in it for the Hindus (unless by implication) since his primary purpose was to tell the Muslims what their religious duty was. He declared that the State was guilty and it was the duty of every individual who claimed to be a Muslim to stand and proclaim this truth, regardless of the consequences of his stand. He then asserted that it was the moral decadence of the Muslims which was responsible for their current situation. This is not a new theme for Azad. It persisted right from the days of *Lisan-us-Sidq*. Similarly, the idea that proclaiming the truth in the face of an oppressive state was an Islamic injunction, a factor which leaves a Muslim with no option, had by now become the basic tenet of his philosophy, expressed in several articles of *Al Hilal* and *Al Balagh*:

> I cannot deny this painful fact that the Muslims themselves are responsible for this reversal. They have lost all the values of an

Islamic life and accepted the debasement of slavery. There is no greater *fitna* in the world for Islam than is their present condition. Even as I write these lines my heart is shattered in a million pieces with shame and remorse. In this very India there are Muslims who make a public declaration of their support for oppression due to their own moral weakness. But the truth cannot be denied because of the bad practices of some human beings. The tenets of Islam are preserved in its Book which does not permit, regardless of the circumstances, that having lost their freedom, the Muslims should continue to remain alive. Muslims should either remain free (*azad*) or perish; there is no third path in Islam.

Thus is the major theme delineated. It was by now familiar to Azad's followers that the struggle for freedom was in accordance with the principles of Islam. Declaring that no Indian heart can harbour loyalty for a government which has perpetrated the atrocities in Punjab and against the Islamic Khilafat, he writes that on 13 December 1916 when he was incarcerated at Ranchi, he wrote to Lord Chelmsford explaining the Islamic injunction regarding Khilafat and Jaziratul Arab (the Arabian peninsula), and warning him that if the British reneged on their promise about the Islamic territories, the Indian Muslims would have only one option—to align with the Islamic countries. Consequently, when, one by one, all promises were broken by the British, the Muslims withdrew all support. This was their duty given the Islamic injunction. He adds that the Muslims were finally convinced that their only path to the attainment of truth and justice lay in the attainment of Swaraj, 'A national government which was of India, in India and for India.'

Explaining his own supreme compulsion to choose this path, he writes the lines which have become a classic expression of freedom:

Is liye ke main Hindustani hoon, is liye ke main musalmaan hoon, is liye ke main insaan hoon.

(Because I am an Indian, I am a Muslim, I am a human being.)

Islam does not sanction any form of government unless it is based on freedom (*azadi*) and democracy (*jamhooriyat*). Islam has been revealed to mankind to restore the lost freedom of the human race. It has established the supremacy of *haq* (truth) and denied the right to any except Allah to hold sway over the human race. It has introduced the concept of equality among human beings and forbidden any differentiation on the basis of race, colour or nationality. The only distinguishing feature which tells one human being from another is *amal* (deed), the best *amal* being the only criterion for excellence. The Koran states:

Yaaa-'ayyuhun-naasu 'inna khalaqnaakum-min zakirin-wa unsaa wa ja'alnakum sbu-uuban-wa qabaa'ila lita-'aarafuu. 'Inna 'akramakum indallahi 'atqaakum. (49:13)

(O mankind! We have created you male and female, and have made you nations and tribes that ye may know one another. The noblest of you, before Allah, is the one who is best in conduct.)

A study of linguistic terminology, he writes, is a useful means of understanding the Islamic spirit. Rejecting the word for personal kingship, Islam favours the word *Khalifa*, which literally means 'deputy', implying that such authority is only a representative one. Similarly the word in the Koran for the organization of the state is *shura*, which literally means consultation. The implication here is that business of the state should be transacted in consultation with the *jama'at* and not by personal ordinance.

The first period in the history of Islam, he writes, was of pure Islamic rule—the Prophet and his four *Khalifas*. The Islamic republic existed then in its pristine form, without the shadow of the autocracy seen in Persia or the Byzantine Empire. The Khalifa was an ordinary 'democrat' who lived in a dwelling with a thatched roof and wore a cloak with many patches. The second period was the dynastic rule of Banu Ummaiyyah, which by its very nature ended the Islamic concept of democracy. The successive Khilafats moved rapidly towards *Shahenshahiyat* (kingship), *takht* (throne) and *taaj* (crown). Azad's purpose in recounting this was to show the Muslims that no matter how oppressive the regime, the *raast go* (truth speaking) men and women did not hesitate to proclaim the truth. The Koran, he says, has enjoined four bases for Islamic life, upon which all human achievement should be built. First, *Iman* (faith), second, *amal-e-salih* (good deeds), third, *tausih-e-haq* (widening the circle of truth), and fourth *tausih-e-sabr* (exhorting upon endurance). The foundation of Islamic belief is *tawhid* (oneness of Allah) which is the opposite of *shirk* (sharing deities with Allah). Therefore, given the fact that only *zaat-e-Ilahi* (entity of Allah) deserves man's *ita'at* (obedience), it follows that to make obeisance to any other power is to be guilty of *shirk* and in contravention with the tenets of Islam.

Azad writes that Islam is a *da'wat* (invitation) for *qurbani* (sacrifice) and *be-khaufi* (dauntlessness). The repeated injunction in the Koran is, 'A Muslim is one who is not afraid of any save Allah, and who speaks the truth in every circumstance'. It further describes the Muslim as *shahid* (witness to Truth) on God's earth. Azad describes the act of *shahadat* (witnessing) as the 'national duty' and 'national character' of the Muslims.[6] The implication here is obvious. Once again he has emphasized that his argument has the sanction of Islam. One of the basic teachings of Islam, which was the motto of his political *jama'at* Hizbullah, is reiterated here: *Amr bil ma'aruf wa nahi anil munkar* (enjoining the good and forbidding the evil). He then quotes a Hadith of the Prophet of Islam, 'Enjoin the good and forbid the evil, because if you do not, the most evil of men will rule over you, and God's affliction will surround you. You will pray for this rule to end, but no prayer will be answered'.

This type of rhetoric when used in current politics is pejoratively described as mingling religion with politics or using religion as an expedient of politics. But in the first century AH 580 (AD) Islam was revealed as a faith which was as much concerned with life on earth as it was with life hereafter. Politics was treated in Islam just as any other aspects of man's life on earth. Therefore the negative connotation attached to any nexus between politics and religion today, did not exist. What Azad was invoking here was the politico-religious practice which existed during the Khilafat-e-Rashidin.[7]

He proceeds to give a few poignant examples from Islamic history about the religious basis of politics. First, he says that the very basis of the case which had been filed against him is negated because there is no Section 124 A in Islam. The implication here is that it is only weak governments which need such instruments for governance. During the period of the first four. *Khalifas*, not a single coercive instrument of state was needed. An old woman could publicly upbraid the *Khalifa*, saying that if he did not dispense justice, 'We will uncoil you like a spindle'. Similarly when the *Khalifa* stood on the pulpit and announced, 'Listen and obey', a man stood up and said, 'We will neither listen nor obey'. 'Why?' asked the *Khalifa*. 'Because your cloak has been stitched using more than your share of cloth, and this is *khayanat* (cheating).' Hearing this, the Khalifa called upon his son to bear witness that he had given his own share of cloth to his father, hence the extra material used in his cloak. This, says Azad, was the forthright attitude of the *quom* towards their Khalifa, the *quom* whose valour overturned the thrones of Egypt and Iran. 'Indeed, Islam had no section 124A.'

The next period of Islam was marked by despotic rule. The first blow of despotism usually falls upon the freedom of speech and opinion; but this could not curb the candour of the tongues and fearlessness of the hearts of true believers, and truth was proclaimed from the darkness of prison cells, between lashes of the whip and under the axe of the executioner. Azad then gives examples of *alims* who did not hesitate for a moment to proclaim the truth even in the jaws of death. One such individual was Saffian Sari, who was summoned to court by Khalifa Haroun al-Rashid. The message-scroll reached him while he was sitting in the Masjid at Kufa, but he refused to touch it saying, 'Whatever has been touched by the hand of a tyrant, I do not want to touch'.

Azad then reminds the Muslims that there have been previous occasions when they have arisen from the depths of despair.

Comparing the British oppression with the savagery of the Tartars in the fifteenth century, he states that just as the last *fitna* of the Tartars resulted in the decimation of the Abbasid Khilafat and concluded with mass killings in Baghdad, so also the last *fitna* of Europe has led to the devastation of the Osmani Khilafat and the killing fields of Asia Kochak. But in the lair of beasts and tyrants such as Halaku Khan, Manku Khan, Abaqaan Khan,[8] there were men like Shaikh Saadi Shirazi, Shamsuddin Tabari, Shaikh-ul-Islam Ibn-e-Taimiyah,[9] whose tongues were more powerful than their oppressors' swords. All of them stood in the courts of their oppressors, called them tyrants, and cursed them to their face.

Having stated this, he carries the argument forward that if this was how the Muslims treated rulers whose rule was sanctioned by *shariah*, then what should an alien ruler expect from them? 'Is British monarchy and the representative status of Lord Reading more worthy than the Khilafat of Abdul Malik and *niyabat* (deputyship) of Hajjaj Bin Yusuf?' Even if we ignore the difference between a 'national and Muslim' and an 'alien and non-Muslim' government, he wrote, still we can do no less than say to them what we said to Hajjaj Bin Yusuf and Khalid Qasri's governments, 'Take heed, fear God, because the earth has been filled with your *zulm* (tyranny)'.

There is a distinct note of regret that Muslims have been made so helpless that instead of engaging in an armed struggle they have to resort to civil protest. The non-violence which they have adopted for aliens would have been more appropriate for the rulers of their own *quom*. The words he uses for the Muslims are *kamzor* (weak), *bebas* (helpless), *badbakht* (ill-fated), all indicative of how frail they have become. His great apprehension is that the Muslims may commit the unpardonable sin of *katman-e-shahaadat* meaning 'hiding the witness'. They are expected not to proclaim *zulm* as *zulm*, for fear of section 124A.

Can you weigh section 124A against the incident in the court of Khalifa Abdul Malik, whose empire extended from Africa to Sind, where an ordinary citizen proclaimed the tyranny of the Khalifa, even while his every limb was being cut off, until only his tongue remained intact to continue giving the *shahadat*.

The court, he writes, has always been an instrument in the hands of repressive and tyrannical governments. Although the fearsome Roman courts of the second century AD and the Inquisitions of the Middle ages do not exist today, he is not prepared to accept that man has been able to rid himself of the sadism that was unleashed at those assemblies. Next he recalls the great men who have graced the convict's dock. Starting with Jesus Christ, he extols the martyrs, paying homage to Socrates and Galileo, his illustrious predecessors who occupied this august place:

> So what a wonderful place is the convict's dock where the most righteous as well as the most criminal of men are made to stand. When I recall the great and meaningful history of the convict's dock and find that the honour of standing in that place belongs to me today, my soul bows in thankfulness to and in praise of God. Only he can understand the ecstasy I experience. In this dock of criminals, I feel that I am the envy of emperors.

On the subject of non-violence, he states that for him it is a matter of policy not of faith. Unlike Gandhiji and within the framework of Islam, he believes that a blow may be returned by a blow. Islam has sanctioned the use of force under certain specified circumstances, which according to *adl* (justice) and *akhlaq* (ethics) constitute the faith of every Muslim. But in the national fight for freedom he is in agreement, not only with Mahatma Gandhi's arguments for non-violence but in the truth behind them as well. This is the reason why he has always advised the Muslims to engage in peaceful struggle. In fact he is one of the very few Muslims who can claim that if they had not kept the Muslims on the path of non-violence, and with a firm hand, there is no saying what horrors could have ensued due to their suppressed emotions for the Khilafat.

The *Quol* ends with the lines which were written in the manner of prophets who asked God for forgiveness for all their persecutors, before proceeding peacefully to the gallows or placing their necks underneath the executioner's sword. That Azad held such men in the highest regard is evident in his earlier writings such as the essay 'Sarmad Shaheed' written in 1910, several articles of *Al Hilal* and *Al Balagh*, and almost the entire *Tazkirah*. That he saw himself standing in the presence of the magistrate in the Civil jail, in the manner of Jesus, Socrates and Galileo, is evident in his thankfulness to Allah for having given him place in such exalted company. The concluding paragraphs are written as if he was watching from a future time-frame, this moment coming into focus on the historical canvas:

> The public prosecutor who is working on this case is my brother and fellow countryman. I have no rancour against him in my heart. I will pray for him in the words of the Prophet of Islam, 'God! Open before them the Way because they know not what they do.' ... Mr. Magistrate! I will not take any more time of the court. This is an interesting and admonitory chapter of history in the arrangement of which we both are equally involved. To our lot has fallen the criminals' dock and to yours the magistrate's chair. I admit that for the completion of the work, the chair is as important as the dock. Come, let us quickly finish our role in this memorable and legendary work. The historian waits and future has been looking out for us for a long time. Let us come back soon and often, and you keep writing your judgement. This work will continue for sometime. Then the gates of another door will be flung open. This will be the Court of the Law of God. Time will be its judge and Time will write the judgement. That verdict will be final. *Alhamdolillah Awwalan wa Aakhirin.* (Praise be to Allah, from first to last.)

The court listened to these final words of *Quol-e-Faisal* in rapturous silence.

This statement was given to the court at his sixth *paishi* (court hearing). The day before the judgement was to be pronounced, Azad gave a statement to the press exhorting the public to maintain the utmost discipline and not to betray any sign of agitation at the announcement of his sentence. He issued four instructions:

(i)   No one should come to watch the court proceedings on 9 February. There should be no crowding on the streets.
(ii)   It is certain that he would be convicted. The public should expect that with the utmost peace and calm. There should be no *hartal* (strike) nor any unusual demonstration.
(iii) People should not flock to the prison or make any effort to see him.
(iv)   They should continue their daily agitation and, if possible, increase its momentum.

Despite the apprehensions of the government, the above statement had a magical effect on the people. Public unrest gave way to public calm. No one appeared at the courtroom, and Azad was sentenced without any fuss. The judgement of the Chief Presidency Magistrate is preserved as Case number 28, 1922. It is entitled, Kaisar-e-Hind *ba nam* Mohiuddin Ahmed alias Maulana Abul Kalam Azad:

> Maulana Abul Kalam Azad stands convicted under Section 124A, Indian Penal Code. On 1 July 1921, at the Mirzapur Square, Calcutta he spoke in Urdu about Khilafat, Punjab and Independence and on 15 July 1921, at the same spot, about Non-Cooperation. He used words through which he tried to spread, in contravention of the law, hatred and loathing among the people against the established government.

The accused has presented a detailed statement which is filled with the story of the government's ill deeds. He has elaborated upon the activities which he claims make him call the government 'oppressive'. He has given an account of those of his own activities which were undertaken against the government. He says that the copy made of his said speeches is totally inaccurate. Regardless, he accepts those portions which reflect his views about the government and those in which an appeal is made to the public to launch a struggle against the government.

I have read these speeches carefully and reached the conclusion that they are seditious. And that through them the accused has tried to spread hatred and loathing for a legally constituted government.

I find the accused guilty as per the declaration of the Public Prosecutor. And under Section 124 A of Indian Penal Code, I sentence him to imprisonment for one year with hard labour.

Signed: D. Swinner, Chief Presidency Magistrate, Calcutta, 9.2.1922.

notes

1 The Karachi Resolution stated that it was against the tenets of Islam to accept civil and military positions with the Government of India, since that would be tantamount to taking up arms against the Islamic nations.

2 Azad claimed that he had mooted the idea for the Karachi Resolution at the Khilafat Conference held at the Calcutta Town Hall on 28 and 29 February 1920. He also gave a press statement, which appeared on 30 September 1921, that at a Jamiat-ul-Ulema congregation in Delhi, he had signed the same resolution in the form of a fatwa.

3 *Quol-e-Faisal* pub. Salahuddin Mazhar, Anarkali Kitab Ghar, Lahore, no date, p. 38.

4 The edition of *Quol-e-Faisal* which I have used is an undated one, published at the Anarkali Kitab Ghar, Lahore. It has an Introduction which is stated to be the translation of the one written by a 'famous Hindu journalist and political leader of Bengal', for the English edition. In my edition it is unsigned and undated. Its title is a Persian couplet, which was Azad's original tide, according to the publisher's footnote. But it was deleted when it was submitted for translation. It is likely that this edition was published soon after it was prepared because the translator's preface is written in an imperative suggesting the recording of a recent event.

5 Italics and brackets are mine.

6 Azad's rare use of the English vocabulary.

7 This refers to the first four Khalifas: Hazrat Abu Bakr, Hazrat Umar, Hazrat Usman and Hazrat Ali.

8 Mongol successors of Genghis Khan.

9 Sufi saints.

7

national politics

THAT ONE YEAR WAS SPENT BY Azad at the Alipur Central Jail. It was there that Malihabadi gathered material for his book *Abul Kalam Azad ki Kahani khud unki Zubani* (Azad's story as told by him) from his conversations with Azad. The book is about Azad's ancestors, particularly his father, and about the formative years of his life. It ends when Azad was fifteen, because when he reached that point in the narrative, he was freed from the prison. Malihabadi recounts that at his insistence, Azad had written several pages about the account of his youthful days. But no sooner had he handed the manuscript to his friend, he took it back with the excuse that he wanted to revise it. Malihabadi regretfully reports that he never saw those pages again.

The other account of these days is found in *Zikr-e-Azad*, which is about the lifelong association of Azad with Malihabadi. Several aspects of prison life are described here; Azad's concern for his fellow prisoners, his effort to cheer them up by playing innocent pranks and fun. Malihabadi recounts how at one stage, Azad shut himself off from everything including daylight and remained cooped in the cell. As a result, his body became inflamed with rash, all of which he bore with amazing fortitude. Both aspects of his behaviour are typical, his compassionate understanding of the mental condition of his companions and his seclusion in defiance of the oppression. Malihabadi gives a vivid account of the prison superintendent's intolerable treatment of the political prisoners which led to the above protest by Azad.

Within a few days of this prison term, the government made an offer to the Congress to reach a settlement, provided the call for the boycott of the Prince of Wales was called off. This proposal arrived before Azad and his colleagues in prison, where a meeting was called[1] to discuss the offer. Azad and C.R. Das recommended accepting the British offer because they felt that Congress had won its point and there was no need to strain the relationship further at this time. Madan Mohan Malavaiya, being one of the few leaders who was not in prison, was the negotiator. He went back and forth between Alipur Jail, Gandhi and the government to affect an agreement. But Gandhi imposed conditions which were unacceptable to the British and the proposal fell through. In *India Wins Freedom* Azad was to write that a golden opportunity for political settlement had been lost.[2]

The first important event that occurred while Azad, C.R. Das, Subhas Chandra Bose and Birendra Nath Sasmal were lodged in the prison, was Chauri Chaura in U.P. in February 1922. About two hundred demonstrators led by Non-cooperation volunteers attacked a posse of twenty-two policemen. The police opened fire but they were overpowered. They ran to the police station and shut themselves there but the place was torched by the protestors. Those policemen who fled were beaten to death. As a protest against this atrocity, Gandhi called off the Non-Cooperation movement. 'The government took full advantage of the situation', sentenced Gandhi to a prison term of six years and 'the Non-cooperation movement slowly petered out'.[3]

The record of his prison days reveals that, once again, Azad used this time to reflect on his past and plan his future strategy. He must have had plenty of time, since there is no record of any writing work that he produced during this period. While he discussed politics with C.R. Das everyday, he also analysed his past and expressed his views on current affairs freely, in the presence of Malihabadi. This time spent in prison, to use his favourite expression, was a *waqfa*, a hiatus which is an essential pre-requisite to a new or a different start. He told Malihabadi about how at the age of thirteen he had rejected the faith of his forefathers. He felt that instead of flesh and blood his body was made up of three questions.

1. Does God exist?
2. If He exists what is the cause of differences in religions?
3. If one religion is accepted as the true religion, then why the differences within that religion?

At this point in his life no amount of reading or discussions with practitioners of other faiths was of any use. The turmoil which raged within him led to a physical breakdown. A temporary respite appeared in the form of philosophy and science, and he tried to understand religion in that light. He became a *murid* (devotee) of Sir Syed. But soon he understood that this also was the route which led to denial. His position hardened further until he became a *dehri* (atheist) reposing his faith only on materialism and rationalism, and regarding religion as nothing but ignorance and superstition. From the age of fourteen until twenty-two, he says, that he gave the outward appearance of a man who wanted to reconcile religion with rationality but inwardly he had no faith or belief.

What he confided to Malihabadi at this time, were random thoughts which were probably written in point form, since Azad spoke much faster than any scribe could write. Azad never intended them to be published, they were written more on the pattern of *malfuz* literature.[4] The importance of this record is that it reflects Azad's views on religion, Hindu-Muslim relations, Swaraj, and which culminates in his address to the Special Session of Congress in 1923. The spirit which pervades the

Tarjuman-ul-Quran flashes through these discussions as well. The points here are the same which form the substance of the preface to *Sura al-Fatiha*, but they are expressed minus the power of Azad's evocative language. Malihabadi had not ventured to show anything to Azad for fear of losing it forever. Regardless of the style, they are useful in defining the time when his ideas crystallized; they were to remain substantially unchanged for the rest of his life.

In the prison, Azad listened carefully to the views of C.R. Das about Gandhi having 'erred grievously' in calling off the Non-cooperation movement. Das was also adamant about Congress participation in the forthcoming, elections and carrying on the fight inside the legislatures. It is evident from Azad's own account of these discussions that he had by this time developed the capacity to take a dispassionate view of things and tried to see one single situation from several points of view. Armed with this capacity, he gave Das the careful advice that as soon as he was freed from prison he should consult friends about the Council Entry programme. He remained sympathetic to Das's point of view until he saw that it led to a split in the party, following the Gaya Congress at which Das presided. The split was most untimely. He felt that the two factions, the pro-changers and no-changers, had to, somehow, be made to see each other's point of view.

When Azad was released from prison on new year's day in 1923, there was not much about which he could rejoice. The party was facing a split between the no-changers which included Patel, Rajgopalachari and Rajendra Prasad, and pro-changers with Motilal Nehru, C.R. Das and Ajmal Khan.[5] Communal riots between the Hindus and Muslims had erupted as a consequence of the suspension of Non-cooperation and Khilafat which had generated immense goodwill between the two communities. It was a critical time for the party, 'like the one after the Surat Congress split of 1907, when the 'moderates' and 'extremists' fought each other'.[6] Azad writes that he was approached by both factions of the Congress but he decided to remain outside both camps. It was probably the result of his non-partisan attitude that he was elected the President of the Special Session of Congress called in Delhi in September 1923. 'It was said that I was the youngest man to be elected President of Congress'.[7]

Azad's address delivered before the Special Congress marks a slight departure from his usual oratorical style. It offers far less challenge to the translator compared with the earlier speeches to the Khilafatists and Jamiat-ul-Ulema-e-Hind. It is true that he was not addressing *uhl-e-zaban* (people who spoke the language), his audience consisted mostly of non-Muslims. But that could not have been the reason for using the simpler language. Had that been a consideration, it should have also applied to Magistrate Swinner, and the Government of India who were at the receiving end of *Quol-e-Faisal*. He begins his speech by congratulating Turkey on her victory and Mustafa Kamal Pasha for infusing a new spirit in his countrymen. Turkey's victory is identified not only with the victory of Asia and the East but the victory of *insaaf* (justice). He says that Britain had capitulated before the might of the sword and not before the power of reason:

> When India protested in the name of truth and honour, it (Britain) turned away in disgust. But when Mustafa Kamal wrote the treaty with the edge of his sword, it bowed like the vanquished do, and could not but welcome it.[8]

This brings him to the question of India's relations with her neighbours, particularly the Islamic countries. He says India cannot neglect her geographical and natural closeness to the Eastern world. Identifying her struggle with theirs, she wants to assure those people that she values their aspirations equal to her own. This is specially true of Jaziratul Arab (Arabian peninsula). India's demand for the protection and respect of the holy cities is not only because of her concern for her own Muslims but also because she is seen as the first link in the chain of slavery which hangs about the necks of her neighbours as well. It was to ensure the permanence of India's slavery that made it imperative for the British to control Suez. And if Arabia becomes the new Asiatic centre of British empire, the boundaries of Indian slavery will not begin at the Indian Ocean. They will start from the banks of Syria on one side, to Mousil and Dayar-e-Bakr on the other.

This concern became a deep conviction with Azad over the years, and acquired a shape after practical Independence. As India's first Minister of Education, Azad was to call the Asian Relations Conference in 1948 and establish the Indian Council for Cultural Relations in 1959. In both entities, Azad established India's role vis-à-vis her near neighbours. He continued to emphasize the close link and common destiny of India and West Asia on one side and India and her Eastern neighbours on the other.

He then refers to the Bardoli[9] decision which was a great disappointment for most people. Urging the members to accept this *waqfa* (pause) with patience and fortitude, he strongly repudiates the notion that Non-Cooperation has failed. Item by item, he lists all the successes of Non-cooperation. He says that in twelve months of its existence, it has changed the mentality of the people:

> The fear of punishment and pain that is natural under these conditions, was so completely rooted out that imprisonment became a sport and law courts became theatres of public entertainment.

The first concrete evidence of its success was the conciliatory position taken by the government in December 1921 on the occasion of the Prince of Wales' visit. It proved the effectiveness of the method. Making a comment on the philosophical underpinning of Non-cooperation, he says that earlier it was a moral pronouncement, now it has become a political programme. He adds that 'Non-Violence is the soul of Non-Cooperation... If it is not accepted as an article of faith, it is enough if it be adopted as a strong policy'.

The decision made at Bardoli to call off the movement (Bardoli *ka faisla*) is referred to as a mistake. But having said that, the question was how to conduct oneself during this temporary lull in the movement? The first issue was the Council Entry programme. Azad addresses the sensitivities involved in taking a position on this matter, by explaining the spirit of Non-cooperation. He starts with the premise on which there was universal agreement—that Independence was the objective, and Non-violence and Non-cooperation the principle. We cannot change the objective or the, principle, but we can make any number of changes in the technique or method. It is in this context, he says, that the Council Entry programme should be looked at. To those who argued that Council Entry was against the principle of Non-cooperation, he said that if the principle was defined in such narrow and unaccommodating terms, it would not endure. The importance being given to this issue he said was disproportionate to its warrant. He then offers the view that under the present circumstances boycott of the Councils was not advisable. He proposes that the Councils should also become forums for the struggle.

The next important issue he takes up is Hindu-Muslim unity. Earlier in the speech he had indicated that the present state of purposelessness had led to the rise in communal tensions. He had also said that Hindu-Muslim unity was the only solid base for the movement. In this context he makes the statement which has become the classic expression for Hindu-Muslim unity:

> Today if an angel were to descend from the heaven and declare from the top of the Qutab Minar that Swaraj (Independence) can be obtained in twenty-four hours, provided India relinquishes Hindu-Muslim unity, I would relinquish Swaraj rather than give up Hindu-Muslim unity. Delay in the attainment of Swaraj will be a loss to India, but if our unity is lost, it will be a loss to the entire mankind.

As a background to the views that he expresses here on Hindu-Muslim relations, there are his comments on the subject which he wrote for Malihabadi in prison. Those were personal reflections which eventually became the basis of his political stand. In these he expressed the respective paranoia of the Hindus and the Muslims. For most Muslims, he wrote, 'self-government' for India, translated to mean a Hindu government. For the Hindus 'self government' entailed the possibility of an attack from the

North, 'They feel that the route of Abdali (Ahmad Shah Abdali[10]) has not been closed yet'.

Muslims being one-third the number of Hindus, feel that rather than be run over by them it would be preferable to let British rule continue. Hindus have visions of hordes of Pathans descending from the Khyber Pass, the moment the British leave the Indian shores. Let us see, Azad quips, 'how long this good fortune of the British lasts?' He attributes this mutual fear between the two communities to a lack of understanding. For this he blames great intellectuals like Tagore and Bankim Chandra Chatterjee.[11] Tagore, he states, implied that Islam had deified Prophet Muhammad and Bankim Chandra was ignorant about the Muslim period of Indian history. Equally to blame, he says, are the Muslims who should have been more open.

On the subject of Hindu-Muslim unity, he makes a passionate plea to Congressmen. He reminds them of the message of *Al Hilal* which was given to allay the fears of the Muslims, who being apprehensive about their minority status preferred to remain aloof from national politics. His stand on this issue earned him censure from all factions within his community but within a couple of years the tide turned and Muslims started joining mainstream politics. In the same spirit, he says, he is now taking a stand against the leaders of the Hindu *sangathan*:

> In place of Swaraj and Khilafat, slogans of *shuddhi* and *sangathan* are being raised. 'Save Hindus from Muslims' says one group, 'Save Islam from Hinduism' says another. When the order of the day is 'protect Hindus' and 'protect Muslims' who cares about protecting the country? The press and platform are busy fanning bigotry and hatred while a duped and ignorant public is freely shedding blood on the streets. Bloody riots have occurred in Ajmer, Palwal, Saharanpur, Agra and Meerut. Who can say how tragic their long-range consequences will be?

At the end he implores his audience from the platform of what he calls the 'cradle of composite India' (Delhi), not to rise from the meeting before deciding whether the country should nurture its hope of freedom or bury it in the blood-soaked earth of Agra or Saharanpur? India is a strange country, he concludes; it is quite possible that the freedom of thirty crore human beings may be stalled for the simple reason that a drum beating procession goes past a mosque, or a branch of a tree is cut off along the way.

The essence of the change in Azad's thinking during the year 1922, which he spent in prison, lies in this address which he delivered after hectic political activity over a twenty-month period following his release. Douglas sees the change in terms of his shift of focus from aspiring to the position of Imam-ul-Hind to accepting the invitation to chair the special session of the Indian National Congress. Offering several plausible reasons which may have caused this change, Douglas concludes:

> The fact is that the founder of the Hizbullah, the author of *Tazkirah*, who had organised his disciples to accept *bai'at* to him as Imam-ul-Hind, no longer sought such a status.[12]

His readiness to take his place in the Congress machinery from here onwards, represents, according to Douglas, not only the recession of his former desire to become Imam-ul-Hind but a new awareness of the significance of daily participation in political activities. This was, he concludes, religion in politics in a new sense; a change from the claim of *Al Hilal* that 'Koran gives special guidance for all political decisions'.

Douglas' oblique criticism of Azad here does not take into account the spirit which informed *Al Hilal*. Its twenty-four year old editor had passed through the agonizing stages which led to *inkaar* (denial). It was then that he 'saw the light' as it were and described Islam as *siraj-i-munir*, i.e. a source of guidance and light in all spheres of human activity. The highest form of this guidance, he said, was that Islam enjoined man to use his intellect and reason and to seek knowledge. Therefore, when Douglas draws the above contrast between the Azad of 1912 and the Azad of 1923 (the former seen by Douglas in *Al Hilal's* exhortations relating to 'apocalyptic expectancy of divine intervention', and the latter in the above address), he fails to appreciate that there is an identical spirit which pervades both phases.

The period between Azad's first address to the Congress in 1923, and his second address as President in 1940, was filled with hectic political and intellectual activity. During his last days in the Alipur prison, he had developed the blueprint of a journal in Arabic, *Al Jamiat* which was to run along the lines of *Paigham*, with Malihabadi as editor and Azad himself as the *nigran* (supervisor). Its purpose would be to acquaint the Islamic world with the conditions prevailing in Nejd where Sharif Husain was the puppet ruler and the British soldiers in their uniforms were roaming freely, desecrating the Harmain Sharifain (*Ka'aba*). Azad's larger objective for this journal was pan Islamism and unity of the East. The journal *Al Jamiat*, ran from April 1923 to March 1924.[13]

According to Malihabadi, it had a great impact on Islamic countries from the Persian Gulf to Morocco and fulfilled its objective of getting King Ibn-e-Saud to take a stand against Sharif Husain and purge Mecca of his presence. Azad remained associated with the work, but none of his articles appeared in the journal. He did, however, strongly object to Malihabadi's intention to publish an article by Syed Rashid Raza in which he had criticized the movement of Young Turks and had branded them as *mulhids* (those who turn back from their faith in Allah). The impact of this article, were it to be translated for the Indian press, he said, would be most detrimental to the cause. He demanded that his name be removed from the cover of the journal if this article was ever published.

By this time, the Khilafat movement had become a pale reflection of its former self. In November 1922, the Turks deposed the Sultan-Caliph and made Abdul Majid the nominal *khalifa* with no temporal powers. In October 1923, the Grand National Assembly declared Turkey a Republic and exiled Abdul Majid. The Khilafat was abolished in March 1924.

These were years of personal hardship for Azad. But Malihabadi records that despite being under severe financial constraints, Azad was unusually cheerful, extolling the virtues of a frugal life.[14] A stream of visitors, such as Motilal Nehru, C.R. Das and Subhas Bose flowed into his Ripon Lane house as usual. People like the Ali brothers who were fond of good eating, were entertained with money borrowed from a Peshawri lender. During these days, writes Malihabadi, another affliction worse than *faqr-o-faaqa* (poverty and starvation) devastated Azad. This affliction was communalism. Malihabadi writes that communalism had strangulated the national movement and Azad was convinced that this was not the time to start anything. He had become withdrawn and spent hours pacing up and down his room. Friends like Syed Mahmud tried to persuade him to jump into the fray and combat communalism but it seemed as if he was immobilized. He told Malihabadi that it had become an ordeal to pass the day; quoting Ghalib:

Subh karna shaam ka laana hai joo-e-sheer ka
(Making the day pass into the evening
Is like carving the rock for a stream of milk)

Malihabdi attributes this state of mind to his financial problems and unwillingness to ask any one for help. In this mood he could neither read nor write. One day he disappeared for a fifteen to twenty day period into *aitekaaf* (a period in which the faithful do not communicate with anyone and only pray in mosques). When he emerged from the seclusion, Malihabadi writes, he was his old self again.

Ever since the Mapila rebellion of 1921 in which the Muslims of Malabar had taken up arms against the British as well as their Hindu landlords, the communal situation had steadily deteriorated.[15] The Muslim League at its annual session in 1925, blamed the Hindus for the communal outburst. In the same year, All India Hindu Mahasaba, under the presidentship of Lala Lajpat Rai, opposed any scheme of communal representation and called for Hindu *sangathan*. Azad tried various moves to heal the wounds and stop the deepening rift between the Hindus and Muslims.

The Unity Conference was held in Delhi in September 1924, to persuade Gandhi to end his twenty-one day fast, undertaken to do penance for the Kohat riots which had taken place a few days earlier. A joint manifesto was issued by Motilal Nehru and Azad in the form of a circular, about the formation of the Indian National Union in July 1926 which was aimed at organizing those sections of Indians who agreed that communalism was the negation of nationalism.[16] All these activities were sporadic initiatives which had a limited impact only. Azad had to find something which would be permanent as well as everlasting. For the Muslims, it was to be his *Tarjuman-ul-Quran*. This was the *quol-e-faisal* (last word), for the development of humanism, he felt, not only among the Muslims but among all human beings.

In November 1925, when Azad addressed the Khilafat Conference at Kanpur, he recalled how the movement had initially worked as a catalyst to unite the two communities. Five years later, all that fervour had been destroyed. What should the new role of the Central Khilafat Committee be, he asked, considering that there was no need left for a sustained struggle for the cause? He suggested that the Khilafat Committees, should now have a much wider scope than implied in their name. They should become the forums for Muslim reform and awakening. For the last five years, he said, the Khilafat Committees had served the cause of the Islamic world and the Eastern nations. But what about matters of national import? What about the reform and progress of the *quom*, for which the committees never had any time? It is as a result of this preoccupation with external matters, he said, that the country has been plunged into the communal dissensions that are renting it apart. The Khilafat committees should now concentrate on this issue. He then outlined the steps that he felt needed to be taken to achieve this objective.[17]

Giving a new direction to the Khilafat organizations is further proof of Azad's positive attitude compared to people like Mohammad Ali who were devastated by the abolition of Khilafat. He redirected the energies of an already established forum to work for the education, social reform and progress of Indian Muslims.

He wrote an article 'Masla-e-Khilafat aur Jamhooria Turkia' (Problem of Khilafat and the Turkish Republic) in seven parts in *Zamindar*, Lahore. In it he argued that any Islamic government could fulfil the functions of the Khilafat; hence the most powerful Islamic government automatically has the Khilafat vested in it.[18]

The appointment of the Simon Commission coincided with the second phase of *Al Hilal*.[19] Its first issue appeared on the tenth of June 1927 and the last in December 1927. Azad did not have time to write regular articles, but the first issue carried an editorial which reflects the state of his mind at that time when communalism was a grave threat to the freedom movement. He wrote that the year 1924 has been spent in the throes of the Hindu-Muslim conflict. At that time he had decided that he would leave Calcutta and move to the capital. Leaving Calcutta, however, was not easy. C.R. Das insisted that he should stay back and together they should work for the cause of Hindu-Muslim amity. Azad writes that among all the Hindu leaders of Congress, he saw Das as the one individual who, if he made up his mind, would not allow any impediment in the way of cementing the relations. We learn that his entire household was packed for Delhi, but he decided to stay and join hands with a man he greatly respected and admired. But C.R. Das' death ended that partnership, and with it ended 'all those hopes that he (Das) had lined up, five months ago, to block my path'.[20]

Malihabadi writes that most of the articles of *Al Hilal* (*ani*) were written by him and that Azad only wrote one good article in which he presented Victor Hugo's hero of *Les Miserables*, Jean Valjean as Hazrat Junaid Baghdadi. He also refers to Azad's article on nationalism, but does not make any comment on it. In an article on the *fatwa* issued by the Jamiat-ul-Ulema and Mohammad Ali on a book, *Rangeela Rasul* (Colourful Prophet), Azad took the view that despite living with the Muslims for one thousand years, the Hindus were still ignorant about the meaning of Islam. Abid Raza Bedar calls this article the best piece that was written in the journal.

Azad's article 'Islam aur Nationalism' responded to the criticism that was levelled at the Muslims in the Hindu circles once the bonhomie of Khilafat had ended. They were accused of being more interested in Pan Islamic matters than in their own national problems. The article also addressed the contention in some Muslim circles that Islam is 'against' nationalism. In passages which echo his explication of the spirit of the Quran in the preface to Surah-i-Fatiha, he describes the Islamic view of nationalism. Islam believes, above all, in humanism:

> But Islam did not stop at these junctures. It denied all these affiliations and their bases, created as it were by the limitations of human knowledge and perceptions. It did not recognize the artificial affiliations of race, country, colour, religion and language. It called man to the one and only relationship of humanism and the natural bonds of brotherhood.[21]

He says that in its simplest form nationalism has existed for ages. But what started as a defence of human rights has turned out to become its greatest threat. Analysing the origin of 'nation', he writes that the word existed only for defining the regions of Europe; as if outside its boundaries nothing else mattered. 'All the principles of liberty and rights were meant for the "superior" and not for the "inferior" nations. Europe and America comprised the "superior" half, the rest, the "inferior" half of the world.' Focusing on the East, he deplores the treatment meted out to Syria by France and the decisions that have been made for Asia by the 'freedom loving' nations.

With amazing foresight he discusses various forms of control, economic or military, which leave the bulk of mankind far away from the ideals of liberty and equality:

> The centuries old domination of royalty and aristocracy over people has now been acquired by the capitalist through the power of money... The destinies of countries and nations have thus passed into his hands.

He says that this is a historical juncture at which one epoch is about to end and the other about to begin. Notwithstanding the uncertainty in predicting the future, he feels that the world is moving towards a broader sphere than the present circle in which it is confined. Will the circle be that of 'humanism' and 'human brotherhood'? Apart from *Tarjuman-ul-Quran* (which is imbued with the spirit of humanism), this is Azad's first avowal of humanism above any other -ism, a concept which was to become the overarching faith of all his subsequent writings and speeches. Islam, he writes, had pointed towards this goal 1300 years ago. 'Has the world reached the goal towards which, some 1300 years ago Islam wanted to lead it but could not?'

The next event of importance for Azad was the release of the Nehru Report in 1928. Azad's role in support of it is significant because it shows his intense dislike of seeing Muslims beg for concessions on the grounds of being a minority.[22] The report accepted two of the Delhi Proposals (1927) which were authored by Raja Mahmudabad, Mohammad Ali Jinnah and Mohammad Shafi, regarding the formation of the North-West Frontier Province and of Sindh. But it rejected the separate electorates and the system of weightage.[23]

A rift was created among the Congress Muslims on the issue of the report. Azad, Ansari, Saifuddin Kitchlew and Syed Mahmud were in support of it, and Mohammad Ali, Shaukat Ali and Hasrat Mohani were vehemently opposed to it. Azad suggested that Malihabadi should launch a newspaper campaign in support of the report. He advised, however, that nothing should be written which makes people suspect that the press is too biased in its favour. His contention, as stated to Malihabadi, was that the principles laid down in the report for ensuring the rights of Muslims were appropriate. They were not inimical to the political and collective progress of the Muslims nor their *azadana jadd-o-jehd* (freedom of struggle). He felt that although the majority could have given the Muslims more rights, but as a rule, no *jama'at* wants to bestow rights on another as a gift. In a country like India, the question is not whether one *jama'at* gives a special dispensation to another but whether any obstacles have been placed in the free progress of the other *jama'at?*

At this time, Azad had completed forty years of his life, and contrary to his natural inclination he was deeply involved in public life. All his avowed intentions to devote his life to scholarship had failed, so pressing were the demands of the times. The communal question had become the most contentious issue upon which India's destiny hinged. Azad's position on the issue was becoming aligned with that of Gandhi and the Congress but with definite individual biases. He supported the Nehru Report but made it clear that it could only be accepted with certain modifications.

Azad was instrumental in establishing the Indian National Union (1926) and the All India Nationalist Muslim Party (1929), but none of the two possessed the charismatic quality of the Muslim League. He participated in the Unity Conferences and tried to negotiate the differences between the League and Congress. Always a believer in settling political issues through negotiations, he had tried to bring the contending parties together on the question of the Nehru Report but the positions on both sides were steadily hardening. Until this time, both Jinnah and Azad had attended meetings of both the Congress and the League. However, this *entente cordiale* ended in 1928. Jinnah is reported to have wept and told a friend, 'This is the parting of ways'.[24] Jinnah's three amendments to the Nehru Report were rejected by the Congress, and the disappointed man left for London in 1930 to restart his law practice and perhaps never to return.

In the years that followed, Muslim communal leaders gained popularity by rousing fears in the minds of their coreligionists about the danger to Islam by a Hindu-majority rule. The Hindu communal leaders made sure that the Muslim demands were not conceded; later Jawaharlal was to admit that there were political reactionaries in the Congress who were 'communalists under national cloak'.[25]

Gandhi launched the Civil Disobedience Movement in March 1930, and was taken to Yeravada Jail in May. During the same month, Azad was arrested in Meerut on the basis of a speech he had delivered there. He was detained in the Meerut Jail for nineteen months. It was there that he completed the Preface to *Tarjuman-ul-Quran*. The manuscript is written in a large note-book in his unmistakably fine handwriting. The last inscription reads '16 March 1930, Meerut Jail'.[26]

The work destined to be completed by the editor, *Al Hilal*, as per the announcement in *Al Balagh* in 1914, was now complete. It was a superhuman effort to bring back to the Muslims the origi-nal message of Islam, uncluttered by the human intervention of centuries of interpretations. Aimed primarily at Muslims but not unmindful of others, it is prefaced by an introduction which explains the basic oneness at the core, of all revealed religions, Hinduism, Christianity, Buddhism, Judaism and Islam.

notes

1 Malihabadi gives an account of this 'conference' in *Zikr-e-Azad*, p. 220.

2 *India Wins Freedom*, p. 20.

3 *India Wins Freedom*, p. 21.

4 Record of conversations of eminent persons are made and pre-served as *malfuz* literature. This is the manner in which Sufi documents have been transmitted to the generations.

5 'Instead of the political struggle against the British, the energy of all Congressmen was being dissipated in internecine warfare'. *India Wins Freedom*, p. 22.

6 V.N. Datta, p. 128.

7 *India Wins Freedom*, p. 12. Azad writes that he was thirty-five years old at the time.

8 All passages of this address are from *Khutbat-e-Azad* ed. Malik Ram. The speech is translated in English in an abridged version in *India's Maulana* ed. Syeda Saiyidain Hameed.

9 After the Chauri Chaura incident Gandhi called a Congress gen-eral body meeting in Bardoli at which an agreement was reached to call off the movement.

10 Malihabadi, *Zikr-e-Azad*, p. 275.

11 Ibid., pp. 275–6.

12 Douglas, Abul Kalam Azad: *An Intellectual and Religious Biography*, p. 191.

13 *Zikr-e-Azad*, pp. 295–303. Bedar, p. 85.

14 Malihabadi describes Azad's eulogies about *arhar ki daal* (boiled lentils) since that was all they could eat, and confesses that he secretly wished that these days of penury would last so that he could be privy to more such delightful discourses.

15 Datta provides the numbers. Eleven riots in 1923, eighteen in 1924, sixteen in 1925, thirty-five in 1926, thirty-one up to November 1927. No source is given for these figures.

16 For a detailed discussion see Datta, pp. 130–5.

17 His educational programme consisted of four measures:

  1. Publication of *navisht-o-khwand* among the people.

  2. For the religious, cultural and social reform of schools.

  3. Reading rooms for the people.

  4. *Juma Khutba* be used for conveying useful information.

18 Abid Raza Bedar, p. 211. Also see Douglas, p. 196.

19 Also called *Al Hilal (sani)*; *Sani* meaning, second.

20 See Bedar, pp. 123–5.

21 Hameed ed., *India's Maulana*. All quotations are taken from the editor's translation.

22 His Presidential Address to Congress in 1940 is another expression of this dislike.

23 Datta, pp. 134–5.

24 Stanley Wolpert, *Jinnah of Pakistan*, OUP.

25 Jawaharlal Nehru *Autobiography* quoted by V.N. Datta, Maulana Azad, p. 136.

26 *Gosha-e-Azad*, Azad Bhavan, New Delhi.

8

tarjuman-ul-quran

the dedication

It was December 1918. I was under detention in Ranchi. I had stepped out of the mosque after the *Isha* prayer, when I felt that someone was following me. I turned around to see a man wrapped in a blanket standing behind me.

Do you wish to say something to me?

Yes, Sir. I have come a long way.

Where from?

From across the Frontier.

When did you reach here?

This evening. I am a very poor man. I walked from Kandhar to Quetta. There I met traders from my country. They took me in their service and dropped me at Agra. I have walked all the way here from Agra.

Alas! Why did you take all this trouble? So that I could ask you to explain some portions of the Quran to me. I have read every word of *Al Hilal* and *Al Balagh,*

The man stayed for a few days, then suddenly returned home. He did not see me before he left because he must have apprehended that

I would try to give him money for travelling expenses. He did not wish to burden me. His return journey too would have mostly been conducted on foot. I don't remember his name. I don't even know if he is alive or dead. Had my memory not failed me I would have dedicated this book to him.

These few lines of *intisaab* or dedication of the greatest work that can ever flow from the pen of a Muslim, are a perfect reflection of the *maqam* or stage Azad had reached when he finished writing *Tarjuman-ul-Quran*.

The preface to the first edition explains several factors which influenced Azad in his writing. The most important was the inner voice which urged that this work was important for the *falah* (progress) of the entire *quom*:

> I could not remain unconcerned about the kind of work which I considered most important at the time for the Muslim community. As the time passed, the thought of the indispensability of the work became unbearable for me. I felt that if not done by me, it may be a while before anyone else would attempt it.

On the one hand there was an acute desire to complete the work, on the other an awareness of other pressing demands on his time which could not stand delay. Then there was the enthusiasm of the *quom* for the promised *Tarjuman*. After Ranchi, he became involved in hectic political activity (for which the 'political invitation' of *Al Hilal* was largely responsible), and despite his desire to remain aloof, he could not stay away from its compulsions. But by 1921, when the demands for the *Tarjuman* started pouring in from all parts of the country, he had to attend to its publication. His self-confessed regret for having combined the life of a scholar with that of a politician is expressed in the Introduction to the first edition:

> The excitement of a political life cannot be combined with the steady pace of a scholarly existence. There can be no peace between the flame and its extinguisher! I thought I could garner both at the same time. Unfortunate that I am, I piled riches on one side, and on

the other, invited the all-consuming fire. Surely, I had full knowledge of what would happen... What right then do I have of uttering one single word of complaint?

His anxiety for completing the work is evident in the fact that the *Tarjuman* was being printed at the same time as it was being written. In 1916, when he was issued extradition orders from Bengal, following the closure of the *Al Balagh* press, the printing of the calligraphed forms was in process. At that time the Government of Bengal confiscated all his papers including the incomplete *Tarjuman*. Upon arriving in Ranchi, Azad still continued from where he had left off, i.e. from the ninth *para* (part). The final completion of the document took place in 1918.

After his release from Ranchi, his negotiations with the government for the return of the original eight *paras* failed. Several months of perservance and hard work reproduced the eight *paras*. By 1921, the calligraphy of the Koranic text was complete and only the translation remained to be calligraphed. At that time occurred the worst calamity that can ever befall a writer; the horrible mutilation of his manuscript, calligraphy sheets, and even the plates by the hounds of the Intelligence Department, during their search for evidence for his conviction under Section 124 A. Azad did not realize the extent of the damage until later, when he wrote to the authorities asking for the return of his papers and received the mess of pulp, which had been his labour of love for almost a decade. He records his anguish in a few restrained sentences in the preface to the first edition:

This was the bitterest sip which the cup of chance held to my lips. I drank it without complaint. But I cannot deny that its bitterness is still clutching at my throat.

After an initial period of near emotional paralysis during which he felt that he could never bring himself to repeat, word for word, what he had completed so meticulously, he felt the stirring of a new life. He records that it was the end of 1927. That was the year when *Al Hilal* (which had been started on 10 June) had closed down after running for five months. Slowly, his pen started moving on paper. And then the flow was unstoppable: 'If I wanted to stop it I could not'. In a little over two years he had re-written the entire work. On 20 July 1930 he had completed the last *sura*.

In the Preface to the first edition, he records that this work was the outcome of twenty-seven years of rigorous study of the Koran. Understanding the essence of each and every *ayat* (Koranic verse) was like drawing blood. In this pursuit, he cut himself away from family, society and traditional education, and ventured out entirely by himself. He used *tehqiq* (research) in preference to *taqlid* (imitation). As always, he veered away from the common road, carving his own footholds along the way:

> There is no conviction of my heart which has not been stung by all the barbs of doubt. There is no belief in my soul which has not passed through all the stages of negativism. I have gulped poison from all the cups and sipped its antidote from all the hospitals. When I was thirsty, my lip-dryness was not like the others'. When I was satiated, the fountain of my satisfaction was not located on the public highway.

Commencing the work, Azad first established the 'Principles of translation and commentary'. He writes that when the Koran was first revealed it was listened to and understood in its natural simplicity. The Prophet's companions had no difficulty in understanding a *sura* exactly in the sense in which it was spoken. But even during the first period of Islam, the winds of civilization had started blowing in from Persia and Byzantium. Concurrently, translations into Arabic of the Greek arts and sciences shifted the emphasis of learning to form rather than content. That had its impact on those who wrote down the text from the oral rendering. Consequently the reality of the Koran receded behind the veils of artifice:

> If we wish to see the Quran in its real form, it is essential that we first remove the veils that have been drawn over its face by the external influences of different ages and different regions. Then one should move forward and discover the reality of the Quran from its own pages.

Azad writes that during the first period of Islam the Koran was committed to memory by the companions of the Prophet. It was written down during the second period, when Imam Fakhruddin Razi wrote his *tafseer* and couched it in dialectical artifices. 'If Imam Razi's eye had been on the reality', he wrote, 'then, if not his entire *tafseer*, at least two-thirds of it would have been rendered useless. It must be remembered that as the moulds of artifice are broken, the reality of the Koran emerges.' When the question arises about the meaning of any treatise, Azad says, the interpretation of those is given preference who have first understood it from the lips of the author.

The Koran was revealed over a period of twenty-three years. During the entire period, the Prophet's *sahaba* (companions) used to listen to it and repeat it in their prayers. Whatever escaped their understanding was explained by the Prophet himself. Unfortunately, the following generations, instead of relying on their understanding, gave new interpretations, which were far removed from the original meaning. The new logic, unreliable traditions, and layers of commentary, created meanings which were nonexistent in the original text. Azad says that the practice of *tafseer bir rai* was the worst outcome of these pedantic exercises. *Tafseer bir rai* means deriving a meaning from the Koran which fits pre-set opinion. It means remaining silent about the Koranic intent, but twisting the words to suit the *muffassir's* (commentator's) intention. He condemns the use of this method by the different schools of *fiqah* (jurisprudence), by some sects of Sufis, by Indian and Egyptian re-interpreters.

These were the obstacles in the way of his own writing, Azad explains, but he has tried to overcome them, and create a path for the discerning student, which is different from all the existing paths. This work, he writes, is comprehensive and complete but still does not permit the reader to stop thinking for himself. He gives the example of his commentary on *talaq*. In the *Sura Al Baqarah*, his explanatory note is brief: 'The assigning of an appropriate period of the *iddat* (the time of probation which must elapse before a divorced woman or a widow can marry again) ensures the importance of the *nikah*, protection of the lineage, and remarriage of the woman'. He admits that if he explained each of the three expedients for the duration of the *iddat* it would run into three pages. But its essence can be expressed in a few lines. It is necessary that the reader ponders over each word.

At the end of this Preface he offers to the reader all he has gathered during his lifelong search:

> Whatever I could gather in this lengthy period of search for my heart's desire, the Quranic truth to the best of my ability, I have spread over the pages of this book.

He ends with the Koranic ayat:

> This is no new tale of fiction, but a confirmation of previous scriptures, an explanation of all things, and guidance and mercy to those who believe. (12:111)

The Preface to the second edition is dated 7 February 1945, written at the Ahmednagar Fort Prison. This was shortly before the time when he was transferred to Bankura and held under detention until 15 June 1945. For this edition, he wrote his famous essay on the concept of God in the *Tafseer* of the *Sura Al Fatiha*. He felt constrained to fill what he considered an important lacuna in the first edition. In doing this work, he says, the path of the dialectician took him nowhere. Once again, the way was indicated by the Koran itself; it was the way of the *salf* (the first generation of interpreters of the Koran).

> The more I dashed my hands and feet against the waves.
> The more woefully perplexed did I feel.
> But when I ceased to struggle and lay motionless
> The waves, of their own free will,
> Drifted me across to the shore.

The core of the Koran is said to be contained in *Sura Al Fatiha*. It is his commentary on the first *Sura* of the Koran which he considered to be the quintessence of the teachings of Islam. He begins with explaining the importance of *Al Fatiha*. This *Sura* of the Holy Book of Islam consists of seven phrases:

Bismillahir Rahmanir Rahim
Alhamdolillahi Rabbil Alamin
Ar Rahmanir Rahim
Malik-e-Yawmiddin
Iyyakanabudu wa Iyyakanastaiin
Ihdenas siratal Mustaqeem
Siratal Ladhina an amta Alayhim
Ghairil Maghdhubi Alayhim wa ladhaalin

In the name of Allah, the Beneficent, the Merciful
Praise be to Allah, Lord of the Worlds
The Beneficent, the Merciful
Owner of the Day of Judgement
Thee alone we worship and Thee alone we ask for help
Show us the Straight Path
The path of those whom Thou has favoured
Not the path of those who earn Thy anger
Nor of those who go astray

So profound is the importance of this *Sura* that Azad defines its relation with the rest of the Koran as the relationship of *ajmaal* (substance in summary) and *tafseel* (detail). He believes that the Koranic verse, 'O Prophet it is true that we have granted you things to be repeated seven times and the exalted Koran' referred to the seven lines of the *Sura Al Fatiha*. If a person cannot read the Koran, says Azad, and only commits the import of these lines to memory, he will understand the basic tenets of Islam.

He then describes the four elements of the Islamic faith:

• correct understanding of the attributes of Allah,
• belief in the Divine law of retribution and reward,
• belief in a life after life, and
• recognition of the right path.

Commenting on the simplicity of this *Sura*, Azad asserts that the closer a subject gets to the truth, the simpler and more appealing it becomes. Every truth which is revealed in this world, until it is hidden, seems complex, but when it becomes apparent, one finds that there was nothing more simple and straightforward. His other contention is that whenever the *wahi* of Allah (Word of Allah) has been revealed it has not taught man anything entirely new. It has just reformulated, the primordial urges of man. This is the special quality of the *Sura Al Fatiha*. Every word of it is the natural expression of his own heart and soul.

The simple prayer format of *Sura Al Fatiha*, Azad writes, reveals the most significant facets of the *Din* (faith):

1. In his concept of God, man's greatest error was to consider Him the object of terror not love. The very first word of the *Sura* corrects this mistake. The word *hamd* (praise) is used in appreciation of good qualities; therefore, it follows, that terror cannot co-exist with *hamd*. The word *rab* signifying *rububiyat* (Omniscience, Omnipresence, and Omnipotence of Allah, the great Provider), the word *rahmat* (the quality of bestowing all that is good), and *adalat* (the quality of being just and temperate) completes the picture of a power that fulfils all human needs.

2. *Rabbilalamin* (Lord of the Worlds) establishes the universal *rububiyat* of Allah, thereby expressing his concern for every individual, group, community and country. This gives the lie to the narrow mindedness which had arisen among the different races who had started considering themselves God's chosen, to the extent of excluding all others.

3. *Malik-e-Yawmiddin* postulates the law of recompense in referring to God as the Master of the Day of Judgement. Requital is the inevitable result of man's own action and his punishment is not a consequence of God's terror or revenge.

4. Combining *rububiyat* and *rahmat* with *malik-e-yawmiddin* establishes that if the attributes of grace and beauty co-exist with anger it is because Allah is *adil* (just) and *adl* is not the negation of benevolence, it is a blessing for man.

5. *Ibadat* (service) is for Allah alone and help is invoked only from Allah. In a word, when *tawhid* (oneness of God) is established all doors to *shirk* (sharing deities with God) are closed.

6. Goodness is identified with *Sir ami Mustaqeem*, the Straight Path, easily discernable by one and all.

7. And *Siratal Mustaqeem* is easily recognizable as the path taken by those who have been rewarded by Allah. For all peoples, nations, times, regions there are only two clearly demarcated paths—one taken by successful wayfarers, the other by failures.

The prayer format is more appropriate for this Sura than the command format because this form of expression rises spontaneously to the lips of a *talib-e-sadiq* (the earnest supplicant).

The manner in which Azad presents the teachings of the Koran to his readers, gives important insights into various aspects of his personality. First, his admiration for the fact that the greatest thought is revealed with straightforward simplicity and his assertion of the symbiotic relation between simplicity and truth, is contrary to his own expression which is often complex and sometimes hidden behind a veil of language. Second, his contention that there is nothing new or startling about the *wahi* of Allah (Allah's revelations), that they are a restatement of the truth which already exists in the heart of every human being. This reflects his general tendency to exalt the human potential (even if it has long been unactualized), which responds to the rejuvenating force of religion. His other creed which is established here is the universal quality of religion, (with a small 'r'), regardless of race, geography, or sect. And finally, his according the highest status to the state of *wajdan*, an intuitive apprehension (of the Truth) as opposed to calculated and reasoned understanding.

The preface to *Sura Al Fatiha* is not the exegesis of one *sura*, it condenses Azad's understanding of the entire spirit of Islam. The biographer can only wonder whether when he decided to assume the title Abul Kalam he was subliminally aware that he would in fact be able to fill the contours of this awesome name by writing a most influential *tafsir* (commentary) of the Koran? He explicates, one by one, each phrase of the *Sura:*

1. *Al Hamdu Lillah* (Praise is for Allah only), the opening phrase of the Koran, is offered to God because all goodness and perfection proceeds from Him. All existence is the work of a consummate artist and the touch of that grace and tender providence is felt in every particle of the universe:

> Those who bear God in mind, standing, sitting and reclining, and reflect on the creation of the heavens and of the earth, they will say: 'Our Lord thou hast not created all this in vain'. (3:138)

The tragedy of man is that he is so dazzled by the artistry of the veils that He throws over His creative beauty, that he rarely thinks beyond what is apparent to his eye. Therefore, says Azad, in one of his most perceptive statements, *the worship of the phenomenal originates with this defect in vision.* The *hamd* (praise) is therefore addressed not to the phenomenal object but to the artist who fashioned it into a thing of beauty.

2. *Rabbilalamin* (Lord of all beings). The word *Rabb* in Arabic means Provider or Nourisher. To visualize God as *Rabbilalimin* is to conceive Him not only as the Creator of everything in the universe but as its nourisher and sustainer as well. Azad then makes a distinction between the divine creation of the provisions of life and the function of *Rububiyat.* The method and manner of providing for the smooth functioning of the machinery of existence is what is meant by the system of *Rububiyat.*

> Ponder over this system of universal Providence ... and it will appear as if it was devised to develop life and protect every latent capacity therein. The sun is there to give light and methodically draw out water from the ocean. The winds are there to produce, alternately, coolness and warmth. Sometimes they waft particles of water up into the skies and spread them into layers of clouds; sometimes they reduce these clouds into water again and bring it down.[1]

Azad explains *Rububiyat* by giving example after example of nurture and the method with which it is measured out to all creation. Sometimes it takes the form of a question. Why does it rain in a certain quantity and why does a portion of it run down the surface of the earth while another soaks into the earth to a particular depth? The Koran gives the answer that it is the *Rahmat* of God which produces water but it is His *Rububiyat* which utilizes this water so as to provide for every living being its means of sustenance. *Rububiyat* is also used as an argument for the life hereafter. In a passage which has direct appeal to human intellect and emotion, the explanation is offered:

> What! Did you think that we had created you in vain and that you should not be brought back to Us? (23:115)

Azad then expounds on the appeal to reason in the Koran. He says that repeated emphasis is laid on the search for truth and on the need for exercising one's reason and insight, of reflecting over the inward and outward experience of life, and then of drawing valid conclusions:

> And on earth are signs for men of firm belief, and also in your own selves: will ye not notice them? (51:20–21)

Since man is endowed with reason and insight he will be held responsible for its proper exercise:

> Surely, the hearing, and the heart sight of man, each of these will be questioned. (17:36)

The Koranic method, says Azad, is not to offer postulates or intellectual surmises and base its arguments on them but to appeal to man's natural instincts. Azad attaches great importance to human instinct and human nature. He deplores that the *muffassirin* (commentators) of the past took little notice of this, and failing to appreciate the Koranic method, lost themselves in far fetched deductions.

Azad raises a question. Is an object, in the shaping of which nature has had to make such prolonged and careful arrangement, just meant to eat and drink on earth for a moment and to be extinguished forever? And then again if the life of man has undergone a series of changes, and appeared as a higher form in every change, why should we not expect the same process to continue in the future?

> Thinketh man that he is to be left to drift?
> Was he not a mere germ in the seminal state,
> And was he not a drop of fluid which gushed forth,
> Out of which God fashioned him and made him perfect.
> (75:36, 37, 38)

3. *Al Rahman Al Rahim* (The Benevolent, The Merciful). Azad writes that the root word is *Rahmat* and whatever beauty or perfection exists in life is an expression of this divine quality. This part is given the longest explanation. When we reflect over the universe, the most important reality that strikes us is the *Nizam-e-Rububiyat*. The objective, of *Rububiyat* is not merely the sustenance of life but the development of beauty in everything:

> We notice that there is a design in the life of the universe and that there is beauty in this design... This aspect of life is greater in its reaches than the orderliness (*Rububiyat*) that dwells therein. And this reality the Koran designates as *Rahmat*, an attribute which displays the qualities of both Rahman and Rahim.

Once again he gives several examples to illustrate his point. He then states that people expect immediate results of their deeds. The Arabs used to taunt the Prophet that if their ways were really evil, why do they not meet with instantaneous punishment. But they forgot that the delay between the cause and effect was only meant to give them time to repent.

> Nor do we delay it but until a time appointed. (11:104)

Emphasizing *Rahmat*, Azad says there is always room for repentance and forgiveness. He regrets that earlier commentators did not stress that the door to guidance is always open. This applies to individuals as well as to nations. But he cautions that the Koran sets a time limit for returning to the Straight Path:

> Every nation has its set time. And when that time is come, they shall not retard it an hour, and they shall not advance it. (7:34)

The moment one feels repentant, he says, the force of mercy is released, 'and every drop of tear one sheds in contrition washes a stain of sin'. He says that the scope of forgiveness is vast and limitless. ·

> Say! O my servants who have transgressed to your own hurt, despair not of God's mercy: for all sins doth God forgive. (39:54)

Azad then states what he considers essential to the understanding of the Koran—that the bond between God and his creation is that of love. 'God in this context does become the Beloved of the devotee.' This intensely Sufi concept is followed by the other important Koranic injunction which the mystics regard as their basic creed. Azad explains it as 'He who desires to love God has necessarily to learn to love His creatures.' He then illustrates it by quoting a Hadith of the Prophet:

> On the Day of Judgement God will address a particular individual. 'O son of Adam! I was sick but you did not attend oh me'. Bewildered, this individual would say, 'How is that possible? You are after all the Supreme Lord of all the worlds (and cannot fall sick)'. God will reply, 'Do you not remember that so and so among my servants was ill and lying close to you, and you did not turn to him in sympathy. If you had but gone near him you would have found Me by his side'.

The entire hadith is quoted by Azad to illustrate the importance that the Koran lays upon man developing the godly quality of *Rahmat*. He says, that this quality of God is referred to most often—in more than three hundred places in the Koran. 'And if we include other attributes which in one form or another are concomitants of it, such as providence, forgiveness, benevolence, protection and forbearance ... the Koran assumes from cover to cover the role of but a single unified message of divine mercy or *Rahmat*.'

The aim of human life according to the Koran, says Azad, is to reflect in one's thought and activity the attributes of God. He says that perfection is to be achieved by expressing in life more and more of His divine qualities. When the Koran refers to the quality of humanity in man, it uses the phrase 'the very breath of God'.

Then shaped him and breathed His spirit into him, and gave him hearing and seeing and hearts. (32:8)

This verse explains two facts; first that man's position is so high that God has breathed His spirit into him and consequently endowed him with the requisite spirit and sensibility. Second, it follows that Allah's qualities such as divine mercy, forgiveness, and all the attributes of *Rububiyat* should also be inculcated in man.

Calling attention to the teachings of a religion as opposed to its practice, he deplores the Christians for not heeding the message of Christ. He says 'History has done great wrong to this teacher of mankind and the unsympathetic critic has made no effort to understand Christ's message'. The Koran, he asserts, attaches to both the Torah and the Bible the same value that it attaches to itself. The basic belief in Koran is that the message of all prophets has been the same. Compared to the passionate rallying cries in *Al Hilal* for the slumbering nation of Muslims, which had spared neither the Christians nor the Jews, there is a remarkable change of tone here. Much greater acceptance of and respect for other faiths which he says is the spirit of Islam, underpins his interpretation.

Interpreting the Christian concept of forgiveness which has caused great controversy, Azad explains the difference between the literal and the figurative. The same spirit has been expressed in the Prophet's Hadith, but—

To take the literal sense of every figurative expression is not the way of the cultured mind. Should we do so, the entire corpus of inspired or revealed literature would straightaway turn into a jumbled mass of incoherent utterance.

While on this subject, he discusses the ethics of punishment. There is no doubt, he says that religion has prescribed punishment for crime; essentially for the safety of society. It is man who has corrupted this intention of correcting man and used it for his destruction instead. The most notable offenders are the custodians of religion and law:

> In fact, more desolation and ruin has been wrought by the exponents of law and religion than by any other. If we ask history to show who has wrought greater havoc to humanity outside the sphere of war, it will surely point its finger at the engines of destruction, the religious tribunals, or the inquisitions which have been set up by the dispensers of religion and law.

The Koran makes a distinction between the actor and the action. Presenting the analogy of a physician and his patient, Azad emphasizes the difference between abhorrence for the disease, and not for the diseased. Even for the worst offenders, the Koran uses the expression 'my servants', the personal pronoun denoting a certain, involvement. Quoting from the Prophet's great grandson and Islam's great jurist Imam Jafar-e-Sadiq, Azad says:

> This form of address bears resemblance to a form which a father usually adopts when speaking to his son … Imam Jafar-e-Sadiq observed, 'Whenever we call our children they run to us without entertaining the slightest fear; for they feel that a parent could never be cruel to them'. More than twenty times the phrase 'Oh my servants or Oh my people' is used in the Koran. This style of address is employed even in the case of the worst sinners. Could there be a better proof than this of the essential mercy of God shown in his dealings with his creatures?

If the essential teaching of the Koran is *Rahmat*, he asks, why is it harsh on those who do not accept its message? In responding to this issue Azad explicates an injunction of the Koran which tends to be politicized from time to time. First, he says that the Koran speaks of the divine attribute of mercy in conjunction with justice. Second, the word *kufr* is used in the sense of denial; simple *kufr* is when a person for whatever reason does not accept the other's thinking. For this the Koranic injunction is *Lakum dinukum walia din* (To you your way, to me mine). Offensive *kufr* is when another's faith is deliberately and violently opposed; it is against this that there is a strong remonstrance in the Koran. 'For to have done otherwise,' he says 'would have been an abject yielding to violence in thought and deed, and would have been against the law of nature. *Rahmat* always goes with justice'.

4. *Malik-e-Yawmiddin* (Master of the Day of Recompense). This attribute of God in addition to *Rububiyat* and *Rahmat* is that of *Adalat* (justice). Azad says that in the Koran requital is the result of one's own action and is not arbitrarily imposed as was the prevalent practice when the Koran was revealed. In this regard the Koranic concept of reward and punishment is different from the Jewish or Christian concept. It does not regard the treatment meted out to man (reward or punishment) Azad says, as something different from the law of causation which is at work in the universe. He gives examples of natural phenomena; it is in the nature of fire to burn, in water to cool, so also the case with every type of human action. 'Every action produces a result which is peculiar to it. That is what the Koran calls recompense, requital or justice.'

Azad underscores the Koranic spirit that it is for the salvation of man that religion invites him to do good and abstain from evil:

He who doth right it is for himself; and he who doth evil; it is for himself: and thy Lord will not deal unfairly... (41:46)

Azad is clear in his understanding that reward and punishment is not dependent upon God's pleasure or displeasure. He adds that sheer terror for its own sake has no place in the scheme of divine attributes. But if the law of requital was not in operation there would have been no sense of balance or justice and the result would have been chaos. *Adl* in Arabic means 'to make even':

> Every planet and every star is at work in space in balanced, or just, or right relation with one another. It is this principle which binds together a society... The term 'maintaining balance' occurs in *Al Imran* and clinches the concept.

5. *Iyyaka Nabudu Wa Iyyaka Nastaiin* (Thee alone do we serve, and thee alone do we ask for help). This part of *Tarjuman-ul-Quran* has evoked the greatest interest and debate because it contains a comparative study of the concept of God in various religions. This chapter has also been expanded to twice its original length in the second edition of the *Tarjuman*. The new part takes into account the concept of God in all major religions.[2] Some critics have decried what they see as 'political motivation' in the comparative study. But when viewed in the context of his overall development it appears to arise from a different impulse. In the Preface to the first edition, he describes the personal anguish of his younger days when he struggled with this concept:

> This was a matter of great anguish for me during my student days. For a long time I remained puzzled. When the reality dawned on me, however, I realized that if there is any path to fulfilment, it is only the one of the Quran.

In the Preface to the second edition, referring to this addition he writes that the concept of God in other faiths, which was briefly discussed in the first edition, has now received much greater attention.

Explaining the Koranic contention that the concept of God underwent a process of retrogression rather than evolution, he writes that the first vision that man ever had was of *Tawhid* (divine unity), which soon degenerated to multiplicity—meaning the association of God with things of His creation. He then surveys the different theories advanced on this subject in the eighteenth and nineteenth centuries. Having done that, he summarizes the conclusion drawn from the survey.

Adam was created with light within himself. His progeny frittered it away and admitted darkness instead. Such is the statement of the Koran as well. 'Mankind was one people, and God sent prophets to announce glad tidings and warn; and He sent down with them the Book of Truth that it might decide the disputes of men (2:209).'

Then he explains that in every age man carved an image of God in his own shape. He calls this 'the first in the series of tragedies which beset the human mind'. To save man from this condition, the revealed word was delivered from time to time. The prophets who appeared in different times delivered their message along three distinct lines.

1. From anthropomorphism to formlessness.
2. From polytheism to monotheism.
3. From awe and terror to love.

The six prevailing concepts of God at the time when Islam was revealed are then discussed; Chinese, Buddhist, Jewish, Christian, Zoroastrian and Hindu. The detail in which he explains the Hindu concept is significant. The explanatory notes on various points reveal that he had meticulously studied several standard works on Indian philosophy and religion. The reasons for this careful articulation are spread over a lifetime's study, as well as the contemporary compulsions. During the Ahmednagar Fort imprisonment, which followed the Quit India arrests, there was enough time to reflect on the course of events, including the distinct possibility of the parting of ways. Before him lay the first edition of *Tarjuman-ul-Quran*, bearing the date 1930.

Ten years had passed. Communal positions had hardened and the gap between Muslims and Hindus had become the widest it ever was. The man in the prison spent his time according to a strict regimen. The day was spent at the desk, the evening in discussions with colleagues, Jawaharlal Nehru, Syed Mahmud, Asaf Ali and others. It is possible that he introduced the part on

Hinduism as a last ditch effort to help his co-religionists understand their compatriots by emphasizing the similarities rather
than the differences. Once again he was seeking the answer to
the problem of the *quom* in the Word of Allah. This was Azad's
memorable *ijtehad* (new interpretation) which he made in the best
tradition of Islam, by highlighting its respect for all the religions
and all the messengers.

The Hindu concept of God, he says has two aspects. The philosophical and the practical:

> The Hindu philosophy presents such deep and intricate problems
> of spiritual contemplation and raises the human mind to such great
> heights that we scarcely find a parallel for it in the religious ideolo-
> gies of ancient peoples. But the religion, as practised, gave to human
> ingenuity a free hand to create demi-gods, so much so, that every
> stone became a god, every tree claimed godhead, and every doorstep
> became a place of worship. Thus the ideology of the Hindus, while it
> attempted the highest flights of the mind in one direction, descended
> to the lowest of depths in another. The former for the elite, the latter
> for common folk.

The entire argument of Hinduism, he says, is based on two
premises, monotheism and polytheism; each corresponds to a
certain class. The *Rig Vedas* reveal the parallel development of
the concept of a higher being and the worship of images. The
monotheistic concept of God, he writes, was gathering so much
strength that the 333 demi-gods were delineated into three
spheres, earth, air, and sky. Finally, the idea of a Supreme Creator
emerges by the name of Prajapati and Vishwakarma. He says
that these ideas became the pantheistic view of the Upanishads.
When the idea of unity subsumed the individual entities, they
became intercessors with God. He likens this condition to pre-
Islamic Arabs who had a battery of intermediaries, to which the
Koran refers:

> They say, 'We serve them only that they may bring us near to
> God'. (39:4)

Association of God with others, gave religion a form which thrived on multiplicity and idolatry. The seeker of truth had to struggle long and hard; only the *arif* (wise) could reach it. Truth could be found in mountains and caves but not in the bazaars and roadside. Al Beruni in the eleventh, Abul Fazal in the sixteenth and Sir William Jones in the nineteenth, all were amazed at this contradictory situation.

Explaining the rationale for the distinction made between the elite and masses, Azad writes that it was due to a practical sense of compromise:

Adaptability was the spirit of life here. A Vedantist knows that communion with Reality is infinitely higher than image worship. But he never sets his face against image worship. He thinks this is the first stage in the journey to God; and that whatever path one may choose, the ultimate goal is one and the same.

But a limit must be prescribed in the case of tolerance as well. He advances the view that unless a limit is defined for every type of activity, canons of knowledge and morality will get disturbed and we will cease to possess any definite sense of moral values. Then follows a discussion about what tolerance means to him. This definition is identical with the Koranic understanding of tolerance. Tolerance, he says, is the right of another to hold his own views and follow his own way, even if his way is clearly wrong according to another. The only proviso is:

If tolerance is given the latitude to water down your own beliefs and affect your own decisions, it ceases to be tolerance.

In saying this Azad takes into account the prevailing social conditions and escalating tensions between the Muslims and Hindus. History is witness, he says, to the ravage caused by violation of the law of tolerance.

Intensity of belief has, at times, led people to set aside all considerations of tolerance and forcibly invade the beliefs and ways of life of others. At other times, tolerance has been given so great a latitude that strength of belief has ceased to bear any meaning.

It is interesting that for forcible imposition of beliefs he should use the example of religious persecutions, and for overdone tolerance the example of Indian history. The compromise between knowledge and intellect on the one hand, and ignorance and superstition on the other, he says, has 'disfigured the Indian intellect; the beauty of the Indian mind and all its great achievements have been clouded by superstition and image worship'. It appears that here he is critical of the corrupting influence of superstition both in Hinduism and Islam. There is nothing more intolerable for one who believes in the fundamentals of all religions, he says, than the ritualism invoked by 'superstition'.

Having discussed Hinduism and other faiths, he comes to Islam. Prior to the advent of Islam, he says, the mind of man was not refined enough to discard the veils of anthropomorphic similitudes and directly behold the splendour of divine attributes. But the Islamic concept lifted the veils and made man stand in the presence of his creator. He quotes the most often repeated *Qul*:

Say, He is God, the One and Only.
God, on whom all depend.
He begetteth not nor is begotten.
And there is none like Him. (112:1–4)

Approaching the study of the Koran with emotion and instinct rather than with philosophy and dialectics, he discusses the different concepts of divine attributes; the dialectic schools of Jahimiya, Batiniya and Mutazila. Denial, in the sense of 'He is not this or this,' as presented in these schools 'cannot quench the human thirst'. Affirmation, in the sense of 'He is this and this' often leads to anthropomorphism. The middle path has, therefore, been chosen by the Koran. The other point that he makes is that man is constrained by the limits of his understanding to look at Reality through the veil of positive attributes, and that the veil has been drawn by us because our eye does not have the capacity to behold Reality.

The middle path of the Koran is the one which not only gives us a perfect vision of a transcendental God, but enables us to counter every kind of anthropomorphic representation. He writes that while the Koran employs every form of figurative expression admissible in literature, for example, 'Nay, both his hands are spread out' (5:64), at the same time it is clear that nothing can be compared to God, 'Nought is there like Him' (42:11). In his last work, Imam Fakhruddin Razi has written:

> I employed all the methods which philosophy and dialectics had provided, but in the end I realized that these methods could neither bring solace to the human heart, nor quench the thirst of the thirsty. The best method and the one nearest to reality was the method provided by the Koran.

Describing the two categories in which the Koran divides its teachings, *Muhkamat* (injunctions) and *Mutashahibat* (allegorical verses), Azad says that the former are clear to the mind, concern practical life and offer no equivocal meaning, while the latter elude complete understanding. The Koran clearly states:

> He it is who has sent down to thee the Book. Some of its signs are of themselves perspicuous ... others are figurative. But they whose hearts are prone to perversity, exploit its figures, craving discord, craving an interpretation; yet none knows its interpretation but God. (3:6)

Azad's attitude towards the rationalists is consistent when he writes, 'All the philosophic disquisitions which our dialecticians have indulged in, are in disconformity with the teachings of the Koran'.

The Koranic concept of the *Wahdaniyat* (unity of God) says Azad is a perfect concept. It presents the positive as well as the negative side of the unity. The positive side is that God is one. The negative is that there is none like Him. The first is unity in essence. The second is unity in attributes. In the pre-Koranic concepts, he writes, stress was laid on the first unity whereas the second was yet to be appreciated. He suggests that this is the reason why in every other religion, the unity of God has existed side by side with image and hero worship. The founder of a faith has often been given the honour and the devotion which is usually offered to God. This has happened in Christianity, Judaism, Buddhism. But the Koran closed the door to all this by offering perfect unity in attributes. It asserted the fact that only God is worthy of worship and if one turns to any other, one ceases to be a believer. All forms of prayers are links between man and God. By associating any other in this worship, the spirit of devotion gets vitiated. Hence the line in *Sura Al Fatiha*, *Thee alone* do we serve and *Thee alone* do we ask for help.

There is the question of the position of the prophets which the Koran defines first in terms of the Prophet of Islam. The basic *Kalima* is 'I affirm that there is no deity save God and Muhammad is His servant and messenger'. No one can enter the fold of Islam unless he accepts the unity of God and the *risalat* (prophethood) of Muhammad (PBUH). Soon after the death of the Prophet, Hazrat Abu Bakr, the first Khalifa ascended the pulpit and claimed:

> He who worshipped Muhammad, let him know that Muhammad is dead, and he who worshipped God, let him know that God ever lives. He has no death.

Azad writes that there is no compromise in the Koran's unitary and transcendental concept of God. This rigidity, however, does not prevent it from teaching tolerance towards other beliefs. He writes that the Koranic concept of God verifies the natural instinct that this universe has been created and it must have a creator. This is all the Koran points out; anything over and above this is left to be thought over individually or to be experienced personally:

> On earth are signs for men of firm belief and also in your own selves. Will ye not then behold them? (51:21)

Azad makes a point about the different levels of refinement in Hinduism based on class, and the absence of such a distinction in Islam. There are, however, three stages in Islam which are articulated in a tradition of the Prophet according to the Hadith literature of Muslim and Bukhari; Islam, Iman and Ihsan.³ But anyone, regardless of class, can aspire to any. stage depending on his aptitude. The first stage is adhering to the doctrinal beliefs: *Namaz, Roza, Hajj, Zakat.* The second is absolute devotion to these beliefs, where 'Islam takes hold of one's mind and heart'. The third stage is that of individual experience or personal enlightenment. Azad says that this stage is epitomized in the expression, 'Pray as if thou seest thy God before thee, and if thou seest Him not, pray in the conviction that God is seeing you'. Azad's definition of *Ihsan* is similar with the highest *maqam* to which the Sufi can aspire:

> It is not a matter either to teach or to learn. He who has reached this stage, if he could say anything about it, he could say nothing but this: become one like me and then behold what you can behold.

Azad says that Islam has made provision for every kind of spiritual thirst. But for the slaking of every thirst, there is only one tavern. He adds that the Koranic verses lend themselves to various interpretations. Shah Waliullah had said that he could prove the pantheistic theory by the very expression of the Koran. But at the same time, Azad is clear, that we should not indulge in far-fetched interpretations. Harking back to the memories of his Sufi antecedents, he hastens to add that the perception of God through *Kashf* (personal revelation) does not conflict with the principles of the Koranic concept. The Koranic concept of Allah, he says, is comprehensive enough to accommodate the unitary concept of God in every religion.

6. *Ihdenas Siratal Mustaqeem. Sirat al Ladhina an amta Alayhim; Ghairil Maghdhubi Alayhim Waladhaalin* (Divine Guidance). The *Sura* ends with a prayer to be guided to the Straight Path, the path of those to whom God has been gracious; not of those who have incurred His displeasure, nor of those who have gone astray. The word *Hidayat* (guidance) is very important in the Koran. Azad specifies that the *Rububiyat* of God has provided each object with a form, with inward and outward talents, assigned to it an appropriate role, and endowed it with a gift of self-direction or

Hidayat. He emphasizes, that he is referring to *self-direction* not to external direction. The other significant point is that it is only the *Hidayat* of revelation which can correct the *Hidayat* of reason. *Al Huda,* he says, is the element in us which responds to the *Hidayat* of revelation.

Then he makes a statement about 'universal guidance', which appears to be the driving force behind his entire thesis. He uses the expression, 'universal guidance of Divine Revelation vouchsafed to one and all from the beginning without distinction'. He writes that what the Koran calls *Al Din* (the religion) is the way of life appropriate to the nature and function of man. He calls this the 'great truth' and 'primary basis' of the Koranic call. He also says that if this fundamental concept is discarded, the entire Koranic message will get skewed. He explains this issue by defining the Koranic view of Revelation and Prophethood and the path along which it desires humanity to proceed. The Koran asserts the unity which originally existed in the human species:

Men were at first one community: then they fell to variance. (10:20)

Mankind was but one people; and God sent prophets to announce glad tidings and to warn them; and He sent down with them the book of truth, that it might decide the disputes of men. (2:213)

The importance of Azad's *tafsir* lies in its closeness to the word of the Koran rather than reliance upon extraneous factors. From the Word he derives the meaning that the divine truth is a universal gift from God. It is not exclusive to any race or people or religious group, and is not selectively delivered in any particular language. It is man who has created national, geographic and racial boundaries; but the truth cannot be thus divided. Using a metaphor for the universality, he then writes, 'The sun shines in every corner of the globe, and shines equally well on everyone'. Later, he was to repeat this expression with personal poignancy in his epistolary collection, *Ghubar-i-Khatir.* Azad writes that the Koran calls Islam the *Din-i-Hanif or* the way of Prophet Abraham. The religion is *Al Islam* because it means acquiescence or obedience or conformity to the way of God, and it follows that this was the religion preached by every prophet:

> And whosoever seeketh as religion other than the way of surrender (Al-Islam) it will not be accepted, and he will be a loser in the hereafter (in consequence). (3:85)

Viewed in context with the Koranic spirit, these lines refer to the meaning of the word *islam* rather than the doctrine. Quoting the famous passage in the Koran invoking man to hold fast to the cable of God and not let go, Azad writes that the Koran brought all those who fought with one another to the path of devotion to God and welded them into a brotherhood. 'It has lined up in a single file those who once hated each other—the Jews, the Christians, the Magians, the Sabians, who all now recognize together the founders of the faiths which they severally professed.' This aspect of Islam makes it universal and Azad emphasizes it to educate his readers about not only the tolerance in Islam but the presence in it of the truth of all other faiths, whether or not they are mentioned by name in the Koran.

notes

1 All quotations are from Syed Abdul Lateef, *The Tarjumanul Koran*, Asia Publishing House, 1962. The original style has a warmth which escapes translation. But Dr Lateef has done a commendable piece of work.

2 Azad's manuscript of the first edition written in his own handwriting is preserved in the 'Gosha-e-Azad', the Azad Collection of the Library of Indian Council of Cultural Relations, New Delhi.

3 *Tarjuman-ul-Quran* Vol. I, p. 201.

9

hindu–muslim unity

THE GANDHI-IRWIN PACT OF 1931 led to a release of political prisoners and to Gandhi's attendance at the Round Table Conference, The British Prime Minister, Ramsay MacDonald, announced the Communal Award which introduced separate electorates for depressed and backward classes and reservation of seats for Muslims in every province. Gandhi, in Yeravada Jail, undertook a fast-unto-death against this award. The award was equally unacceptable to Azad, being contrary to everything he had ever wanted for the Muslims. Civil Disobedience was launched throughout the country, even as Gandhi was marched back to prison in January 1932. People in large numbers courted arrest. Azad was arrested in February 1932 and detained in Delhi Jail. This was his fourth prison sentence.

The Government of India Act 1935 was promulgated, paving the way for the first elections. It provided for provincial autonomy while reserving special powers for the governors. This effectively meant that democracy could function in the provinces only so long as, and to the extent that, the governors permitted.

In *India Wins Freedom*, Azad writes that at the centre the position was even worse. It was a weak federation, sharply inclined in favour of the princes and others with vested interests who would be expected to side with the British. Regardless, he felt that the Congress should participate in the elections. General Elections were held in February 1937. Over 54 per cent of the electorate went to the polls and out of the 1581 seats in the Provincial Assemblies, Congress won 711.

Having secured 'an overwhelming majority', Azad wanted the Congress to form governments in the provinces because its failure to do so would result in less desirable elements assuming power and then speaking on behalf of the Indian people. While Congress was sorting out its internal differences, interim ministries were formed in the other provinces by non-Congress and anti-Congress parties. Finally the various Congress factions came together, accepted Azad's view and their ministries were formed.

Azad writes that he was in charge of parliamentary affairs in Bengal, Bihar, UP, Sind and the Frontier. This was the first time the Congress had become responsible for governance and people were waiting to see whether or not it would live up to its professed national character. The Muslim League did not miss any opportunity to criticize the Congress severely for being a national party only in name. It accused the Congress ministries of committing atrocities against the minorities, the Muslims in particular. While Azad denied that there was any truth in these allegations, he was chagrined at two incidents which smacked of communalism. They are referred to in *India Wins Freedom* as involving F.C. Nariman and Syed Mahmud, two stalwart leaders of the Congress. The incidents are given as examples of the communal character of some people in the Congress.

In one case, Nariman, a Parsi, was the obvious choice for leading the Provincial Legislature Party in Bombay. In the other, a Muslim, Syed Mahmud was the obvious choice for becoming the Chief Minister of Bihar. In both cases the Congress compromised, with the preference given to Vallabhbhai Patel for Bombay and to Rajendra Prasad for Bihar. These instances prove, writes Azad, that 'Congress did not come out fully successful in its test of nationalism.' There is wistfulness in his words that 'Congress had grown as a national organization and given opportunity of leadership to men of different communities', but it did not live upto its professed ideals.

There was, however, one individual, besides Gandhi, who Azad felt could have prevented this trend had he lived longer: Deshbandhu C.R. Das. What C.R. Das did in Bengal to solve the communal problem is seen by Azad as a model which should have been replicated in the rest of the country. His high regard for Chitaranjan Das is expressed in several of his writings. The problem of minorities was handled by Das in a manner that the Muslims of Bengal had no hesitation in recognizing him as their leader. Azad writes how Das was able to overcome their fears and apprehensions. He recognized their need to feel economically and politically empowered. First, he said that unless the Muslims were properly represented in public life and services, there could be no true democracy in Bengal. Second, he announced reservations in various spheres for the Muslims until such time that they could compete with other communities on equal terms. This announcement evoked a hue and cry, and many Congress leaders accused Das of partisanship and opportunism. But he did not budge from his original stand, and ultimately the strength and sincerity of his purpose won him the support of the Bengal Congress.

'I am convinced', Azad writes, 'that if he had not died a premature death, he would have created a new atmosphere in the country.' By implication, then, there was no one else in the Congress who had the sensitivity on the one hand and the clout on the other to champion the cause of the Muslims. The Muslim League and other communal parties were now working on fertile ground. The vessel of a united India which was to flounder ten years later was beginning to show cracks; and although Azad may have seen it coming, he was hoping that the tide would turn.

Although Azad had presided over the Special Session of the Congress as early as in 1923, surprisingly, it was not until 1937 that he was elected a member of the Congress Working Committee. This was, presumably, to fill the seat vacated as a result of the death of Dr Ansari in the same year. With Vallabhbhai Patel and Rajendra Prasad, he was appointed to the Parliamentary Board, known as the Party High Command.[1] He was elected as the Congress President in 1940 due to several reasons. He had played a pivotal role as a negotiator and mediator first between the No-Changers and Pro-Changers in the 1920s, and then between the rightists and the leftists in the 1930s. Above all, the growing alienation of the Muslims made him a natural choice for the post of President.

It was as the Amir of the caravan of Muslims, leading his followers on the path of Congress, that he spoke to the *quom* (nation) in the speeches and writings of this period. With the exception of *Tarjuman-ul-Quran*, Azad did not write anything during the decade of the thirties which had a literary or philosophical import. Two of his speeches which are preserved in *Khutbat-e-Azad*[2] are to Jamiat Tabligh Ahl-e-Hadith (1934) and Hindustani Committee, Bihar (1937). One manuscript of an unpublished article 'National Tehrik' is all the material that is available from this decade.

From his position at the helm of decision making in Congress, Azad saw, with growing consternation, the justifiable alienation and fear of the Muslims. In an unpublished and undated manuscript of an article entitled 'National Tehrik' Azad discusses several current issues concerning the Muslims and the Congress.[3] From internal evidence it appears that the document was written in the first half of 1938. In it he first traces the origin of the Muslim League and the Hindu Mahasabha; the latter, he writes, was established as a reaction to the former. Prominent Hindus like Pandit Madan Mohan Malaviya declared the Mahasabha a 'deadly movement'. Regardless, it gathered strength during the post-Khilafat period, when Hindu-Muslim unity started to wear out.

He repeats his original advice that in this struggle, the Muslims should join forces with the Hindus. He suggests that while they maintain their unique identity as Muslims as well as Indians, they should not allow the bond that connects them with crores of Muslims of the world to become submerged in any other identity. It is imperative, he writes, that every moment they should be vigilant of protecting their dual identity namely that of being Muslims and Indians simultaneously. Referring to Sampoornanand's statement in the U.P. Assembly, in which he had said that he wanted to see no distinction between the Hindus and Muslims in matters pertaining to education and culture, Azad declares it to be unacceptable for the Muslims, and against the Congress' principles. In support of his argument he uses the Protection of Minorities Resolution of the Karachi Congress 1931, in which the Muslim identity was recognised as a distinct factor in Indian polity. The Calcutta Congress Resolution which fortified the Karachi Resolution, he says, was written by him. The import of this was to assure the Muslims that the purpose of Congress is not to submerge the Muslim identity in the composite Indian nationality.

In keeping with its avowed objective, he writes, Congress I has declared that it will promote the language and the culture of minorities. Accordingly, Urdu will take its place by the side of Hindi wherever it is the official language. One may, an as aside, recall that the issue of language, which became increasingly important to him from now on, was raised a year earlier in his address to the Hindustani Committee, Bihar. In that he identified Urdu as the language which, since the end of the seventeenth century, was spoken in all parts of India, and consequently used by the British for the army. Calling it the *quomi zuban* (national language), he said that until that time it was called Hindvi, and there was no difference between Hindi and Urdu. The difference was between Hindi and Rekhta, the former was the everyday spoken language and the latter was the Persianized scholarly language. It was Mir Amman, who distinguished Urdu from Hindi when he was called to Fort William College, Calcutta, by John

Gilchrist. He evolved a clean and flowing language in which he wrote the classic, *Baagh-o-Bahar*. The importance of Urdu, as a national language is a dominant theme in both the speeches. That until this point he had the confidence of receiving his party's support on this issue, is evident from the statement that if any province not accord Urdu its rightful place, it could be compelled to do so.

The question before the Muslims, he writes, is: what should they do given the current scenario? First, they should 'shout aloud' that they are not prepared to become submerged in Hinduism. Second, they should recognize the fact that the years of living together have created certain common features between them and the Hindus. Third, they should operate from a base of confidence rather than from suspicion and weakness. Referring to the British ploy of convincing the Muslims that they need a third force to protect themselves from the Hindu onslaught, he says that it is hardly necessary to tell the Muslims that this 'third force' will not be an impediment to the Hindus gaining power but certainly will cause harm to their own progress. He expresses confidence in a bright future for the Muslims in India, by virtue of the fact that they 'occupy every inch of the road between Khyber and Constantinople'. According to Azad:

> So far, the Muslims have generally left the impression that if they participate in the freedom struggle they are somehow obliging the Hindus. Murmurs are heard—'during the Khilafat, we made the Congress', or 'during Non-Cooperation Muslim boys left the educational institutions (Aligarh) but what did the Hindu boys (Benaras) do?' As if the benefit of that sacrifice has accrued only to the Hindus and now they should somehow pay for it.

Azad suggests here, that the benefits accrued to both Hindus and Muslims, but the Muslims asserted that they had done all the work and others were reaping their harvest! So far as the Muslim League is concerned, he writes, he tried to offer them a share in the provincial governments, provided they accepted three conditions. First, the goal of complete independence, second, joining

forces with the Congress, third, assigning to the League the protection of the Muslim rights.

The presence of Jinnah, he wrote, was inimical to the League's
acceptance of the Congress proposals. His own efforts at affecting
a reconciliation between the two parties, he confesses, were not
acceptable to a majority of the Congress Working Committee:

> Only Gandhiji supported me. At last we began talks with Mr Jinnah,
> about including the League members in the governments and, there-
> by, removing a great obstacle from the path of a unified struggle.
> It is a pity that the League brought up the question of status and
> ruined the negotiations. How could we accept their idea of declaring
> the League and the Congress as communal parties of Muslims and
> Hindus respectively? Congress is a national party and wants to
> remain national... We (Muslims) should also take into account
> whether it is better for us that Congress calls itself secular rather
> than calling itself communal?

From the above it becomes clear that Azad was not getting much
support from his colleagues, Patel, Rajendra Prasad and others.
Regardless, he commanded seniority and respect, given the fact
that he had been associated with older veterans like Motilal
Nehru and C.R. Das. He was, therefore, able to carry his motion
in the teeth of opposition. The Congress did not fall into the trap
of declaring itself a communal party.

The other aspect of his concern was: what would be of the
greatest advantage to the Muslims, a communal Congress or a
national Congress? In terms of what was best for the Muslims, he
did say that if their rights could be better protected by separating
from the Congress he would not hesitate to do so. His presence
in the organisation was for the benefit of the Muslims. And he
was convinced that outside the Congress, their rights could not
be adequately safeguarded. He reminded them that there was a
time when the Muslims considered the Congress a band of rebels.
They had never thought that this outlawed party could one day
form the government. There was a time when they had aligned
themselves with the British for fear of the Hindus.

But the ground reality today was different:

> Even if all the Muslims of India say to the Britisher, do not leave this country, we will help you, he won't stay... When his own vessel is caught in a whirl, how can he help another's sinking ship?

For this reason, he writes, even the powerful and titled *zamindars* (landlords) today are sympathetic to the freedom struggle. Although their's were the sticks that were raining blows upon the heads of the freedom fighters, while they sat smugly in their *mehfils* and poked fun at freedom struggles.

What Azad intended to do with this piece of writing is not clear. It was never published in a journal nor distributed as a pamphlet. Was it meant as an analysis of the options available to the Muslims and of the implications of each option? He admits to having received complaints during the recent party elections that at the lower levels of the organization, all kinds of machinations are at work to keep the Muslims out of Congress. But he asserts that despite the fact that there were certain communal elements in it, at the *markaz* (apex) the Congress was entirely non-communal. He therefore concludes that it is in the Muslim interest to align itself with the Congress.

On the question of forming governments in the provinces, he explains that the Congress has done so as part of a much larger purpose. If the establishment of a democratic government had been the sole purpose, then Muslim League members would have been admitted at any cost. But the goal being *purna swaraj* or *mukammal azadi* (complete independence) it is possible that the burden of ministries may be cast off at any time. At such time, if people who have been taken in are undisciplined or weak, they may become an impediment in the realization of the goal. At the same time, he strongly advocates the principle that Congress should form the government only if it has a clear majority. For example, in the case of Assam, he writes, he opposed the formation of the government although he was told that 'Congress would get the majority later'. He said that he wanted to 'tell the world that we do not want to run after offices. If the League wants to form the government, let it. We have not taken a contract for forming governments'.

The same situation arose in Sindh. The Muslim League's provocative behaviour had spoilt. the atmosphere to the extent that the Congress wanted to support the Allah Bakhsh government. Even Patel had promised to support it. But Azad writes that he stuck his ground, saying that the League could go ahead and make 'one lakh governments'. This was a time when the Congress could impress upon the world that it had agreed to form governments on the basis of certain avowed principles. Azad himself always respected the show of majority. Aruna Asaf Ali recalls that when the communists won the elections in Kerala in 1955 Azad was adamant that they should form the government, regardless of the slim majority with which they had won. He said, '*Agar ek vote sey bhi unki aksariyat go to hukumat unhi ki honi chahiyé* (Even if they get a majority by one vote, they should still form the government).[4]

Despite the dissensions within the party, so far, Azad had been able to affect a reconciliation without compromising any of the principles. The two instances he gives in this article are about matters in Punjab and Sindh concerning the cultivators who happened to be Muslims and the landlords who happened to be Hindus. In the case of Sindh, the Hindus were opposed to asking for statehood because they felt that it would not be able to bear its own financial burden. After it got statehood and the question of levying taxes arose, the Hindus refused saying that the Muslims should take the responsibility for their decision. Sir Ghulam Husain conceded the Hindu demand and increased the *aabpaashi ke narkh* (charges for irrigation). The cultivators revolted and his government fell. Next, Allah Bakhsh faced a similar situation; aided and abetted by the Governor and communal Hindus he too declared an increase. The Congress decided to withdraw its support because Allah Bakhsh's move to burden the cultivators was against its principles. The Muslim League saw this as a golden opportunity to form the government in Sindh. At a meeting in Karachi, it communalized the issue and made such provocative speeches that the Hindu members of the Congress were thrown into the lap of the communalists.

The view gained ground that no matter what, the Muslim League should not be allowed to form the government. Supporting Allah Bakhsh, however, would have meant taxing the poor cultivator and deviating from the principle espoused by the Congress. But even principled men like Sardar Patel were convinced by the Congressmen from Sindh that Allah Bakhsh had to be supported. Azad writes that regardless of the rumblings within Congress, he could not accept compromise on the principle. Ultimately, Congress had to concede his point and the increase in *mehsul* (tax) was postponed forthwith. He ends this part on a note of regret that no one applauded this decision of Congress; neither the f press nor the public. While the Muslim League continued its slander, the communal Hindu remained infuriated with the Congress stand.

Besides the Hindu–Muslim question, the document contains Azad's views on the Muslim princely states, Wardha scheme and religious education for Muslims, and the false propaganda of Muslim League. It ends abruptly with the comment that the Muslims must not lose sight of the *markazi taqat* (central power) of the Congress. The import of this article as stated earlier, was to vindicate the Congress in the eyes of the Muslims and impress upon them that staying with it would be to their greatest advantage. It was a fitting prelude to his address to the Ramgarh Congress in March 1940.

War was the topical issue when Azad was elected the President of the Congress in 1940. At the Tripura Session in March 1939, Congress had passed a resolution dissociating itself from both imperialism and fascism, and thereby from Britain which has 'consistently aided Fascist powers and helped in the destruction of democratic countries'.[5] Gandhi's growing despair at the impending disaster and the consequent rift in the Congress is recorded in *India Wins Freedom*. Azad writes that Gandhi pressed him again and again to lend support to non-violence at any cost, even at the cost of India's freedom. But Azad could not bring himself to endorse non-violence as a matter of creed: 'For me non-violence was a matter of policy, not creed'.[6] On 3 September 1939 Viceroy Linlithgow announced that war had broken out between His Majesty and Germany. 'In the case of India, the Viceroy on his own declared war on Germany, without even the formality of consulting the Central Legislature', writes Azad. Thus India was 'unceremoniously dragged into the war', causing mental distress to Gandhi which brought him to a 'breaking point'.

The Congress Working Committee met in Wardha a few days later and passed a resolution which was a clear statement of its attitude to war. It asked the British government to specify its war aims with regard to 'democracy and imperialism and the new order which it envisaged'. Azad felt that this resolution would one day occupy an outstanding place in history because while it originated in India it represented a larger populace. In October, Linlithgow made a statement which Azad found 'long-winded' and 'tiring' and which declared Dominion Status to be the goal of the British policy in India as stated in the Preamble to the 1919 Act and now embodied in the Act of 1935. The Congress Working Committee rejected the statement and called upon the Congress Ministries to tender their resignations in eight provinces. By November the Ministries had resigned and Jinnah had declared 23 December 1939 as the 'Day of Deliverance and Thanksgiving'. Azad summarizes the events of this period in his address to Ramgarh Congress, in March 1940.

The fifty-third session of Congress was held one day later than scheduled, due to heavy rainfall. Azad faced the critical task of affecting reconciliation among the warring factions within the Congress. Without losing sight of the ultimate goal of *purna swaraj* (complete independence), the question of participation in the war had to be addressed. Azad spoke in simple language to hundreds of delegates who had thronged to hear the President speak at a moment when the country seemed poised on the hinge of freedom. Azad began by reviewing the War Resolutions that had become an integral part of the annual Congress proceedings, due to the impending clouds of war. The first such review, he said, had taken place at the Lucknow Congress in 1937. All these resolutions stated India's rejection of Nazism, Fascism, and Imperialism. They had been despatched to the British Government.

The British, he said, had always excelled in the art of political expediency. In the first war, which started in a corner of the Balkans, Britain and France raised the slogan for the rights of small nations. After the war, flushed with victory, they changed their tune. They watched in silent approval, while unrestrained dictatorships, based on brute forces, challenged the peace and freedom of the entire world. When the small nations began disappearing from the map as free countries, due to the Nazi ambition, they readily assisted in their burial. It was only when the menace approached their own territories that they raised slogans of freedom, world peace and democracy.

When India asked the British to declare their war aims, it became evident, he said, that their lofty objectives of freedom and democracy were confined within the geographical boundaries of Europe. The people of Asia and Africa were not expected to have similar aspirations. Reiterating the stand he had taken earlier, he declared that this exclusivity has always been a creed of all of Europe:

> Although these war aims were articulated by a British spokesman, they represent the mentality of entire Europe, which the world has known for two hundred years. In the 18th and 19th centuries, the principles of individual and collective freedom were regarded the exclusive rights of European countries and that too only of the Christian nations.

The fact that the British denied self determination to India, he says, proves that all their claims that the old order of imperialism has ended are counterfeit and false. When India placed on the table her demand for determining her own faith, the British raised the communal question.

At this point in the address Azad appropriately introduces a discussion of the most trying questions facing the country, the communal issue, rights of minorities and the Indian Muslims.

This discourse which has become a classic of minorities literature, is Azad's ultimate argument for a united India. He starts by stressing the seriousness of the communal problem and emphasizing that the British have used it as a ploy against according India her right as a nation. Congress, he says, has always been a national party, 'representing India as a whole and every move it makes is in the interest of the entire Indian nation'. As regards its stand on minorities, he says, it has stood by two basic principles. First, any constitution that is framed for India must contain the fullest guarantees for the protection of the rights and interests of minorities. Second, the safeguards for the protection of minority rights should be left to be formulated by them and not by majority vote.

Having said this for the Congress, he turns to the Muslims and asks if they consider themselves a minority in the sense of fearing for their survival? Referring to what he had said in *Al Hilal*, twenty-eight years ago, he condemns the widely held fear that the Muslims constitute a political minority and should, therefore, be wary of losing their individual and communal rights in a democratic India. This false image, he says, was created by the genius of the British sixty years ago, to use the Muslims to counter the new political awakening that was stirring among Indians. The two false premises which they used in weaving their design were: first, that since there were two communities in India no demand could be made on behalf of a united India; and second, since Muslims were a smaller number, the establishment of democratic institutions would lead to the rule of the Hindu majority and jeopardize the very existence of the Muslims.

He then defines the term 'minority'. Discounting the simple arithmetical definition of minority, he describes it as a group of people who find themselves both numerically and 'qualitatively' ineffective. By this definition, he says, the Muslims of India cannot call themselves a minority.

They number between eight and nine crores. Unlike other communities they are not divided on cultural and racial grounds. The powerful bonds of equity and brotherhood informing the Islamic life have, to a large extent, saved them from the weaknesses that flow from social segmentation. True, their fraction is no more than one-fourth of the total population of the country, but the question is not of the fraction, but of the number and of its quality. Can such a vast mass of humanity have any legitimate reason for apprehension that in a free and democratic India it may not be able to protect its rights and interests?

Thirty years ago, he continues, when he started work on this issue he found that the Muslims still nurtured the attitude of political indifference which was engrained in their psyche in 1888 (by Sir Syed). Within a short time he realized the fact that India was 'marching ahead towards its future' and the Muslim community could not remain indifferent to this course. In 1912, he says, he launched *Al Hilal* and placed his conclusion before the Muslims. The resultant political awakening which occurred from 1912–16 was astounding. It became apparent to him when he was released from prison in 1920 after almost four years.

Twenty years have passed since. Today, he declares, he can speak with the confidence of one who has participated in every event which has occurred since that time. He still believes that the one and only course of action which is in the interest of the Muslims is the one he had exhorted them to follow in 1912. He implores the Muslims not to be swayed by passions since they are dealing with the destinies of men and nations. 'Let them even today examine the issue from beginning to end; they will find no other path open to them but the one indicated by *Al Hilal*.'

One can be a Muslim as well as an Indian at the same time and with equal pride in being both, says Azad, not for the first time but with greater poignancy than expressed in any other speech or writing. There is an urgency in his tone which may have been an expression of his growing apprehension for the future. He was never to speak in this manner again. This was almost the end of his lifelong mission to reconcile the perceptible tension within his *quom* (nation) whether to regard itself primarily Muslim or primarily Indian, and how to order its loyalties. He gave his own prescription to them in these lines:

I am a Muslim and profoundly conscious of the fact that I have inherited Islam's glorious traditions of the last thirteen hundred years. I am not prepared to lose even a small part of that legacy... As a Muslim, I have a special identity within the field of religion and culture and I cannot tolerate any undue interference with it. But with these feelings, I have another deep realisation, born out of my life's experience, which is strengthened, not hindered by the spirit of Islam. I am equally proud of the fact that I am an Indian, an essential part of that indivisible unity of Indian nationhood, a vital factor in its total make up without which this noble edifice will remain incomplete. I can never give up this sincere claim.

Having given them his creed of harmony between their two identities, overlaid with the vastness of their numbers, he sees no reason why they should have any external or internal apprehension about their position in this emerging nation state.

The last part of this discourse contains the famous passages about composite nationhood in which he reminds the Muslims and the Hindus that having lived together for eleven hundred years, they have imbibed influences from each other and have now become one, an 'Indian nation, united and indivisible'.

If there are any Hindus among us who want to bring back the Hindu life of a thousand years ago and more, they are just dreaming and such dreams cannot become real. Likewise, if there are any Muslims who wish to revive their past civilisation and culture, which they brought a thousand years ago from Iran and Central Asia, they too dream and the sooner they wake up the better.

The next passage which seems to echo the sentiments that Tagore expressed in his poem *Bharat Tirath* (which Azad had undoubtedly read), describes how the languages, art, culture, dress, manners and customs of Hindus and Muslims, bear the unmistakable stamp of the life they have shared together for a thousand years:

Such moulds cannot be artificially constructed. Nature's hidden anvils shape them over centuries. The mould has now been cast and destiny has set her seal upon it.

On 31 December 1940, a few months after the Ramgarh Congress, Azad was arrested and sentenced to Naini Jail while he was engaged in Individual *Satyagraha*, which had just been started by Gandhi. The mutual respect between Gandhi and Azad did not mean that there was perfect agreement between the two. *India Wins Freedom* gives a blow-by-blow account of their differences pertaining to the War Proposals. Azad was to recall the polarity of some of their views in 1948, on the occasion of establishing a memorial to Gandhi, a few days after his assassination. Gandhi wanted no part in the war, even if it meant freedom; Azad wanted freedom, even at the cost of participating in the war effort. But this and other differences, he was to recall, did not cause any permanent distance. Gandhi drafted the Congress Working Committee resolutions according to Azad's wishes and Azad agreed to fully participate in Gandhi's individual *Satyagraha*.

Azad was released in December 1941, and immediately called a Working Committee meeting in Bardoli. More differences on the war front arose between Gandhi and the committee members. When, as President, he summarized the meetings, Azad pointed at Gandhi and recited this couplet:

Dilbar se juda hona, ya dil ko juda karna
Is soch mein baitha hoon akhir mujhe kya karna

To part from my beloved or part from my heart
Lost in the torment of choice, I wonder?[7]

The account of Azad's tenure as the Congress President is described in detail in *India Wins Freedom*. It becomes evident from this account that he had to reconcile the differences among all the Congress leaders. He writes that in addition to differing in principle, differences arose between his and Mahatma Gandhi's reading of the political situation. Gandhi believed that if India cooperated in the war, the British would be willing to concede India her freedom. Regardless, he would stick to his original principle that nonviolence was a creed which should not be abandoned under any circumstance. Azad felt that despite their anxiety to enlist India's cooperation, the British were not ready to concede freedom. In matters such as this, writes Azad, it was to Gandhi's credit that he was always ready to understand even a contrary point of view.

A substantial part of Azad's tenure as the Congress President was taken up with the mission to India of Sir Stafford- Cripps, a high ranking minister in the British Cabinet. Azad writes that he had spent several days with Cripps when he had visited India for the first time, soon after the outbreak of the war. The gist of their talks was that Cripps would persuade the government to declare India a free country as soon as the hostilities ceased, provided India agrees to participate in the war. Cripps returned to England via Soviet Russia, where he secured a diplomatic victory by affecting to some degree the distance between Hitler and Stalin. This increased his standing in British public life, so much so that when the American pressure mounted on Churchill to settle the Indian question, it was Cripps who was selected to handle the mission to India.

The account of Azad's negotiations with Cripps on the one hand and his handling of Congress on the other reflect his consummate artistry in politics. Notwithstanding his initial reluctance to enter active politics, he appears as one who played it as the art of the possible. In theatrical terms, in this enactment, there were several players with different motivations. Azad was the protagonist who would have accepted the British offer provided it led to the freedom of India. Cripps was the antagonist who wanted to secure a diplomatic victory in India like the one he got in Russia. By dangling the promise of freedom before Congress, he hoped India would enter the war. The other players included Gandhi, who was adamant about adhering to his creed of non violence, no matter what the cost; and Nehru, who was anguished because of his commitment to democracy and antipathy to fascism, both of which militated in favour of the British, whether or not they conceded India's independence. The rest of them, minor players, looked up to Gandhi for guidance.

When asked by the press about his efforts to hammer out an agreement between various parties, he answered by quoting a couplet from the poet Ghalib:

Koi ummeed bar nahi aati
Koi soorat nazar nahin aati

No desire is fulfilled
No direction is visible

Apart from the general question of transfer of power, the major difficulty with Cripps' proposal, says Azad, was the definition of the power of the Commander-in-Chief and the Indian Member of the Executive Committee in charge of Defence. He had, on Cripps' suggestion, met Commander-in-Chief Wavell to discuss the matter of the power of the Indian Member, but gained nothing from the meeting except the knowledge that the member would have responsibility but no power. The other part of Cripps's proposal, which Azad calls the 'greater snag', was about the communal problem, i.e. after the war the provinces would have the option to decide whether to join the Union or not. Gandhi 'reacted violently' against this and Azad told Cripps that 'the right given to the provinces to opt out meant opening the door to separation'.

The Working Committee in its meeting of 10 April 1942 concluded that the proposals as they stood were unacceptable. Azad wrote two letters to Cripps in which he gave the reasons for rejection, the most important being that they laid much greater emphasis on the future than on the present. During the war, he wrote, defence overlooks every sphere of civil administration and is, therefore, of paramount importance. To reserve it for the Viceroy or the Commander-in-Chief was to deny Indians the de facto power. There was nothing in the proposals, he asserted, which infused new faith in the Indians:

The picture, therefore, placed before us is not essentially different from the old one. The whole object which we, and I believe, you have in view—to create a new psychological approach to (sic) the people, to make them feel that their new national government had come, that they were defending their own newly won freedom—would be completely frustrated when they see this old picture again, with even the old labels on. The continuation of the India Office, which has been a symbol of evil to us, would confirm this picture.[8]

He frankly states that the Indians cannot assume responsibilities when they are neither given the freedom nor the power to shoulder them effectively, and when the old environment continues to hamper the effort. Stressing that the demand for a 'truly national government', meaning a government with full powers and not merely the continuation of a Viceroy's Executive Council, is the unanimous demand of the Indian people, he concludes his letter on the following note:

It would be a tragedy that even when there is this unanimity of opinion in India, the British Government should prevent a free National Government from functioning and from serving the cause of India as well as the larger causes for which millions are suffering and dying today.[9]

Cripps wrote a defensive reply, assigning the blame for the breakdown to the Congress camp. He brought up the communal question with reference to Azad's suggestion of a 'truly national government', saying that if such a system were introduced by convention, constitutional changes being impossible in war conditions, the nominated cabinet would 'constitute an absolute dictatorship of the majority'. He said that all minorities would reject this suggestion since it would subject them to a 'permanent and autocratic majority in the Cabinet'. In a sentence which was specially hurting to Azad, he said: 'In a country such as India, where the communal divisions are still so deep, an irresponsible majority government of this kind is not possible'. This statement seemed a negation of everything for which Azad had fought all his life. He patiently answered all Cripps's allegations, explaining the Congress stand, but on the communal question he spoke with barely suppressed anger. Reminding Cripps of their previous understanding that as soon as the British transferred power, the communal question would be tackled by parties concerned, he spoke words of harsh reproval:

> We are convinced that if the British government did not pursue a policy of encouraging disruption, all of us, to whatever party or group we belonged, would be able to come together and find a common line of action. But, unhappily, even in this grave hour of peril, the British govt., is unable to give up its wrecking policy. We are driven to the conclusion that it attaches more importance to holding on to its rule in India, as long as it can, and promoting discord and disruption here with that end in view.[10]

The events following the failure of the Cripps Mission centred on the war. In *India Wins Freedom* Azad refers to the period between Cripps and Quit India as the 'uneasy interval'. The fear of Japanese attacking India was imminent. Azad was adamant that Japanese aggression should be resisted. The general public, however, was so embittered against the British that even the Japanese were considered tolerable. Azad said to Gandhi that it would be unthinkable to 'exchange a new master for an old one'. It was at this juncture that Gandhi decided that it was time to launch an organized movement, and mooted the idea of Quit India. Azad's immediate reaction was, once again, different from Gandhi's. He felt that with the enemy at the Indian frontier, the British would not tolerate an organized movement of resistance. Moreover, if the British withdrew, he could not trust that the Japanese would stop their victorious march into India. From the account in *India Wins Freedom* it appears that this was the 'mother of all clashes' between the two. Gandhi asked for his resignation. Due to the intervention of Patel, however, the crisis was resolved and on 14 July 1942, the Working Committee passed a resolution which became known as the Quit India Resolution.

The Resolution was published. As predicted by Azad, the government refused to receive Gandhi or his emissary, Mira Behn on the ground that it would not tolerate any protest during the war, whether it was violent or non-violent. The All India Congress Committee was called in Bombay on 7 August 1942 to consider the situation which had arisen due to the government's attitude. Rumours about the Government's decision to arrest the leaders were flying around. Azad left Calcutta after having prepared Congress leaders from different parts of the province for the eventualities that might arise. He writes that he had a premonition that he was leaving his home for a long time. He reached Bombay on 3 August, and as usual, stayed with Bhulabhai Desai. On 8 August, after two days of intense discussions, the Congress passed the Quit India Resolution.

The events of Azad's arrest are recorded in the first letter he wrote from Ahmednagar to his friend Habibur Rahman Khan Sherwani. Nine members of the Working Committee formed the Ahmedabad band of prisoners: Nehru, Patel, Asaf Ali, Shankar Rao Deo, Govind Vallabh Pant, Pattabhi Sitaramiyya, Syed Mahmud, Prafulla Ghosh and Azad. *Ghubar-i-Khatir* is the most complete and unusual account of those days in prison—complete because it describes in great detail the daily life of the *zindanis* (prisoners); unusual because it strictly avoids any political analysis, regardless of the politically charged environment. The political discussions that took place in prison can be reconstructed from Azad's account in *India Wins Freedom* and letters of Jawaharlal Nehru written to family and friends during these years.

In *India Wins Freedom*, Azad writes of the violent reaction of the country to the 'government's leonine violence', something he says he foresaw, since a movement can remain non-violent only so long as the leaders are there to guide it. During the total period of his imprisonment, which lasted for three years in the two prisons Ahmednagar and Bankura, there were some momentous events, which he describes, including favourable signs of victory for the Allies. Each day the group of nine prisoners met for political and other discussions, the meetings were informally chaired by Azad. They met twice each day, after lunch and after dinner in sessions that were always held in his room. His reactions to national and international events, and the responses of the others which he records in *India Wins Freedom*, were a consequence of these discussions.

The general tone of his personal comments is that whatever happened was more or less what he predicted and that Gandhi by not heeding his advice made some serious mistakes. He provides examples, such as Gandhi giving undue importance to Jinnah, or his miscalculating the government's attitude when he launched the Quit India Movement. He asserts that all Working Committee members, with the exception of Nehru, blindly followed Gandhi. When one becomes familiar with Azad's writings, this blatant expression of 'I-told-you-so' is difficult to attribute to him. Judging from all that he ever wrote or said, the smugness projected by these comments, does not resemble any aspect of his personality. This and several other statements in the book create doubt in the reader's mind about *India Wins Freedom*. It is unclear whether or not Kabir understood the refined nuance of Azad's words. It is equally unclear whether or not Azad bothered to make him understand the working of his mind or the fineness of his expression. This problem, which throws a cloud over this entire autobiography, is discussed later.

notes

1 See V.N. Datta, p. 146.

2 *Khutbat-e-Azad* edited by Malik Ram.

3 The manuscript is preserved in the archives of the Azad Library of the Indian Council of Cultural Relations.

4 Aruna Asaf Ali 'Reminiscences' in *India's Maulana* ed. Syeda Saiyidain Hameed.

5 Tripura Resolution quote in *India Wins Freedom*, p. 26.

6 Ibid., p. 32.

7 Mohammad Yunus, 'Wit and Wisdom' in *India's Maulana* ed. Syeda Saiyidain Hameed.

8 See Azad's letter to Cripps, 11 April 1942. *India Wins Freedom*, Appendix 3, p. 259.

9 Ibid.

10 Azad's letter to Cripps is dated 11 April 1942.

10

the man within: *ghubar-i-khatir*

GHUBAR IS A VAPOUR WHICH RISES due to high precipitation. *Ghubar-i-khatir* is an expression used for the unburdening of the soul; in other words, permitting the 'vapour of the soul to rise'. As much as Azad was capable of allowing his tightly reined-in emotions to flow into a written expression, is what *Ghubar-i-Khatir* is all about. In his brief preface dated 6 February 1946, Azad states that these were personal letters, not written with the intention of publication, in fact handed to the press 'without a second glance'.

The letters, written during the first two years of his incarceration in the Ahmednagar Fort Prison (1942–5), were addressed to his friend Nawab Sadr Yar Jung, Habibur Rahman Khan Sherwani, Rais of Bhikampur, Zilla Aligarh. In his Introduction, Ajmal Khan, Azad's secretary of many years and the 'Fazluddin factor' of this work, writes that Azad had a very restricted circle of friends of which Nawab Sahib was one of the oldest, whom Azad had known since 1906. He also specifies that the epithet, *siddiq-i-mukarram*, which is used to address his friend in all the letters, should not be read as *siddiq-i-mukarram* (double emphasis on 'd' is wrong), the meaning changes from 'friend' to 'the true' with the use of the double consonant. It is not difficult to guess whose would have been the moving spirit behind Ajmal Khan's meticulous directive to the reader.

Azad's sensitivity to his friends is evident in the letters themselves; Ajmal Khan draws the reader's attention to one such instance. Recognizing that Nawab Sahib's interest in active politics was no more than what was customary among the feudal classes of the time, Ajmal Khan writes, that Azad does not burden him with politics; instead, he makes him privy to other areas of his mind. If something political slips in, he apologizes:

> I should not have started this topic here. Mine and your *majlis* (gathering) is not arranged for relating these tales. My storehouse of expressions is not restricted only to one commodity. Whenever I take anything out for you I carefully strain it in the sieve of caution, so that no trace of political adulteration remains.

The other quality to which Ajmal Khan refers is Azad's capacity to keep separate the various compartments of his mind. The apolitical correspondence with the Nawab at a time when he was immersed in politics, is a prime example of that capacity. Once he reportedly told Ajmal Khan that he kept the bases of his friendships with individuals distinct and intact. He did not 'contaminate' one base with other bases. Surrounded with the tumult and uncertainty of political life, not knowing whether the next day would bring imprisonment, banishment, or something worse, suddenly the memory of a friend's face would float in, and for a few moments everything else was forgotten. He could pick a subject as remote as possible from the present crisis—literature, art, philosophy, religion, ethics, anything except politics. Azad used to refer to this quality of quick change as *tehmiz*, the Arabic word for 'changing the taste of the mouth'. He told Ajmal Khan that if he did not indulge in *tehmiz*, his brain would stagnate. '*Tehmiz* provides for my mind the relaxation necessary for it to become refreshed and rejuvenated.'

The extraordinary capacity he had developed to control his feelings and change himself, writes Ajmal Khan, was an amazing phenomenon. Only those who have seen it with their own eyes can appreciate its magnitude.[1]

The arrangement of the correspondence probably owes little to Azad. It has a bureaucratic logic more likely attributable to Ajmal Khan. The background events were as follows. Following the Quit India call on 8 August 1942, the leaders were arrested from Bombay and sent to various prisons. One band of prisoners, which included Azad, was sent to Ahmednagar Fort. After they had served their sentence, they were disbanded and transferred to various other prisons. Azad reached Bankura, from where he was finally released on 15 June 1945. It was then that he handed his file of unposted letters to Ajmal Khan for making copies prior to mailing, as was his customary practice. Included in it was one letter which he had written a few days before he was arrested, while he was travelling by train from Calcutta to Bombay. The portfolio thus contained twenty letters, nineteen from Ahmedabad and one from the train, Bombay Mail. This would have made a perfect volume, but Ajmal Khan following a certain logic added three more letters—one written from Simla, and two from houseboats in which he was staying while holidaying in Srinagar and Naseem Bagh, both post-Ahmednagar. The logic was that they were also addressed to Sherwani; their inclusion and placement, however, creates some confusion in the reader's mind whether they were a continuation of Azad's earlier state of mind and environment.

Two other pointers from Ajmal Khan's Introduction are important; first, Azad's endless capacity to store information in his mind, and second, what he calls the writer's *dimaghi pas manzar* (mental perspective). The obvious proof of memory is Azad's lavish use of poetry to illustrate or substantiate his thought, when he was miles away from the use of any library. He uses poetry sparsely in religious and other intellectual discourses; but in giving a free play to his feelings, in other words, in ventilating his own *ghubar-i-khatir* (pent up feelings), couplets appear almost unbidden and slip in naturally, becoming intrinsic to the present discourse. Similarly the attention to detail with which he records history, not leaving out dates, names, or places, makes it appear as if he was sitting in the reference section of a library. Ajmal Khan, then, refers to what he calls the *dimaghi pas manzar* of an individual (Azad), who is woken up one morning to discover that he is under arrest and being taken to an unknown destination. Twenty-four hours later he wakes up inside the prison walls, picks up his pen and begins to write. The pattern repeats itself every few days; the question is: what 'mental perspective' enabled him to recreate another reality and turn into prison life as if it was his normal life of reading and writing?

The best account of the *raison d'etre* for these letters is, in Azad's own words, in the letter of 3 September 1945 written from Srinagar, two and a half months after his release. What Ajmal Khan has called his *dimaghi pas manzar* is substantiated by Azad's own description of his superhuman strength of will, although he never seems to regard it as anything out of the ordinary. On 10 August, the day after his arrest, he woke up as usual at 3 a.m., made his special light jasmine tea, and saw the unposted letter lying among his papers. Suddenly arose the desire to continue correspondence with the one to whom that letter was addressed, 'A letter thus came to be penned'. For one who was by now used to being imprisoned and who had developed rigorous self-discipline, the fact that the letter would remain unposted, or as he says in his poetic-prose, 'people have despatched letters through messengers or on the *kabootar's* (pigeon's) wings ... to my lot has fallen *unqa* (zero, also an imaginary bird)', was not a serious deterrent. Every two three days the letters were written, until the sequence suddenly stopped in May 1943, a month after he received the news of the death of his wife.

> After the event of 9 April 1943 ... the work on manuscripts[2] continued as usual and there was no change in the daily routine of Ahmednagar. But I do not want to hide the truth that this expression of peace and tranquility was purely external. It had nothing to do with what was going on inside. I managed to save my body from the blow but I could not save my heart.

The letter of 3 August 1942, may be read as a preamble to the Ahmednagar series. Its spontaneous beginning shows that Azad was in the habit of writing frequently to Sherwani,[3] whom he always referred to as *sidiq-i-mukarram* (Dear Benefactor), sharing the smallest detail, even of personal indisposition so long as he was able to work it into a linguistic conceit. He starts, 'The attack of influenza in Delhi and Lahore has tired me out. I can't seem to get rid of a heavy head. How can I free myself (*subuk dosh*) of this dead weight on my shoulders (*wabal-i-dosh*)?' The fun he has with language is matched by the fineness of expression which is possible only when one is addressing a kindred spirit. The letter is about sensuousness, albeit in a manner that one barely suspects it to exist. First, the description of the cool breeze from the open train windows is a purely physical experience. Then follows the account of the preparation of tea, which was later much discussed, praised and maligned by literary critics, as a metaphor for wine.[4] The pleasure of sipping tea with a simultaneous drag of a cigarette is described in the language of ceremony, almost like a Far-Eastern tea ritual with which he was undoubtedly familiar. The combination of the delicately fragrant tea with the aromatic bitter tobacco is pleasing to his senses; and the precision of timing: the last sip of tea with the last puff of the cigarette is satisfying to his mind.[5]

The description of a sensuous experience, makes him wonder about its morality. To his friend he admits that these 'self created habits' are 'mistakes', but whenever he has thought about them he could never convince himself of 'making life innocent' of mistakes'

> Just think! What kind of life is it whose dry garment cannot be dampened by any mistake? What kind of gait is it which has never known the pleasure of unsteadiness?

The commonly used metaphors in Urdu of dry garment being dampened and of gait becoming unsteady would normally be understood as directly referring to drinking. Here Azad refers to them as 'mistakes' of a kind he would be too happy to condone as part of a *bharpoor zindagi* (full-blooded life).

The metaphor of the dampened garment (wine spilled over clothes during drinking), however, has much wider meaning in Urdu as well as Persian poetry. Azad has often quoted the couplet of the Urdu poet Mir Dard:

Tar damini pay shaikh hamari na jaiyo
Daman nichor dein to farishtay vuzu karain

O, objector (in the name of morality) do not judge me on the evidence of my 'wet garment'.
For what this wet garment (made wet with tears of repentence) would yield when I squeeze it, would be pure enough for angels to wash themselves (ablution) as required before saying their prayers.

The poet Ghalib, who was held in great esteem by Azad, says in one of his ghazals:

Darya-e-ma-asi tunak abi say hua khushk
Mera sar-i-daman bhi abhi tar na hua tha

The sea of the world's sins ran dry
Before it had dampened even a small part of my garment.

This hyperbole used by Ghalib, which echoes Azad, means that in leading a good life, good people accumulate more than a sea-ful of what are considered as sins by conventional morality.

So what is Azad's prescription for a life that is to be lived fully and without fear of making mistakes? The next few lines in the same letter, allow a glimpse into aspects of his ethics and morality. They may be read as his spontaneous expression, considering the circumstances in which they were written. Taking his cue from the scholars of *tariqat* (the Sufi way), he writes:

Renunciation and resumption … on this path the problem is not the entanglement with the thorns, but when the thorns pin you down. It is not necessary that for fear of getting it wet you should keep your garment gathered up. If it becomes damp, so be it. But your hand should have the strength that, whenever necessary, you should squeeze it so hard that not a drop of liquid remains.

With characteristic economy of expression Azad makes a cinematographic cut to an incident which illustrates where he stands in relation to this dilemma. In 1921, when he was being taken to the Presidency jail, he freely offered his cigarettes to the accompanying policemen and on reaching the prison, presented the remainder along with his cigarette case to the jailor. For two years after this, he did not taste a single cigarette, despite the fact that fellow prisoners received supplies. Tins arrived from his home only to be distributed among the inmates. But the point of recounting this experience was that on the day of his release when the superintendent offered him his first cigarette in two years, the willingness with which he accepted this offer was no different from the determination with which he had quit in the first place:

> No lamentations at the deprivation, no celebration at the acquisition. The pleasure at the bitterness of renunciation is now matched with the pleasure at the sweetness of possession.

Azad's philosophy of sin and morality may be compared with that of some of the greatest seers of the world of Islam. He distantly approaches the great heights reached by men such as Bu Ali Shah Qalandar (b. 1185) and the renowned Persian poet the Hafiz of Shiraz but does not reach them. The former, embodiment of the popular slogan *mast qalandar*, is buried at Panipat and according to legend, simultaneously, at Karnal and Budha Khera. He went around town completely naked as a *mast* (one living in the 'other world', the 'exalted one') and appeared to ordinary men in a state of ecstacy. He made statements and composed verses that attracted the penalty of death. Some orthodox ulema had no hesitation in decreeing death. The Sultan of Delhi, Ghiyas-ud-din Balban, then sought help from other scholars who would absolve the *qalandar* of the alleged crime. The latter, the Hafiz of Shiraz, was acknowledged as a saint and a poet of the highest order. He expounded his version of religious truth and worldly wisdom in more than six thousand verses seeking and describing the pleasure of proximity with the Creator. He liberally used flesh and blood metaphors associated with wine and beloveds, and cursed the mullah for his hypocrisy in stopping people from drinking and enjoying life. Addressing the mullah, the petty moralist, Hafiz says:

Tu wa tuba wa ma wa qamat e yar
Fikr e har kas ba qadr e himmat e oast

While you seek the pleasure of *tuba* (the tree found in Heaven described in the Holy Koran, which gives delicious fruit and shade), I long for the truth which radiates from the tall stature of my beloved;
 How true it is that each one of us can only think and dare within one's limit and capacity!

While Azad saw no sin in drinking or enjoying the commonly indulged pleasures, the only evidence he has left of his own indulgences is the twenty page confessional statement in *Tazkirah* which refers to the brief seventeen month period after his father's death after which he launched *Al Hilal.* For the rest of his life he was to conform to the middle class moral code. The fact that he drank was known to his close associates but remained a strictly private matter. Did he lack the courage to publicly indulge in what gave him pleasure or was it a case of compromising with the requirements of common moral standards in the interest of maintaining his public image as a leader of the Muslims? These are questions to which writers on Azad would continue to seek answers.

The first letter of the Ahmednagar series is entitled *Dastan-i-Be-Sutoon-o-Kohkun* (The Story of Be-Sutoon and Kohkun). Of the total of nineteen letters, only three have titles. According to Ajmal Khan, Be-Sutoon is a relic in old Persia, which means 'Place of the gods'. Storytellers have connected it to Kohkun (Farhad), the lover of Shirin, who was ordered by Khusro, the Emperor of Iran, to carve a canal of milk into the stony boulders leading to the royal palace. He is, therefore, the symbol of strength of the common man pitted against state power which stands in the way of his achieving his life's most cherished desire, Shirin. It is appropriate that Azad should have chosen to write his first letter against the background of the Farhad story. It clearly shows that he counted himself in the category of those lovers who are prepared to bear the maximum possible hardships to secure what they love the most, *in his case the freedom of India.* He recognizes that the struggle to win freedom is as hard as that which fell to the lot of Farhad, the lover.

The letter relates the story of his arrest in Bombay, transportation to Ahmednagar, the first impression of the Fort and the first night in prison. The fact that the letters are considered the finest examples of Urdu prose is evident from the first few lines. The straightforward version of the events may have been, 'I was so busy in Bombay that I did not have time to ask Ajmal Khan to post this letter. Now I have so much time that I can write volumes'. Azad wrote:

> Yesterday, in the vast city of Bombay, the poverty of my limited leisure was such that I could not even hand my 3 August letter to Ajmal Khan for mailing. Today within the narrow walls of Ahmednagar Fort, just look at the luxury of timelessness! I feel like writing volumes upon volumes.

Despite the literary diminution due to translation, the point about his prose is evident from the above passage.

The account of the circumstances of his imprisonment takes up most of the letter. Descriptions are sharp and tight. Images rise to the mind as they are described on paper; his host's son Dhiru bending over him at 4 a.m., the early morning sight of the ocean, and the sea breeze laden with the fragrance of *champa* flowers which remind him of lines from Hafiz Shirazi. The Victoria Terminus Station, and railway platform scenes of companions showing signs of a rude early morning awakening by the police. Finally the train's last whistle which evokes this popular verse from Hafiz:

> *Kas na danast ke manzil gah-e-maqsood kujast*
> *Ein qadar hast ke bang-e-jarase mi ayad.*

I do not know where my desired destination lies
I do know that the caravan bells are calling me.

History then preoccupies his mind. Ahmednagar Fort, unrivalled for its strength except, according to the Duke of Wellington, by the Fort at Vellore. This was where the valour of Chand Bibi[6] became a legend of sacrifice and bravery, where Abdul Rahim Khan-e-Khana,[7] when asked where he would be found in case the enemy routed his armies, spoke his famous words, *'Zer-e-Lashaha'* (underneath the dead bodies), meaning he would be the first to die. From history to architecture, the narrative moves on relating the details of the moat, walls, courtyard, stopping at an old grave in the corner of the court. This relic comes to acquire special significance for him later, as described in his letter about the death of his wife. Here he makes the conjecture that this could be the grave of a 'possessed' individual, otherwise when all other inside the fort structures were razed why should this have been saved?

> The wilderness of this miserable existence of ours contains the seed of the miracle of habitation. This old grave had to be ravaged by time, so that it could be rehabilitated by the noise and excitement created by us, a bunch of *Kharabati* (wicked creatures).

The second letter, written the very next day, uses the subject of imprisonment for introspection and philosophizing. First he counts the number of days of his life which he has spent in prison—one out of every seven days in a total of fifty-three years; i.e. seven years and eight months. Why? The answer is the same as was given in all the earlier Writings, *Al Hilal, Al Balagh Quol-e-Faisal*, and various other speeches and addresses. He restates his conviction that there are only two alternatives available for the people of this land, to live a life of callousness or a life of awareness. The first can be lived anywhere, for the second there is no place but the prison cell. For him this way of life began as early as 1916. The Farhad in Azad has no alternative but to dig the canal in to the mountains to attain the object of his love.

Azad recounts that at the age of twenty-seven, when the work of *Al Hilal* and *Al Balagh* was at its peak and the Darul Irshad had been established, suddenly one day he had to give up everything, and exchange for a full life a life of isolation and detachment. Initially, the transition from one to another, did not cause him much pain but later he realized that it was not as easy as it appeared. The rest of the letter explores this experience of forced renunciation and, for him, its deep philosophical implications. We learn that the willingness with which he first walked out on life was a result of the initial spurt of bravura which soon wore out. He had to 'fashion a protective shell' around himself which was strong enough to withstand this periodic onslaught. Twenty-six years later, he used the very same shell which had by now become so invincible that it would sooner break than bend.

In a situation such as the one in which he found himself at the Ahmednagar prison, his past readings in philosophy evoked a certain stoicism but could not give him any lasting satisfaction. Like the wise bird of *Kalilah-o-Dimnah,*[8] it could advise him not to lament for what was lost but had no answer for the nagging question, now what? Science expressed only proven realities and informed the mind about physical determinism. But it too offered no satisfaction. The question then arose, where should one look for sustenance during these trying moments? Azad's answer to this is *in religion*. Religion, he states, is the only wall against which an aching back may be rested.

> Philosophy opens the door to doubt but cannot close what it has opened. Science gives proof but cannot offer faith. Religion gives us faith.

At this point he gently lifts the curtain on his own life. We learn that he could not remain content with the religion he had inherited from his forefathers. The incident of his *inkaar* (refusal to follow the faith of his ancestors), described earlier, is based on this intimate revelation. At the age of fifteen, he experienced torment when he could not make himself rise to offer his prayers. With the passage of time, when his faith was restored, it is important to remember that what he lost was inherited and what he gained was self-achieved. Backing up to the original argument, he claims that it is this *haqiqi* religion which is the 'wall against which an aching back could rest'.

Having said this he becomes aware of his surroundings—the four walls of the prison and all the consequential uncertainities. Characteristically he makes no reference to these conditions, but the very next lines are a rationalization of why he (or anyone for that matter) should put up with this ordeal called life? The justification he finds is that this is the demand made by the overpowering *maqsad* (purpose) of life. One can fulfil this *maqsad* by following the path strewn with thorns. However, there are two other concomitant considerations. First, *alam* (pain) and *raahat* (comfort) are neither permanent nor objective states of mind, and secondly, in his case, they are not inflicted externally. He says that we impose our own injuries and apply our own unguents.

The next few concluding paragraphs of the letter are concerned with the pleasure of a dynamic and free, versus a uniform and ritualistic existence. He quotes from a *rubayi* of his favourite poet Sarmad:

Zahid ba namaz-o-roza zabtey darad
Sarmad ba mai-o-piyala rabtey darad

The ascetic lives by self control, *roza* and *namaz*
Sarmad lives by connecting with the wine and cup

Then he goes on to describe two types of temperaments, one derives its satisfaction from keeping busy. For the other, simply keeping busy is not enough, it needs constant flux, movement. Azad further explains the second type, in which he includes himself, by stating that the need for change has a psychological dimension. He uses the same expression that was used by Ajmal Khan in the Introduction to *Ghubar-i-Khatir*, *hammazwa majaliskam*, the Arabic phrase for 'keep changing the taste of your congregations'. Nothing is more irksome than a placid existence. The elixir of life is its unevenness. Only those who have lost can understand the pleasure of gain. He who has never lost cannot understand. And, finally, stillness is death; the wave in the ocean lives only so long as it agitates.

At the end he reminds himself not to allow any diversion in the pursuance of the one paramount goal. In this passage, the turn of his phrase, though almost untranslatable, is so unique that even a watered down version needs to be quoted:

> The dust which lies along the path of the *maqsad* (purpose) is a very proud commodity. It snatches from the forehead of the wayfarer all the concealed *sijdey* (prostrations), so that there is nothing left in it to be offered at any other doorstep.

The symbolism of the passage is most revealing. In a memorable verse Mirza Ghalib, a favourite poet of Azad, says:

> *Oos naqsh e pa kay sijdey nay kya kya kia zalil*
> *Mein koocha-e-raqib mein bhi sar kay bal gaya*

> Woe to the humiliation inflicted on me by my beloved!
> I had to prostrate myself following her every footprint. Even in the street where my rival lives I went with my head bent (kissing the dust).

Azad uses the metaphor of *sijda* (prostration in prayer) somewhat differently. In the course of the *namaz* (prayer), as the Muslims prostrate themselves before Allah, their forehead touches the ground. In some cases, years and years of praying leaves a mark on the forehead, which is called *gatta*. Azad hints that in the arduous journey towards the destination of India's freedom, the layer of dust kicked up from the path has covered his forhead and concealed the mark formed by the years of his prayers. The distinction that was awarded by the traditional prayer in the shape of the mark, has been superseded. No other objective for the attainment of which he could now prostrate himself is now left for him. The unstated implication in this passage is that the cause of India's freedom is now the holiest of all the causes.

The third letter of the series is written four days later on August fifteenth. If this letter was to have had a title, it may have been called, *Sehr Angezi Ki Aadat* (The habit of waking up early). The mood is upbeat when he starts writing, a feeling which is conveyed by the remark that all of life's problems have only one solution—a *finjan* of tea! This early morning habit which began during his childhood became a lifelong characteristic because of the overpowering desire to be awake when the world slept and thereby enjoy a few moments of complete privacy.

> When I think of it, in this matter, too, I walked in the opposite direction from the rest of the world. What constitute the most precious moments for everyone else to enjoy the sweetness of sleep, are my most treasured moments of wakefulness... My advantage is that no one can interfere with my solitude. I have not allowed the world to take liberties with me. I sleep when it wakes, and I wake when it sleeps.

These letters reveal how in his private thoughts Azad was conscious of acting differently from the rest of the world. Seeking the solitude of the early hours of the morning when the world sleeps is understandable as any introspective individual may just want to be all by himself, undisturbed, perhaps to think, to plan, to meditate. But what were the 'opposite directions' he took in defiance of the rest of the world he leaves unspoken. Although his entire life's struggle was to move along the path of his personal convictions, in the opposite direction to the popular tide.

Conditions of prison life continue to be oppressive but there is a lightheartedness in his account of the day to day events. Only on the question of asking the government for any privileges is there a discernible irritation. When he is informed that the privileges accorded to murderers lodged in jails, like meeting with and writing to their families, are to be denied to them, he decides that he will refuse the government's offer of sending for books and papers from home. His companions follow suit. The couplet quoted in this regard has a strange poignancy:

Zaban jalayee kiye qata haath puhnchon tak
Ye bandobast hue hain meri dua ke liye.

My tongue is burnt, my hands amputated till the wrists.
This is the rearrangement my oppressor has made for saying my
prayers [which require the raising of palms].

But good humour dominates the account of the prisoners'
encounters with the jailor, the cook, the barber, the washerman.
The jailor, one Major Sendak, has been nicknamed Cheeta Khan,
after a keeper of the Fort during Chand Bibi's times. The conflict between the cook and the jailor is compared with the confrontation between determinism and free will in the writings of
Schopenhauer. Problems of the prison are tackled by the bumbling
jailors and warders, Cheeta Khan (true to his name), is described,
'always sharpening his nails while the knots in the operation
became too complicated for anyone to successfully undo!'

The fifth letter has a title, *Hikayat-e-Bada-o-Tiryak*, meaning
'The story of wine and the antidote'. Here Azad describes his
dual life—one inside and one outside the prison—one the *bada*
the other the *tiryak*. The question is: which is the wine and which
is the antidote? Can confinement in prison be defined in these
terms? Can it be reconstructed in terms of a 'cocktail of *bada* and
tiryak' He uses the word 'metamorphoses' (a rare use of English
vocabulary) to describe his manner of coping with every visit to
the prison, which is often in an unknown place, and always of
uncertain duration:

> If you see me at this juncture you will imagine that my previous life
> has escorted me to this new doorstep, from where a new life has
> taken over.

He arranges his prison life on the basis of the contradicting
philosophies of stoicism and epicureanism. 'I have emptied both
bottles into my cocktail', he writes, 'and my thirst and desire
cannot be satisfied without this blend. Try to understand this
according to an ancient analogy—I have revived the *hikayat* of
the *bada* and *tiryak*.'

This letter, which reveals an intimate aspect of the man, invites us to take a fresh look at the individual called Mohiuddin Ahmad, for whom the tendency among scholars is to cast into a certain rigid mould which fits his adopted name Abul Kalam Azad. Certain stylistic devices he uses are important in this regard. First, it is evident that while writing prose, he was thinking poetry. His prose is profusely sprinkled with similies, metaphors and stylistic innovations as if it were poetry. Second, he was using wine as analogy for whatever challenged him and gave him pleasure. This was quite in line with the greatest of Muslim poets for whom the *zat* of Allah was the object of love and worship, the simile of the state of intoxication with wine was used for a state of total forgetfulness, indeed, of sublimation into what may be unsatisfactorily translated as communion with the Creator, *Kashf.* Third, he was expressing views on religion and philosophy within the broad aesthetics of literature. This letter is used to express three ideas; first, that happiness is not an external commodity—it resides within individual perception; secondly, nature is indiscriminating in the distribution of her bounties; and thirdly, to live life happily is man's highest achievement and happiness is in having a true, genuine and full blooded religious attitude, such as he himself had.

In elaboration of the above, he says that the happiness we seek here and there blooms and wilts within the recesses of our own heart but our problem is that we know everything except what is most important, ourselves. The Koranic injunction he quotes is the original source for this belief.

Wa fil ardi ayatul-lil-muqineen
Wa fi anfusikum aafala tubsiroon (51:20, 21)

And in the earth are Signs for those who have certainty of faith and also in your own selves. Will you not see?

The peacock of the jungle, he says, does not need a garden. Wherever he opens his wings he creates a garden of myriad colours. For Azad, the recognition of the self is supremely important. One has to be quite independent like the peacock, a bird full of beauty, grace and majesty which cares not for the presence of the audience and displays itself in the wilderness of the jungle. Apart from what one can recognize by looking around, one can discover the certainty of faith by looking into one's own self. In the process one achieves personal freedom and independence. To be happy, it matters little if one is in Calcutta or Bombay or in the Ahmednagar prison.

Confined within the walls of the prison he then details the bounties of nature which are bestowed alike on the insider and the outsider:

Everyday the sun shines inside the four walls of the prison. Moonbeams make no distinction between a prisoner and a free person. During dark nights, star-torches in the sky not only brighten the world outside the prison walls, they create bright pools of light around the prisoners as well. When the day spreads sunshine, its light is not exclusive to those who live in pleasure houses. This visual feast is equally displayed for the benefit of those whose eyes are glued to the holes in the walls of the prison houses. Unlike man, Nature never makes favourites in bestowing her favours. When she lifts the veil from her face, she invites one and all to savour her beauty. It is we who are to blame, never glancing at the breath-taking vision presented by Nature, always immersed in our narrow world.

The secret of happiness in these conditions, he says, is to keep alive the enthusiasm of one's heart. He knows that all the pleasures of life are essentially derived from this 'tavern of solitariness'; if this is ravaged nothing remains. Armed with this talisman for happiness he begins his day at three or four in the morning. Several *finjans* of tea, like Hafiz Shirazi's cups of wine, then circulate in his tavern. Undoubtedly this is the best time to savour his solitude. The absence of an attendant to perform the tea-ritual is almost a relief because this gives his 'eager hands' an opportunity to move between the tin of Chinese tea and its accoutrements. Finally having arranged the cup and *surahi* (wine carafe) on the right hand and the writing materials on the left, he sits down and allows himself to be transported to a state which he believes was not enjoyed even by the 'connoisseurs of Champagne and Bourdeaux who tasted the preserves of hundreds of years old wine cellars'. The ritual of tea is described in a state of trance, while savoring every sip, deriving utmost pleasure from whatever is strewn around. Politics recedes from his mind, 'I don't know what happened after the morning of ninth August and what is happening now'.

The next period of *kaif* (the word in Urdu means 'exhilaration' and is used often in the context of intoxication that overwhelms a man) is the afternoon when he indulges in the second round. The sight of the clear sky washes off the lurking mental cloud and he philosophizes on human happiness:

An old Chinese adage questions, 'Who is the wisest man?' The answer is given, 'He who is the happiest'. The Chinese have understood life better than any other race, he claims, although the French writer Andre Gîde has taken it a step further by his contention that a cheerful temperament is our moral responsibility to the rest of the society. Philosophizing along the lines of Gîde, Azad uses the word *aaina-khaana* (a house lined all around with mirrors) for life, in which one image appears in a thousand mirrors. Therefore, we cause a ripple of happiness all around by remaining happy ourselves, and the happiness that thus gathers around us becomes the cause of our own happiness.

Azad maintains that strangely enough, the three disciplines which have endeavoured to solve life's riddle, namely, philosophy, religion and ethics, all three have developed an anti-life bias. The person who has the most morose expression and melancholy temperament is easily identified as a philosopher, a theologian, a moralist. As if a sorrowful look is a prerequisite for 'respectability' and 'learning'. In ancient Greece it was not only the cynics and the stoics who derided life; the peripatetics did no less. Gradually an overarching sadness and a wry expression became a distinguishing mark of a philosophical temperament. A laughing face cannot be associated with *zuhd* (asceticism) and *haq* (truth).

A gathering of tasteful people has room for everyone, except—
and by saying this Azad makes a very important revelation about
himself—for those who wear the pretentious robes of the *zahidan-
e-khushk* (ascetics who do not drink). The 'wet' *zahid*, Azad
himself, then carries this argument to an extreme, by saying that
if we wear the arid face of a *zahid*, a sadhu, or a philosopher we
cannot find our place in the scheme of this exquisitely designed
universe.

> In this cosmic design which displays the sun's shining forehead, the
> laughing face of the moon, the wide-eyed stars, the dancing trees, the
> song-birds, the harmony of waterfalls, and the coquetry of myriad
> coloured flowers, we, of a morose and wry countenance are not
> deserving of a place. Only those who are integrally harmonious with
> this spectacular composition of nature may hope to fit in.

Most of the stereotyping of Azad, as stated earlier, must now
be revised in the light of the intimate revelations in *Ghubar-i-
Khatir*. The man who gave the highest priority not only to inner
happiness but to an external expression of it, who said that
those who display a morose expression and temperament such
as the *zahids*, sadhus and philosophers are not deserving of a place
within the exquisite cosmic design, has often been branded as
the Mullah. Understanding of Abul Kalam Azad has been on the
whole somewhat deficient and simplistic. This one-dimensional
view has no place in the Azad rubric, as is evident from other
letters of *Ghubar-i-Khatir*.

The next letter, written only two days later, is in itself a significant fragment of his autobiography. Certain factual details
from it have been used in biographical accounts, but the spirit
in which they have been revealed by the author has been given
little attention. At the beginning, once again, there is the preoccupation with being under detention. This time the conditions
in prison were quite different from the ones that prevailed in
previous sentences, when more consideration was shown by the
authorities to political prisoners. But he was still able to adjust
and establish a normal routine within a few hours of entering the

prison gates. This was due to a childhood trait of preferring his own solitude to the company of other children. Several memories are invoked, allowing the reader a glimpse into life in his father's home, led according to the strict rules laid down by the patriarch. In the recounting of his childhood, there is one incident which says volumes about the boy who would grow up to become the *daiyee*, and *musleh* of the *quom*. It has been quoted earlier in chapter two:

> People spend their childhood in fun and games. But from the age of twelve or thirteen, I used to retire in a corner with my book, trying my hardest to hide from the rest of the world. You must have seen the Dalhousie Square in Calcutta, right across from GPO (General Post Office) which is popularly called Lai Duggi. Inside, there was a cluster of trees which hid a fair size clearing and a bench. Whenever I went for a walk, I took a book along and sitting down on the bench became engrossed in reading. Father's special servant Hafiz Waliullah, who always accompanied me, paced around the cluster of trees saying, 'If you had to read a book why did you ever leave the house?'[9]

This desire for seclusion was part of a psyche created by the atmosphere of *piri-muridi*, an aspect of which was excessive adulation by murids in his household. The passages pertaining to this are perhaps the key to understanding his attitude to leadership.

This adoration of the *murids* is a part of his childhood that he recalls with distaste. He believes that this trait is often the cause of great temptation, and corrupts impressionable youth, turning them into spoilt sons of rich fathers. He writes that this type of behaviour irked him from the beginning, and all he wanted was to distance himself from it unlike his brother and cousins who seem to thrive on it. This trait persists in later life when, unlike his political contemporaries, he cannot bring himself to become a man of the masses. His attitude to leadership was thus conditioned by his temperamental reserve, a point which has been discussed. The other effect of this trait was his indifference to the kind of popularity which politicians long for. In the course of every day political life, whenever people moved away from him, he felt grateful instead of resentful. His own description of this bent of mind is candid:

> If I tolerate the attention of the crowd, it is not by choice but by compulsion. I have not sought and found politics, politics has sought and found me.

This temperament, he confesses, has caused him much hardship. People have attributed it to pride and snobbery. Regardless, he is content with his own company, and values the fact that his colleagues respect his routine and desire for privacy. What does it matter, he asks, if all the external means of keeping busy are snatched away?

> I have brought, hidden in my heart, all of life's accoutrements which no one can seize. I arraign them before myself and become engrossed in their viewing.

The three letters that follow contain perhaps the most important segments of autobiography. They were written during a one-week period, 12, 17 and 18 October 1942. The questions he raises are addressed to himself. Who am I? What made me the way I am? What do I believe in and why? The answers are amazingly simple and candid. Unlike *Tazkirah*, there is no attempt here to use language as a protective device. Although these letters have been available to Azad scholars since 1946, little attempt was made to explore the deeper meaning of *Ghubar-i-Khatir* in order to understand the multifarious personality of Abul Kalam Azad. The first letter of the series of three is about himself. It fully articulates the sentiment one encounters as early as the *Al Hilal* period, that he was born before his time or at the wrong time. He calls himself *na waqt ka phal*, a fruit out of season, precious, because it is rare, tasteless because it is against the law of nature. If such personalities come into existence, by the very definition of being unnatural, they cannot keep pace with their times, nor can their time keep pace with them. In the passage that follows, he explains that he was forever swimming against the current, and for that reason he always found himself alone:

> In the marketplace, only those commodities are kept which are in popular demand... But my case was diametrically opposite. Whatever commodity became popular could not find a place in my shop. In the marketplace of life, people usually bring things which are commonly used. I strove to collect only those things which no one wanted. People usually set up their shops only where the crowds of shoppers gather, I looked and looked until found a place where the fewest shoppers passed by.
>
> In religion, in literature, in politics, on the paths of philosophy, wherever I went, I went alone. The caravans of the times did not support me on any of my journeys.
>
> Whenever I went on a journey, I found that I had travelled so far from the popular destinations, that upon turning around to look, I saw nothing but the dust of the road. This dust, too, was raised by the rapidity of my own pace.

Having expressed all this, he writes, is liberating—like the unfastening of a bolt. What follows is a natural corollary.

The story of his youthful vagaries, as told here, is corroborated in the last part of *Tazkirah*. It is clear that he considers, as any true believer is expected to when looking back on a part of his life, that it was the loss of faith which resulted in waywardness, for which he uses the expression *awara-e-dasht-e-vahshat* (vagabond of the valley of unrest and depression). For ten years, from the age of fourteen to twenty-four, even as he was at the peak of his journalistic career, he confesses to having become an emotional vagabond.

> At the age of twenty-four, when people usually start their journey of sensuousness, I had completed my wanderings and was picking the thorns from my feet.

Once again, repeating the statement made in *Tazkirah*, he confesses that the hand which 'dragged me from the grip of my environment' was the same which ultimately steered him off the paths of self-forgetfulness. When he caught his breath, he was standing before his destination, and, by implication, it was the same guiding spirit that led him there. Of the two paths open before him, the choice was obvious. To follow the path of compromise was not his creed. Courage was the only way. With full awareness of its implications, he strode along the path and since he could not walk in step with time, he, and people like him 'soared above the time, and ultimately soared with complete detachment'.

The second letter of the series is about his concept of God which has been discussed at length in *Al Hilal, Al Balagh* and *Tarjuman-ul-Quran,* besides being continuously referred to in most of his speeches and writings. This is the last written account we possess on this subject. The fact that these two letters contain the essence of a lifetime's thought on the subject, imbues every word with a special significance. It is important that the reader realizes that there is nothing here which has not been stated in the *Tarjuman.* But what makes it significant is that these letters were written almost ten years later, and the events of the intervening period had left their mark on the writer.

The concept of God discussed by Azad is not of the God of any one religion. The concept is of a universal God. Thirty years earlier, in the pages of *Al Hilal* the God was *Rahman, Rahim* as well as *Qahaar* (wrathful) and *Jabbaar* (forceful). But there is not much in these letters which reflects the rhetorical style of invoking and explaining God which had characterized the writings in *Al Hilal.* He writes that there is no solution to the business of life unless man is able to recognize the existence of God. But how does that happen? When man tries to unravel a mystery he first tries to rationalize. It is only when his reason is satisfied that he accepts the outcome. Giving elaborate examples of the application of reason he then asks, what about *tilism-i-hasti* (mystery or magic of existence)?

Since man opened his mind to consciousness he has been looking for the solution to this mystery. But the first and the last page of this ancient tome has been lost; no one knows how it began, nor is there any indication of how or where it will end.

Then begin the questions:

What is life and what is motion? Why does it exist? Does it have a beginning? Will it ever end? What is man? This thought yours 'what is man?', what is this thinking? And then, behind all the veils of *hairat* (astonishment) and *darmandgi* (vagrancy) does anything exist?

From the start of human civilization when man looked out of the caves and saw the rising and setting sun, until today when he looks out of his laboratory and sees many forms of nature exposed before him, this mystery has remained unresolved. Although the more we try to unravel it, the more it gets tangled, but our thirst for truth is insatiable. Sometimes we delude ourselves into thinking that we do not need a perfect solution. But this self-deception gets shattered when it comes up against life's relentless demands; and the questions arise.

This entire commerce of existence, its every mode and form is gathered into one single question. 'What is this?', 'Why is all this?', 'What for, all this?' We take the support of reason, and in the light of what we have named learning, we keep moving along which ever path becomes visible. But we do not find any solution which can slake the thirst for discovering the ends of this tangle… As we turn towards the old solution that, 'An embodiment of knowledge and strength is the Presence behind the veil', we suddenly emerge into the light. Now radiance floods in. Every question finds its answer, every demand finds its fulfilment, every thirst is slaked—as if the perplexity was a vice like grip which opened at the gentle touch of the key.

The solution to man's dilemma about the existence of God is further explained in two ways. First the inner recognition of the Presence, *Ek Sahib-i-Idrak-o-Irada Quwwat, pas-i-parda maujud hai* (An all-knowing and all-doing Power exists behind the veil) that makes all the pieces fit. In nature, he says, there is a perfect pattern which is at once lofty and aesthetic. Its loftiness impresses us, its aesthetic absorbs us. How can we then presume to think that there is no intelligent force working behind this perfect display of nature? Our understanding is limited by the scope of our mind. We want solutions which will end all confusion. But the dilemma of man's concept of God requires a different mind, a different language, a different measure. Secondly, man has always sought a higher goal towards which he should strive. And who else (but God) can be the destination of the human soul which soars towards those limitless heights?

Azad explains why. Everything that exists in the universe is of a lower stature than man. He cannot look up to anything. He cannot posit the sun as life's goal. He cannot adore the stars. Towards what, then, is his desire to soar at the highest level directed? At the end, quoting the German philosopher Riehl, Azad brings his narrative towards its final conclusion:

> Except God, what can be the goal of man's desire to achieve great heights? If this goal is removed, he will have no choice but to look downwards. Once he looks down, his greatness begins to plummet. This state of affairs convinces us that faith in God is the *natural* outcome of human need. And since it is a *natural* need, there was, at all times, a natural place for it inside every human being. It was not something which evolved later.

The universality of his concept of God is nowhere more evident than it is in the last lines of this letter when he states, that from the primitive tribes of Australia to the advent of civilized man, no one has been without desire for this concept—the ancient Vedantists, the Hittites from the dawn of history, the pre-Christian Egyptians, and the Caledonian artisans, all expressed it in different forms.

The issue raised in the last letter of the series pertains to man's inability to accept an abstract God, devoid of any shape or form. It explains man's continuous effort, in accordance with his capacity, to give a concrete shape to what essentially comes through as a personal God. The most ancient cradle of *Wahdat-ul-Wujud* (the doctrine held by Sufi saints that nothing really exists except as an emanation from the Divine Being, was India and probably it was from here that this concept reached Greece and Alexandria. Its only description of the Divine Being is that *it is*, nothing else. This is why the Upanishads took the negative attribute approach, i.e. *neti neti* ('not this, not this'). But the thirst for a personal God had to be slaked and according to Azad, Brahma began to be seen in the form of Vishnu. 'Idols of stone had to be carved to give the heart the solace of attachment.'

Azad describes the Judaic view of God as a despotic and oppressive monarch and the Christian view of God as that of the Father. He contends that since the Islamic view was essentially abstract, it allowed no room for personal definition. But ultimately the vague contours of a form could be felt and the doors to miracles started to open. Azad interprets the Islamic experience as the final proof of the fact that man's desire cannot be fulfilled without an anchor to which his imagination may be hitched. Man cannot easily grasp a supra-natural or transcendental concept. He needs a *jalwa-e-mahboobi* (vision with which he can fall intensely in love) which can engage his heart, and in pursuit of the elusive beauty of which he can become oblivious to what exists around him. He needs a Being towards whose exalted garment he can extend his humble hands and with whom he can spend nights of love and confidences.

Azad writes, that He (God) should be placed at the highest pinnacle. The Koran states that His glance always follows man's every movement. *Inna Rabaka la-bil-mir-saad* (Your Allah is always looking at you from a vantage point, 89:14). He says further, that the descent from an impersonal and an impervious God to a personal God in the Upanishads is reflected in the Sufi concept of *Ahdiyat* and *Wahidiyat Ahdiyat* implying unique and *Wahidiyat* implying the first. The concept of the first requires that there be a second, third and fourth. According to Azad, the signs of reality are scattered all around us. If we stop to think, our existence itself is a Sign. The real guiding light for man is not of *dalil* (argument), but *kashf-o-mushahida* (witnessing and revelation).

Azad rejects the theory of evolution put forward by science and says that the phenomenon of evolution is neither self-explanatory, nor can it be explained in purely material terms. If matter is the only reality, Azad says, then where does human *fikr-o-idraak* (thought and intelligence) come from? Why does man have an evolutionary urge which compels him to greater and greater heights? Why should there be such an urgent desire for ascent, that his ladder's reach appears to be unending? Was this ladder built without the presence of any *bala khana* (top storey)? Azad relies on the work of biologist, Lloyd Morgan, who had concluded that a 'creative principle' is at work; it is a *la zaman* (timeless) reality in this temporal world, says Azad. If we cannot locate an explanation for this within the world of matter, Azad believes, we should not think we are on the wrong track. The explanation lies in spiritual configurations. And finally he voices his conviction that the explanations pertaining to matter which were developed in the eighteenth and nineteenth centuries are being rejected in the twentieth century. Intellectual explanations are once again being sought in subjective rather than objective terms, an order reminiscent of the trends which emerged during the rennaisance.

These three letters are the last written evidence of Azad's concept of God. The trajectory thus traced from 1912 to 1942, reflects his changing views and widening horizons. First, there was the inherited God of his ancestors, with a brief interlude with the *Mutaliza*; secondly, the 'godless' period of his teenage years; thirdly, the inception of a personal God, and finally the closeness to a universal God. His narrative focuses on scientific evidence, until he is able to deconstruct it in favour of a philosophical explanation and spiritual acceptance.

The tenth letter, written at four o'clock in the morning, after a six-week gap, introduces a subject which has found expression in almost all his earlier writings, but had not been touched so far in *Ghubar-i-Khatir*: the causes of the decline of Islam. Tracing the history of the conflict between the Crescent and the Cross during the Crusades he focuses on the strengths and the weaknesses of each. First, he explains why he considers the memoirs of a French crusader, Jean de Jeanville, more authentic than any other account of the period. But at the same time, he cautions the student of history to be wary of *rivayat* (oral tradition) because well intentioned individuals sometimes invent traditions for what they consider a good cause or to set a good example, believing in the adage that the ends justify the means. In Islamic history, he says, there are people who went as far as fabricating Hadiths. They were usually the ones who were honest and virtuous and believed that there was nothing wrong with presenting an exemplary life (of the Prophet) to the public, even if it meant inventing a few Hadith. Therefore Imam Hambal had to say that among the *waiz* (recounters) of Hadith, such men were the most dangerous. Azad's intolerance of any kind of tampering with history is expressed in *Al Hilal* and *Al Balagh* as well, and he condemns it all the more when it is reflected in the most pious literature of Islam.

Azad establishes the authenticity of the accounts of Jeanville and his (Jeanville's) source, *La Brettan,* by verifying their facts. Then taking a *dastan-go's* (story-teller's) elaborate route reaches his point. What was the position of Muslims *vis-à-vis* the Christians then, and what is it now, he asks:

> The crusades caused medieval Europe to stand face to face with the Middle East. Europe represented the Christian thinking of the age... It led the century's religious obsession. On the other hand, the Muslims heralded the wisdom and learning of the age. While Europe wanted to fight the enemy with prayer, Muslims fought with weapons of fire and iron. Europe had reposed its faith only in God. Muslims reposed their faith *also* on God and equally on the means created by God. One believed only in spiritual power, the other on spiritual as well as material power. The first waited for the appearance of miracles, the other for the appearance of the results of their labour. Miracles never appeared but the fruits of labour appeared and declared who was the victor and who the vanquished.

This describes the respective positions of the Christians and Muslims in the thirteenth century. But a few centuries later, there was a total reversal. Once again, both parties faced each other but with what different results!

In the eighteenth century, when Napoleon attacked Egypt, Murad Bak collected the ulema of Jamia Azhar and asked them for their advice. Their unanimous view was that the recitation of *Sahih Bukhari* (one of the two most authentic collections of Hadiths) should be commenced at the Jamia, since its effectiveness at such moments was infallible. This was done but even before the completion of one round, Egypt was defeated in the battle of Ahram... Similarly when the Russians surrounded Bokhara in the first part of the nineteenth century, the Amir of the city ordered that all the *masjids* and *madrasahs* should start a recitation of *khatm khwajgaan.*[10] While the Russian canons were blowing up the bastions of the city, people were sitting and chanting in circles of recitation ... and the result was as expected in a situation where on one side was heaped canon and powder and on the other *khatm khwajgaan*. At the end he writes:

> Prayers help. But only help those who have courage and determination. For the weak, they become an excuse for inaction and inertia.

Azad's contempt for inaction is a theme that recurs in all his writings. It is primarily directed at the Muslims although when the need arises, he does not spare any other community. The letter is a dirge for the downfall of the Muslims, a sentiment which flowed in all the contemporary Urdu writing, both prose and poetry. Azad had started, by directly confronting his co-religionists with this issue in his articles of *Al Hilal* and *Al Balagh*; later, as this letter demonstrates, his technique charges but his theme remains the same.

The letter of 17 November takes off in an entirely different direction. The subject under discussion is the delicate art of drinking tea which is Azad's highly individual device for philosophizing about the aesthetics for living. It also reveals several hidden facets of his personality. What kind of an individual would write twenty pages on the subject of tea with the same seriousness as twenty pages on the decline of Islam? What was his order of priority? One wonders. Pressing national and international concerns must have been weighing on his mind especially, in his capacity as the President of the Congress. Then what caused him to apply his mind and energy to a subject which is considered trivial by many? A study of the letter reveals the importance of the subject for Azad.

The time is 4 a.m. The moment has arrived when the *finjans* of tea with which he started his mornings, have to be filled, but now they must be filled with an inferior liquid. Instead of the white jasmine tea which was imported from China, stocked in the Calcutta stores and which appeared at his table every single morning no matter where it was laid, he now had to contend with something inferior. In this indulgence of taste he finds himself alone. Jawaharlal, he says, is a tea drinker. 'Conforming to the Western elite, he drinks it without milk, but cannot get away from the plebeian habits of the "Lopchu" tea drinkers'. Of his other fellow prisoners, he regretfully says, 'Several gentlemen are addicted to milk and yogurt. And you can imagine how far is the world of milk and yogurt from the world of tea? A lifetime may be spent but that distance cannot be covered'.

He then proceeds to expand on the subject of tea? To the Chinese who have now used it for fifteen hundred years, he says, goes the credit of discovering tea. No one in China could dream of corrupting the taste of tea by using milk. The credit for this lack of taste goes to the British. And since they introduced tea to India, the malaise was introduced here as well. To them also he attributes a second corruption; when the demand for tea became global, they started experimenting with transplanting Chinese tea in Indian and Ceylonese soil. 'The soil here refused to produce tea, but produced something else of the same shape and form.' The tragedy, however, was that the commodity became affordable and everyone started indulging in it. The most painful part was that coastal Chinese were also caught in this web of universal lies and drank the potion of these leaves imagining it to be tea. Generalizing from this, Azad makes a comment which reveals the exclusiveness of his temperament:

This is usually what happens when decisions are made according to the majority opinion. In a congregation of human beings, the intelligent ones can be counted on one's fingers, while the crowd consists of fools. If they start believing in certain things, even the cow becomes God, but if they start disbelieving, even Christ is hung on the cross.

Tea should never be contaminated with milk, he writes, and be sweetened only very slightly with sugar—sugar that should be 'unblemished like alabaster and clear like ice'. His own taste, he writes, was never for sweet things. His friends used to tease him by saying that he should chew *neem* leaves, and once they made him a paste of the bitter stuff.

His description of his own tea is written in the kind of language which has led to the epithet *nasri-nazm* (poetry in prose), being applied to the style of *Ghubar-i-Khatir*. The ritualistic manner in which he prepares for the event of tea drinking is like a pagan rite:

Its fragrance is so dainty that I have no words. Its intoxication is proportionately potent. What can I say about its colour? People have used the analogy of *aatish-i-saiyyal* (white fire) but the vision of fire is still tied to this world, and the ethereality of tea demands something else. I try to capture the sun's rays in my hand and say, it is as if someone liquefied the rays of the sun and dissolved them in an alabaster *finjan*.

The story of tea is narrated with undisguised enjoyment, which affects the readers to the point that they cannot drink their next cup of ordinary tea without a mental apology to Azad. With the same engaging detail, he then describes the ritual of stirring sugar. And finally, chortling, he describes the jailor's predicament when the servant he has sent for jasmine tea to the Ahmedabad market, comes back empty handed, but leaves behind him plenty of speculation about who could have the taste and finesse to ask for White Jasmine. The next day the 'who' is identified in the gossip corners as 'Madame Chiang Kai Shek' who is 'reported' as coming to visit the prisoners of the Ahmednagar Fort prison.

The next letter starts with the theme of tea but soon digresses to the weather best suited to his temperament, that is, winter. The account of his love for winter, no matter how severely cold it might turn is expressed as an invocation to the senses. Throughout *Ghubar-i-Khatir*, he expresses his intense love for four things which relate to his four senses; tea (taste, smell, sight), music (aural), flowers (smell, sight), and winter (feeling). If these four sensations were available to him, even his prison sentence would become tolerable. Azad is rarely given to over-statement; therefore behind his words that winter is the 'real treasure' and when it ends, it is as if life has been drained of all feeling lie deep feelings, rarely exposed before the world. Similarly, his description of what is for him life's greatest luxury—a freezing cold night, a flaming fireplace next to which he is sitting (having discarded all the couches) busy reading and writing—reflects an intensely romantic temperament. Then snatching himself away from this reverie and to divert his reader's mind from this intimate view of himself, he adds:

I wonder what will be the condition of paradise? I hear a lot about its streams. It frightens me that it may have everlasting summer.

With a play on words and concepts, he adds that the sight of flames quenches the thirst of his heart. The normal expression is that the flames are quenched by water which in turn, quenches thirst. The linguistic conceit of fire quenching thirst is quite unique. Carrying this conceit further, he recalls the pleasure of swimming in Hoogly river in Calcutta, the memory of which thrills him even to this day. He then dwells on the contradiction between water and fire, both of which he says are reflections of his temperament.

Subhan Allah (Glory be to Allah)! Observe the changeability of temperament. On the one hand this desire to be one with the river, on the other, this thirst for the blazing flames. Perhaps the reason for this is that water flows on the surface of life and a fire rages at its pit.

The letter ends with a vivid description of one winter spent at Mousil in Iraq. The severe winter that gripped Ahmednagar is regarded as a gift from heaven, since it normally has a temperate climate all the year round. When people around him surmise about the causes for this intense cold wave, he says quietly to himself, 'What do they know, how effective are the prayers of the condemned and the sentenced?'

Two days later, when he was writing the first draft of a book (he does not reveal the name nor is there any other record of what he wrote during those days), the question of Egoistic Literature (his own use of the English vocabulary) arose. How can a writer get around 'himself in his own writings? He asks, what is the ego of a writer, a poet, an artist? Without delving into philosophy of *ana* (egoism) or *khudi* (I-am-ness), (parenthetic English vocabulary is his own), the common explanation offered for ego is that it is a natural upsurge of individualism; the more the artist tries to suppress it the more it rebounds. Although we are never specifically told why he has started writing on this subject, by implication, the letter reveals why. Is Azad suggesting that he is writing something which (he would have been ashamed to reveal) is essentially nothing but egoistic literature? Is he also saying that no matter how skillfully a self-portrait is drawn, where is the eye of the 'true beholder' which would appreciate the artist's skill? This sentiment is not unusual in Azad's writings. Time and again the reader encounters to his regret that for him the beholder's eye has never existed. He was not meant for his times:

> This is where all the troubles start for an author who desires to say something about himself. Given the fact that he cannot belie the reflection that he sees of himself in his 'internal' mirror, he realizes that all the external mirrors are giving him the lie. The 'I' that holds the greatest importance for him is becoming singularly insignificant in the eye of the others. He sees himself as the artist, who lifts his brush with the full realization, that no matter what artistic skill he uses, no eye but his very own would understand the beauty of his creation.

These lines provide the overwhelming reason why Azad always avoided the subject of writing his autobiography.

He then proceeds to describe the personalities which are unique in the sense that their egos are as large in the eyes of the world, as they are in their own eyes. Whether in the 'external' (world's) or the 'internal' (their own) mirror, the 'dimensions' (Azad's word) of their egos remain unchanged. Such people have to be separated from the common standard, and it must be admitted that each time they say 'I', it is infinitely more pleasing than when they say 'they' or 'you'. These lines convey the unmistakable impression of his own yearning to be counted among that category of writers, and autobiographers. He refers to them as men with naked egos (*be-parda anaiyat*), but whose spontaneity of expression holds their readers in a state of rapture.

The examples he cites are, St. Augustine, Rousseau, Strindberg, Tolstoy, Anatole France, Andre Gîde, whose autobiographies have acquired the status of immortal literature because they are spontaneous and candid. From literatures of the East he cites the examples of Imam Ghazzali, Ibn-e-Khaldun, Babar, Jahangir, and Mulla Abdul Qadir Badayuni. We may not admire or appreciate all of them, 'or see them with their own eyes', but we cannot but be attracted by the naturalness of their narrative. The outstanding example of egoistic literature, he feels, is Tolstoy's autobiography, which appears as powerful to the reader as it does to the author, meaning that in this matter the two are one. No writer could say 'I' with the confidence with which Tolstoy uttered the word. His autobiography is no less riveting than his *War and Peace* and *Anna Karenina;* in fact the two novels also resound with his 'I's. He calls Tolstoy '*ajeeb-o-gharib Rusi*' (the strange Russian), because he was able to achieve the impossible—transfer his own vision of himself to his reader.

What about Azad himself? He was an accomplished writer, speaker, and a communicator *par excellence*. But his ego would not permit him to say anything about himself unless he could speak with the confidence of Tolstoy. But did he have the same degree or kind of confidence which he found so attractive in Tolstoy?

Would he have been able to transfer his own vision of himself to his reader? His own assessment seems to be 'no, he could not'. He therefore continues to dodge all the proposals of 'autobiographies' (Fazluddin, Malihabadi) because he feels that he may never be able to achieve the heights to which Tolstoy rose and transfer his own vision of himself to his reader.

In this regard, Azad almost startles the reader when he says that naturalness, is an essential ingredient in an autobiography that survives in the true sense of the word. Otherwise the world gives it a place in its libraries, but never in its collective human mind.

> There is a certain attractiveness about 'being real' which is why the eyes of the world become naturally riveted towards it.

The question is: why did Azad, given his confidence in himself, hesitate in going all out writing or even talking about himself in the 'natural' manner of Tolstoy?

There is every reason to believe that since his childhood days, Azad was satisfied with his image in the 'collective human mind'. It was the image of a child progidy who would grow up to become a brilliant scholar, courageous freedom fighter, principled political leader and a highly respected gentleman. He was far from keen to alter that image. But was Azad afraid that if he were not to reveal what was his natural or spontaneous self, he would be relegated to 'libraries'? And here lies the paradox. Azad's private image of himself was not in any way lower than his perception of the image he held in the public mind. And yet he did not care to reveal his private image of himself to the public. Why? Was it because he considered the public not educated or qualified enough to appreciate those fine attributes that the story of the inner moorings of his life would reveal? Probably so.

But, more importantly, Azad's reasons for having a high opinion of himself were, in important respects, at variance with the reasons for which the public held him in the highest esteem. His understanding of a good life and a good man were intimately related to his faith as a follower of Islam and an interpreter of the

Koran in his own unique way. His understanding and devotion to his faith was not based on any blind acceptance. He had arrived at it not merely through observation but also through the mysterious processes of the *kashf* (inner illumination).

Common minds are said to be incapable of understanding the links that connect and prop that special breed of beings whose knowledge emanates from illuminations or inner revelations. Instead of understanding they would have misunderstood Azad. Was it not better, he must have thought, that he should continue to present to them the image of the man that they had come to like and follow. His inability or unwillingness to present a spontaneous image of himself is also evident in the entire collection of his photographs which are available. These mostly project a self-conscious rather than a candid image. Undoubtedly, there is a hidden note of regret that he could not summon the courage to show his natural self to the world. His superhuman effort to keep the appearance of outward calm when he received the news of the illness and death of his wife, Zuleikha, is part of this self-consciousness.

The letter ends with a brief lesson on the etymology of the word 'ego' and the rationale for allowing it to enter the Urdu lexicon without any phonetic change. Despite his pride in the perfect use of language, whether Urdu, Persian, Arabic, English, French, Turkish or any other, which qualifies him as a purist, there is an irrepressible desire in him to see the languages live and breathe by imbibing new vocabulary. This desire is later manifested in his policies as India's first Minister of Education.

The next set of letters are grouped under two titles, derived from Persian folklore, *Hikayat-e-Zaagh-o-Bulbul* (Story of the Crow and the Nightingale) and *Chidya Chidey ki Kahani* (Story of the Male and the female House Sparrow). The Persian classic *Manteq-ut-Tair* of Fariduddin Attar provided the title and the framework of these letters. For the inmates of the Ahmednagar Fort, the only visitors from the outside world were the birds who freely flew in and out as if flaunting the authority of the prison. It is these winged creatures around whom he weaves his story.

Similarly, the only aesthetic pleasure available to these *zindanis* (prisoners) was what they could derive from the bounty of nature, in the form of growing seasonal flowers. This provided Azad with the most fertile ground for philosophizing about beauty and the ephemerality of human existence. Whereas birds become metaphors for the human species, flowers represent the cycle of life itself.

In the letter about the crow and the nightingale, the former refers to Syed Mahmud's lavish hospitality to the *muniyas* which had built their nests in crevices of the high ceilings. Unfortunately, the plan backfired and its real beneficiaries were the entire crow population of Ahmednagar which arrived in droves to feast at Syed Mahmud's hospitable board. However, when a pair of vultures started eyeing his hospitality from afar, Syed Mahmud had to abandon the idea. The second part of the *Hikayat* is about the nightingale. To start with, however there is a major digression. It is this part which constitutes the essence of the letter.

When they arrived in Ahmednagar, the prisoners were dismayed at the bleakness of their surroundings. To liven up the place, the idea of a garden was mooted. The monsoons were in full swing which made it a fruitful exercise. Jawaharlal, Azad writes, who was always enthusiastic about such schemes, became all set for the task. The work began with different people displaying different talents, and Azad's pen capturing the humour of the situation with delectable literary flavour. For example, when the ground which had many old graves was dug up, he wondered what bones of mighty rulers and courtly beauties were mixed in the upturned soil?

Azad leaves the reader with some memorable images of the prison garden; the image of Jawaharlal armed with spade and axe, morning and evening, 'digging the mountain' like the legendary lover, Farhad, the Kohkun; the suggestion given by a scientifically oriented Bengali colleague, that the plants should be watered with animal blood. The idea of using chicken blood from the kitchen of the Officer's Mess, inspired Azad to compose a couplet, a skill he had abandoned long ago. All these incidents evoke a sense of camaraderie and fun which removes the sting from the prison sentence, and turns it into a bed of roses, not only in the metaphoric sense but in the literal sense as well! This is demonstrated in a spectacular description of the flowers that bloomed in the spring as a consequence of the toil of the prisoner-gardners:

> One flower was a bowl of rubies, another, a cup of sapphire. One flower was etched with gold and silver penmanship, and yet another was printed like a chintz cloth in myriad tints. Some flowers were sprinkled with colour in a manner that seemed as if Nature's paint-brush had become so drenched in colour that it had to be jerked clean before use and the paint-flecks that flew around, caught the mantle of the bloom.

Forty varieties of flowers are described in the order in which they appeared that season. He mentions a few, giving some of them new names. First, morning-glory (*bahar-e-subh*), then zinnia, hollyhocks (*gul khatmi*), asters, cornflowers, sweet-peas, phlox, calliopsis, cosmos, salvias, petunias, pinks and pansies. Zinnias are described as standing on guard, each one sporting a turban, tied with utmost care and meticulousness, Hollyhocks appeared as wine glasses of every colour, in fact each branch balances so many glasses that the 'poet' fears that the breeze would knock them over and the glasses would be shattered. There are numerous such descriptions, displaying a botanist's mind with a poet's skill. In the same breath there is acute awareness of the ephemerality of spring, reflecting the ephemerality of life, a theme found in all Romantic poets such as Keats, Shelley, Wordsworth, Byron, poets with whose work Azad was undoubtedly familiar.

> These flowers are called seasonal because their birth and death is restricted to the season. Once the season ends they too say farewell. As if only one garment of life has fallen to their share, which also serves as their winding sheet.

Nature's dispensation is perfectly logical in the way she arranges the life-cycle of flowers. His description of the plant *Gloria Superbia* is a perfect illustration of this point. This view of Nature is characteristic of all Azad's writings, including, most notably, of the *Tarjuman-ul-Quran*.

The *Hikayat-e-Bulbul* has to do with his finely trained ear which can pick from the cheerless noises of prison life the notes from the song of the Bulbul, and derive intense enjoyment from it. First he says that the Indian Bulbul (*Pycnonotus cafer*) is not the *Bulbul Hazar Dastan* (*Luscinia megarhynchos*) 'Bulbul of the thousand-tales', from Iran, but nevertheless, it is sweet-throated. Next, in a rare betrayal of sensuousness, he writes that in a moment of intense joy he has drained the last 'cup' at the last note of the bulbul's song. He then remarks to a companion that he has just heard a bulbul singing. The gentleman cocks an ear to catch the sound and says 'Yes a cart seems to be going past and I can hear its wheels creaking'. Azad's exasperation is evident in the remark:

> *Subhan Allah* (Glory be to Allah)! The woes of trying to discern! Here there is no difference to the ear, whether it is the song of the Bulbul or the *reen-reen* of cartwheels! What would you say in all fairness, if two such ears were locked up in the same prison? One filled with the Bulbul's song and the other with the wheel's *reen-reen*.

Is Azad making a general remark about the world being out of tune with his sensibility? He finds himself locked up with people unable to discern the song of the bulbul over the unpleasant grating noises of a passing cart. Here his tuneful ear (and all that goes with that particular capability) seems entirely out of place. Or, extending the analogy, is he in fact saying that the 'Bulbul', cannot be heard in an environment which is filled with harsh and grating noises. India has always been identified with the parrot and mynah and not with the exotic nightingale. *Tooti-e-Hind* rather than *Bulbul-e-Hind* was the title given by Hazrat Nizamuddin Aulia to his favourite disciple Amir Khusro.

Azad says that the people of Iran have been gifted by God with an ear for the nightingale's song because Iran is a region which has the pleasure of experiencing extreme winter. Here, the first sign of spring is heralded by the song of the bulbul. How can warm lands ever understand this feeling? Once again he returns to his love of winter which he had recounted earlier, and identifies Kashmir as one region in which one may catch a glimpse of the world of the Bulbul. Once again, he is out of step with the rest of the world (or the rest of the world is out of step with him). He remarks on the crudeness of the people who visit Kashmir during the season of fruit rather than of flowers.

> I cannot imagine why the world has turned into such a glutton. Although, along with the stomach, man has also been endowed with a heart and mind.

Chidya Chidey ki Kahani, narrated in two letters, has turned Azad in the eyes of many of his admirers into an ornithologist. By the same stretched measure he should also be called a horticulturalist, botanist, musician, physicist, besides being a philosopher, poet, essayist, historian, educationist, scholar, and politician. Rather than give pedagogical titles to his talent for a keen observation of life, it may suffice to say that it was the combination of wide reading on many subjects in at least five languages, a phenomenal memory, a keen eye and extraordinary skill as a writer which made him appear an expert at whatever subject he selected. Therefore though not an ornithologist, he appears in these letters to have acquired some expertise in the subject.

The high beamed ceilings of the prisoners' quarters were the ideal spot for the *goraiyyas* (*Passer domesticus*) to build their nests. The evidence of their house-building activity was the constant dropping of building material on the bed and other furniture, including the wash-basin which stood in a corner. With brilliant flashes of humour and gentle irony, Azad recounts his battle with these denizens of the air! Finally, when he realizes the futility of confrontation, he calls a truce and relations become cordial to the extent that they get bold enough to pick grains of rice from his naked palm. The bird story is written in the heroic style of an epic, with all its ingredients—adventure, war, love and a triumphant ending.

First there was war, and various weapons were devised, such as an umbrella and a bamboo meant to clean cobwebs. The enemy, however, was impervious to such humble instruments. Therefore wisdom called for a truce in which the two parties could co-exist peacefully. The next step was not just a truce but a friendly truce. The kitchen was asked to provide a daily ration of grains of rice. Thus began the arduous period of courtship during which the birds would feign indifference to the grain, and Azad would feign indifference to the birds. Mutual indifference broke down, when one robust *chida* (male bird) decided to take the plunge and devour the scattered grains. Azad had named this particular bird Qalandar; one who is possessed by love of God and indifferent to all worldly things, hence the bold and daring, is called a *qalandar*. The moment Qalandar took the initiative, others followed, until there were no holds barred. Azad writes:

> If one was to borrow the English idiom, 'the ice broke' (vis-à-vis the birds). In this world, all the 'steps' seem to be listening for the sound of that *one* single step. Until such time that its sound is heard, all the potential little steps are stuck in the ground. When that one step is taken, it seems that the entire world of steps wakes up... The cup of victory, in this world of profit and loss is not won by hesitant hands. It has always been won by the hand that has the courage to reach out for it by virtue of its own strength.

Slowly the distance between man and bird was reduced; because the latter was convinced that this form, which was always visible on the sofa, despite being human was not dangerous like the others of his species. The extent of the familiarity shown to him by the birds is reflected in the experience that sometimes, while writing, if an exclamation escaped his lips or if there was an involuntary movement of his body, suddenly there was a flutter of wings at his side. Azad explains the commotion:

> When I looked, I realized that a band of budgies was at my side busy playing around. As soon as they felt the 'stone' shudder, they flew off, startled. I would not be surprised if they said among themselves, 'A stone lies on this sofa, but sometimes it becomes human!'

The Man Within: Ghubar-i-Khatir   231

Another bird displays such characteristics that he merits the appellation Mullah. Yet another one is called Sufi, and the prettiest one who may have won the crown in a bird beauty contest is called Moti. He gives reasons why Mullah has been given this name:

> One bird is very well-fed and quarrelsome. Whenever you notice him he is chattering away with his head high and chest puffed up... Whenever there is a gathering on the carpet, he struts in, darting a look first to the right, then to the left. Then he jumps on a raised object and in his special manner starts *choon-chaan*. This is like the speech of the *waiz* (preacher) of the Jama Masjid described by the poet Qa'ani.

The bird story ends on an extraordinary note of tenderness. The occasion for it is Mori's baby, who she is trying to launch into flight. Even as Azad watches, pen in hand, Moti flies out of the nest with a tiny fledgling tailing her. Unable to sustain the flight, it falls in a small heap, eyes closed, form inert. Moti brings grains of rice and drops them into its open mouth. But no matter how much she tries there is no urge for flight in its lifeless body. For two days it appears to be half dead; the third day it drags itself towards a pencil of sunlight which has appeared in the room. Suddenly, it shudders once or twice, thrusts its neck forward, gathers the fallen wings, spreads them out, and soars into the skies. What was it that gave the baby bird the strength to take the ultimate leap upward, Azad asks? It is the same principle, he answers, which works in human beings as well:

> What did this 'new inmate of the prison of life' lack for the commencement of his flight? Nature had sent him equipped, the mother was coaxing him to take wing. But until and unless the reality revealed itself to him, that he was a bird meant to soar in the skies, all the accoutrements of flight were useless. Similarly, so long as self-awareness remains asleep in a human being, no external commotion can awaken him. But once his inner self wakes up and he recognizes his own hidden *haqeeqat* (reality), then, in the flash of an eye, the

entire transformation takes place. In one leap, he springs from his lowly bed of dirt, and reaches the loftiness of the heavens.

The intervening period between letter 16 and 17 was a time of great anxiety because of the news that he received about the serious condition of his wife. Azad, as said earlier, could never bring himself to reveal his intimate feelings. It was much more characteristic of him to leave them unspoken. The fact, however, remains that he did reveal (albeit a small fraction of), his anguish to his friend, in the letter dated 11 April 1943, two days after her death.

From this letter we learn that this was the sixth consecutive night that sleep eluded him, so he began writing well before his usual hour of 4 a.m. Here we need to take account of the fact that Azad liked to record exact times, days etc. Therefore, the figure of six nights is precise. The mental stress is extreme. But the letter, except for a chink here and there which reveals emotion, is written with extraordinary self-restraint. We get a glimpse into his relationship with his wife, which was one of wordless understanding and support on her part, a relentless demand of being married to a man like Azad. On his part, there is an implied regret at the strictness which he had imposed on the marriage. He writes about their last parting eight months ago:

How well she understood me. She knew that if she betrayed her emotional distress at a moment like this it would intensely displease me and its bitterness would linger for a long time. In 1916, when I was arrested for the first time, she had not been able to contain her anguish. For this reason I had remained displeased with her for several days. This incident had changed her way of life forever and she always tried to gracefully compromise with the conditions of my life.

His quality of restraint had influenced her to the extent that she did not communicate to him the details of her failing health, although she continued to write regularly. He heard about her condition from the newspapers. But being a prisoner of his self-imposed restrictions, Azad could not make the slightest deviation from the daily routine of prison life. Although his internal equilibrium had disappeared the day he received the first intimation that she was dying his routine was unchanged:

> As soon as I received the first news of her critical condition, I began to probe my heart. How strange is human nature! We spend our lives trying to comprehend it yet the mystery continues unabated. My circumstances had been such that from the beginning I had many opportunities to use self-restraint and self-control, and so far as possible, I utilized every such opportunity. Yet I felt that my equilibrium had been shattered and I had to struggle to restore it. This struggle exhausts not the mind but the body, and it begins disintegrating from within.
>
> I do not want to conceal die state of my heart and mind during those days. I tried to endure my pain with patience and forbearance. Superficially, I succeeded but internally I felt shattered. I realized that my mind had begun to play the usual games of duplicity and affectation that we find ourselves resorting to when we want to prevent our inner feelings from showing through.

Regardless of the news of the grave illness of his wife and the anguish that overtook him, he still continued to leave his room four times a day for his meals, punctual to the minute, and 'forced a few morsels down his throat'. His colleagues realized that he did not wish to discuss his personal grief so they continued to respect and follow his routine. Jawaharlal tried to persuade him to accept the jailor's offer to appeal to the government for special dispensation, but he refused saying that he wanted no favours from the British. His studied indifference to the jailor's footsteps as he walked to his room through the long verandah carrying the newspaper which had begun to publish daily bulletins about Begum Zuleikha's health, speaks volumes about the man. His own comment on this attitude shows stark honesty:

> I confess, all these affectations were part of a role played by a proud temperament; the reason being to keep its dignity and forbearance free from the tarnish of anguish and despair.

The final note of dirge is a total of a dozen words:

'At last, on April ninth the goblet of my pain brimmed over'.

Then in the manner of classical tragedy, which he knew well, there is a comment that establishes the universality of grief and the resumption of life which must continue to be lived regardless:

Thus ended twenty-six years of our married life. The wall of death stood between us; we could still see one another but through the barrier of the wall. During those first few days I had to traverse the path that usually takes years. My will was still steadfast but my feet lost their sensation. There is an old tomb inside the enclosure. I don't know whose it is but since coming here I must have looked at it hundreds of times. Now whenever I look at it I feel a new affinity. Last evening I looked at it for a long time and recalled the *marsia* (dirge) written by Mutammim bin Nurida at the death of his brother Malik.

After his wife's death there is a noticeable change in the tone of his letters. Later on when he reflected on the change, he wrote to *Sidiq-e-Mukarram* that at that time his interest in letter-writing just waned. One month after the letter about his wife, two short letters were written on two consecutive days, 14 and 15 June. The first one was about the basic principle of nature: the cycle of life, death and regeneration. This principle is manifested in all creative processes; unless the flowers of one season wilt, the next season does not see its blooms. As if the garden of the world is so limited, he writes, that it has space just for one season at a time.

Whatever treasure she had to squander, Nature squandered away. Now it's arrangement will only have to be changed around. Things from one area will be displayed in another area.

What is *banawat* (order) and what is *bigar* (disorder) he asks? In this world, he says, every order is the result of some disorder, and every disorder is a new kind of order. Examples abound. We are delighted at the sight of the gardener's basket full of flowers, but we do not stop to think of the flower bed that must have been devastated. We enjoy the luxuries but do not pause for a moment to ponder over the sweat of the labourer whose labour has provided us with the luxuries. Only the eye of a poet and artist can discern the tragedy inherent in creating the order. Concurrent with the cycle of life, death, and regeneration, is the principle that a thing is nurtured only so long as it retains its usefulness. Once it outlives its utility, it is mercilessly destroyed.

The next brief letter of 15 June is about the shortness of life. It becomes increasingly evident that he would not allow his intense grief at his wife's death to reveal itself. It was successfully hidden from the eyes of the world in the rigorous self discipline of maintaining the daily routine of prison life. He wrote neither elegy nor dirge. What he says simply in this letter is that life is as short as the stretch from morning to evening.

> The entire period of human life is no more than from one morning to one evening. Eyes open in the morning, the day is spent in hope and desire, and when the night falls, the eyes close again.

The abruptness with which this letter ends is quite uncharacteristic of the writer. There is much more he could have written on the subject, especially since he begins with a reference to the Arab philosopher, Abu'Ala Mu'arri, and it would have been quite natural for him to have proceeded to describe at length Mu'arri's concept of Time. But it seems that there was not much philosophy that he wanted to discuss, and what he felt, he could not bring himself to express. Silence was the sole option.

The last letter of *Ghubar-i-Khatir* was written three months later and ran into twenty-six foolscap pages. It is the longest and the most unusual letter of the series. The letter is entirely about aesthetics, especially music; what it means to him personally, what it meant to people in the course of history, and how India's composite culture is reflected in her music. Important details about his own life are scattered throughout the letter, which biographers have picked up and tried to piece together. Most of what he reveals about himself here, has been expressed before in

Tazkirah, but in a highly suggestive and evocative language. The expression in *Ghubar-i-Khatir* is more spontaneous.

We learn that as a child he was fascinated with balloons filled with helium gas. What intrigued him more was the *betaabi* (restlessness) of the gas to escape, which became apparent when he pricked the balloon with a needle. The title of this epistolary collection, *Ghubar-i-Khatir*, was probably inspired by this single childhood memory. He then says that his present state of mind is similar; as if now he is filled with some potent substance which eagerly waits for the prick of the needle. One night it seemed as if the vapour (*ghubar*) of the self (*khatir*) would condense and start flowing (in tears) but that did not happen. The cause was the sound of Mendelssohn's 'Song Without an End' being played on the violin (a jail officer was listening to the BBC). The words he uses to describe his feelings are, 'As if a carbuncle was about to burst.' The choice of words to describe his feelings is unusual and has not been used in any of his other writings.

The music raises a strong wave of memories from a time when, as a youth, he had started learning music. The story of what got him started on music reveals several facets of Azad's temperament—especially his desire to attain perfection in whatever he undertook. At the age of sixteen, he was one day browsing through *Rag Darpan*, a Persian translation of a Sanskrit treatise on music by Saif Khan, an amir of the court of Aurangzeb. The Principal of *Madrasa-e-Aliya*, Denison Ross, challenged Azad to explain the meaning of a certain page. Much to Azad's embarrassment, although he could understand the words, he could not make out the meaning. Since childhood, he writes, he had understood everything he read with the greatest of ease, but this' particular field demanded help and guidance from an expert practitioner. So he decided to get that kind of help no matter what it entailed. For a *murshidzada* (son of the respected 'teacher'), it was nearly impossible to find anyone willing to give him lessons in music.

Among his father's disciples, however, there was a man Maseeta Khan, a musician of the Jaipur Gharana (Jaipur school of music), who used to teach music to the prostitutes of Calcutta. Azad's description of Maseeta Khan, reflects his sympathetic understanding of this humble *murid*. The man's only purpose in life seemed to be to attend at the daily discourses and supplicate Azad's father, Maulana Khairuddin, until he agreed to bestow upon him the favour of making him his disciple. Although Azad does not say in so many words, it appears that he secretly hoped that his father would allow Maseeta to enter his circle, regardless of the fact that his life had been spent in pursuits considered undesireable, including that of earning his livelihood from educating the 'nautch girls' of Calcutta.

Azad learnt music according to his own private method; Maseeta could not impose upon him his traditional mode of teaching music. His revulsion to traditional practices for the one and only reason which were adhered to that they had had been in existence for long, extended to music as well. At the age of seventeen, he devised his own method of learning the sitar, and spent every afternoon in music practice. The key word was perfection; nothing merited doing unless there was a will to achieve the pinnacle of perfection. This was the case with music as with all other pursuits:

> I was no older than seventeen. But even at that time my temperament was such that whatever field of endeavour I undertook, it had to be done fully and taken to the farthest limit. No matter what the task, it was never possible to leave it half-done. The last pebble of the *kucha* (way) had to be turned over and examined in detail. Neither acts of piety nor of sin were left unfinished. I always remained at the forefront of life, whether as a *rind* (sinner) or a *parsa* (saint). The only *shart* (condition) was that one should never appear defective or incomplete in anything. If contact was to be kept with anyone it should be only with those who have achieved perfection.

The rationalization offered for the discontinuation of music offers another interesting insight. Music, he writes, is essential for developing the aesthetic sense as well as for creating a sense of balance. Once he had learnt what was to be learnt from it, further indulgence would not only have been useless but also a hindrance. In this case he likens his passing interest to that of a honey-bee:

Tuk dekh liya, dil shad kiya, khush kam huey, aur chal nikley
(Had an eyeful, was filled with joy, tasted and drifted away.)

Therefore it was logical to move on, leaving music behind as a means to an end. But this momentary indulgence created in his heart a lifelong love for music. So much so that depriving him of music was tantamount to depriving him of every enjoyment that life had to offer.

This avowal of his undying love for music is followed by recalling an experience which probably represents the best example of poetic prose in the Urdu language. During a visit to Agra he had arranged to take his sitar to the Taj Mahal on a moonlit night to see what the combination of the two would produce. A translation of the entire passage (however difficult it is to catch the flavour of the original), would still give the reader a slight of the language flavour:

As the moonlight bathed the monument, I would start a *raag* on my sitar and become fully engrossed in its melody. How can I express what fantastic sights and sounds used to dance before my eyes? Dead of night, shimmering stars, waning moon, dampness of April, and the minarets of the Taj raising their heads. All around me the arches sat holding their breath, and, in the centre, the marble dome sat motionless on its base. The silver waves of the Jumna gently lapped around its base, and, above, innumerable stars looked on with wide-eyed amazement. In this chiaroscuro, a wordless lament emerged from the strings of my sitar and wafted effortlessly on the waves of the air. Stars started shooting from the sky and from my bleeding fingers a melody was born.

For sometime, the whole environment remained motionless as if it were listening with rapt attention. Then slowly, very slowly, the entire, audience, sprang into motion. The moon started her celestial journey until it reached right over my head. The stars gazed with dazed eyes and the branches of trees swung in ecstacy. Behind the black curtain of the night, the elements could be heard whispering to one another. Often the arches of the Taj moved their shoulders. You may not believe it but often I have talked with the arches and whenever I looked up at the silent dome of the Taj, I found its lips moving.

This is offered as background to an enormously well-informed essay about music. If one were to read it as a separate piece, it would be impossible to think of the writer as anything but a poet. It is an essay on history and aesthetics. Azad was born with the sound of music in his ear. His first music was the sound of the *tarheem* which precedes the *azan*, which was heard day after day at the house he was born, in Qidwa, near Bab-es-Salam, Mecca. 'The lamps in the minarets were clearly visible from the terrace windows and the Sehr sounded as if someone was calling it (the *azan*) from our roof.' This also resulted in his developing a life-long interest in Arab music, which was further explored during trips to Egypt and Iraq.

The erudite discussion revolves around the interchanging musical influences between Arabia and Iran and the fact that the original source of this music was ancient Greece and its arrangement of the 'twelve *raaginis*'. This was attributed to the twelve *burj* (terraces) of the heavens. Despite the changes, he says, the *oud* (a musical instrument) still produces the same music which was heard at the music halls of Haroun-al-Rashid. Azad writes that he sought the company of masters with whom he could discuss the intricacies of the art. He has no hesitation in admitting that this love of music made him seek the company of women whose music was a match for their beauty. The name of Umm Kulsum, who was the most renowned singer of Lebanon in the 1940s, is mentioned as the watershed of Arab music.

Indian music he claims has much greater depth than any other music. As for Western music, although our ears are not tuned to it, we cannot help acknowledging its greatness. European music of the eighteenth and nineteenth centuries, especially German music, is an extraordinary example of the human genius. It is surprising that the Arabs showed interest in all the arts and sciences of India, except music. Although Al-Beruni did not pay any attention to Indian music, that was the time, Azad says, when Indian musical instruments were heard being played on the streets of Ghazni.

The composite music which evolved as a result of Muslim contact with the native Hindu inhabitants is then described with reference to the occupation of North India and parts of Deccan by the Muslim rulers. The point of this discussion is that the Indian arts did not remain foreign to the newcomers; they became a part of their own culture. In the seventh century AH (fourteenth century AD) the genius of composite music created by the fusion of the two cultures is reflected in the work of Amir Khusro. With him Indian music finally became the music of Indian Muslims and Persian music began to be regarded by them as foreign. Amir Khusro's creation of *raags* like *aiman, saazgiri*, and *khayal* has immortalized him, as also has his work on *quol, tarana, sohla*, all of which are great musical inventions.

Azad writes about how music was patronized by the Muslim divines as well as by the rulers. The Khanqahs at Multan, Ajodhan, Gaur and Delhi attracted the most accomplished musicians. Muslim rulers throughout the length and breadth of the country became renowned for their love for this art. In the courts of the Khilji and Tughlaq sultans music reigned supreme. At the same time, Deccan and Malwa became the centres for music, hence the ruler of Deccan, Ibrahim Adil Shah was regarded by the poet Zuhuri as the 'Jagat Guru'. The sultans of Gaur became patrons of local language and local music and, in Malwa, Sultan Baaz Bahadur became a poet and musician for the love of Rani Roopmati.

Abul Fazal's account reveals the names of the artists who assembled at Emperor Akbar's court. His son Jahangir's book *Tuzuk-i-Jahangiri* reflects his interest in music, poetry and painting. The important change that occurred during this period, Azad writes, was that the theory and practice of music entered the realm of knowledge, that is, no education could be considered complete without the study of music. The demand for teachers grew, and singers of Delhi, Agra, Ahmedabad and Lahore were employed at enormous salaries by members of the elite class for rounding off the education of their children. During those times, visitors from Iran and Turan, immediately on arrival, realized the importance of learning Indian music. One example is that of the historian, Ferishta whose book on Indian music, Azad says, is part of his library collection.

Even some of the *alims* became extremely knowledgeable about music. For example, when Akbar made Mullah Mubarak, the great connoisseur of music, listen to Tansen his only comment was, 'Yes! He does sing a little!' An orthodox and prejudiced individual like Mullah Qadir Badayuni was an expert on the flute. Abdus Salam Lahori, whose fame had spread to Samarqand and Bukhara and who was selected by Shahjehan to tutor the young princes, was as well-versed in music as he was in texts like the *Hidaya* and *Buzduvi.* During the last days of the Mughal rule, great Sufi masters like Mirza Mazhar Jaan-e-Janan and Khwaja Mir Dard were presented with compositions of expert musicians for correction and the slightest movement of their heads was considered the greatest testimonial that a piece of music could achieve.

In the Mughal court, the patronage that was extended to musicians by military men like Abdul Rahim Khan-e-Khana rivalled the favours that had been given by Emperors Akbar and Shahjehan. In contemporary accounts the names of musicians are mentioned along with those of the ulemas and poets who were connected with the General. This included Indians and Iranis, Hindus and Muslims. Prince Khurram (Shahjehan) had a Rajput mother, Manmati, the daughter of Raja Uday Singh. When she came to Jahangir's palace as a bride, the emperor, being an expert and connoisseur first examined her musical skills in which he found her highly proficient. Her son became so well-versed in music that Tansen's successor Lal Khan used to touch his ears at the mention of his name, and contemporary historians recorded his mastery of the Dhrupad *raag.*

Nasir Jung Shaheed, the son of Nizam-ul-Mulk Asif Shah, learnt Sanskrit to be able to read the ancient music texts, and is mentioned in *Shahadat Nama* as an expert in music and conversant in Persian. When the Sufi saint Shaikh Saleem Chishti's grandson, Aslam Khan was appointed the Subedar (provincial chief) of Bengal by Jahangir, he spent 80,000 rupees a month on the patronage of music and dancing. While his table was laden with the choicest food for his artists, he ate nothing more than millet *roti* and spinach with boiled rice.

During the days of Aurangzeb, Azad writes, music was severely curtailed in the court but he could not reverse the tide among his subjects:

> Whatever happened was restricted to the Durbar. The waters that had started flowing, as a consequence of previous efforts of irrigation, were not such meagre trickles that they would dry up as soon as the royal favours were withdrawn. Undoubtedly, during the Alamgiri reign the royal *karkhanas* (manufacturing plants) were shut down, but who could have turned off the *karkhanas* in the hundreds of thousands of private households?

An incident from Aurangzeb's life is then recounted from the contemporary source *Ma'asir al Umra*. One day, while walking in Ahukhana, the name of a garden in Burhanpur, Aurangzeb fell madly in love with Zainabadi, a maid employed in the household of his aunt. Azad's comment on this incident, reflects the romance of his own *mizaj* (temperament):

> The story of Aurangzeb's love affair is very interesting. It shows that although his boundless ambition turned him into iron and stone, at one time he was a man of flesh and blood. Having acquired Zainabadi from his aunt, Aurangzeb's love for the maid drove him to the extreme of offering her cups of wine for the pleasure of seeing her beauty enhanced by her intoxication. One day Zainabadi offered the cup to the prince, and persisted despite his pleas not to test his love on this basis. Just as he was about to succumb, she dashed the cup to the ground. Zainabadi was unparalleled in her singing skills.

Aurangzeb himself was not untutored in musical skills but the asceticism which became his distinguishing characteristic alienated him from the arts. When the singers took out the *janaza* (funeral) procession of music, the Emperor ordered them to bury it in such a manner that it never rises from its grave. But it did. This austerity ended with Aurangzeb and the mood of the Empire returned to normal. Azad asserts that the excessive indulgences of Mughal rulers like Farrukh Sair and Mohammad Shah Rangeela were a natural backlash of the astringency of Aurangzeb.

Music was regarded in the ancient Indian tradition as a powerful instrument for taming animals. The Mughal emperors' royal hunts were heralded by bands of musicians who sang and danced in the wilderness to attract the game. Al Beruni in his *Kitab-ul-Hind* writes about the island of Serendip which abounds in monkeys. If a traveller gets caught in their midst, he is advised to recite the *chhaands* (verses composed in a certain form which have a prescribed way of recitation almost like singing) from the epic *Ramayan*, which are in praise of the monkey-god Hanuman. The power of music, Azad writes, is all pervasive.

Balancing his praise for music, Azad recalls that unless it is judiciously used, the very thing which is the cause of *fazal-o-kamaal* (well-being and excellence) becomes the cause of a hundred wrongs. Mohammad Shah Rangeela was the descendant of the great Emperor Akbar. But his excesses were such that unless the women of the palace pushed him out from the *Zenankhana* (women's quarters) he would not enter his *Deewankhana* (Audience Hall). Similarly, Wajid All Shah was a descendant of the Nawab Safdarjung of Oudh, the great administrator who summoned his musicians only when he became tired of working for the state. But Nawab Wajid Ali Shah was known to permit an audience to his Vizier, Ali Naqi, Azad writes, only to refresh himself when he became tired of playing the *tabla*.

The above are a few highlights of Azad's essay on music. The question one asks oneself is what was Azad's purpose in recording these incidents. Was it to dispel the prevailing notion that Muslim rulers had no use for music and certainly not the music that they encountered upon their arrival on Indian soil? Secondly, was it to correct the impression that music, implying an indulgence of the senses, was anti-Islamic? It seems likely that both these considerations were on his mind while writing this particular letter.

At the end he makes an important statement. He says that the reason that the ulema became unyielding about music was due to their considering it a drain on the limitations of *sadd-o-saiyal* (resources). Their severe strictures were imposed by using the instrument of *qaza* (law) rather than *shara* (practice). The scope of *qaza*, says Azad, is broad. Should anything become a source of *fasad* (unrest, evil) by usage, it may be stopped by *qaza*, but this has no impact on the injunction of the *shariat*. To prove the argument Azad quotes a line from *Sura al Araf* of the Koran, 'Say, God's graces which he has created for his creatures, and the delectables for eating and drinking, who has forbidden them?' Although he says that he does not want to engage in this argument here, but the point is transparent. Music is one of God's graces; it cannot be forbidden to man because it has been created for man.

This essay on music reveals an important dimension of Azad's personality which runs counter to some of his earlier protestations about his abhorrence for *taqlid*. First, with disarming frankness he expresses his love for music. Having done that he sets about exploring spiritual and temporal sanctions for music, such as, it was part of the Sufi tradition, it was patronized by the ruling elite, even the ulemas and the *fuquhas* could not stay away from it. Therefore he was following the best of tradition, right from the time when as a child the sound of the *tarheem* preceding the *azan* touched his ears. The dichotomy is between his self-avowed abhorrence for *taqlid* and the urge to carve his own individualistic path even if that meant a lonely trail, and his invoking worthy precedents to justify his love for music. He has always taken pride in recalling that his path was separate from the public thoroughfare and that he never drank from the fountain to which others came to slake their thirst. But this letter consisting of '26 foolscap sheets' is a 'justification' of his love for music, given that it has the sanction of some of the most respected individuals in Islamic history. This contradiction is an important aspect of his highly complex personality.

Ghubar-i-Khatir has not received the attention it deserves from scholars of Azad, literary critics, or historians. The analysis which has been offered in this chapter breaks the ground for further exploration. In terms of its placement in time, it is wedged between two crucial periods in Azad's life. Pre-partition and post-partition. He was never to write anything substantial again. This in effect is his final written word.

notes

1 *Ghubar-i-Khatir* 1946 edition, third printing.

2 What manuscripts was Azad engaged in writing during the Ahmednagar days will forever remain a mystery. It was alleged by several close associates like Ajmal Khan and Syed Abdul Latif that a trunk of manuscripts was shipped out of Ahmednagar. The author tried to locate it during her visit to Azad's nephew Nuruddin Ahmed in Calcutta but could not discover any clue to the whereabouts of Azad's prison writings.

3 *Karvan-i-Khayal* is a collection of letters from Azad to Sherwani and vice-versa. It is edited by Mohammad Abdul Shahid Khan Sherwani.

4 There are no two views about Azad's taste for good spirits. Several of his contemporaries like J.B. Kriplani and John Mathias have referred to it. It seems unlikely that he would have wanted to perpetuate a lie that he was a teetotaller.

5 'The pleasures of tea and prison life', a chapter in *India's Maulana*, Vol. 2. Selected Speeches and Writings, ed. Hameed, is a collection of Azad's thoughts on this subject as expressed in *Ghubar-i-khatir*.

6 *Ghubar-i-Khatir*, p. 52. Chand Bibi was the sister of Burhan Nizam Shah of Deccan.

7 Ibid.

8 *Ghubar-i-Khatir*, p. 112.

9 Ibid.

10 A *dhikr* formula recommended for its efficacy in invoking divine help.

11

president and negotiator

THE MOST CHALLENGING TASK FOR ANY biographer of Azad's life is to reconstruct his years as Congress President from the recollections found in *India Wins Freedom*. The question that arises is: what to do about this so called autobiography of Azad? There are many reasons for doubting its authenticity. For example, the language of the narrative is so uninspired and so unlike anything that Azad ever wrote that no matter which way one interprets it, it refuses to yeild to any enquiry other than a one-dimensional account of the history of his term as Congress President. The book (its title was suggested by Jawaharlal Nehru *post facto*) was to be released on Azad's seventieth birthday, 11 November 1958. It was, however, preponed and posthumously published, hurriedly it may be safely presumed, in March 1958.

In his Preface, Humayun Kabir, who wrote the book from Azad's dictation, writes that in 1957, when Maulana had read the complete draft, he decided to hold back thirty pages and to place a thirty-year moratorium on them. There is no written evidence of Azad's thirty-year ban on the thirty pages. Memos in Urdu handwritten by him as Minister of Education, which are preserved in the National Archives, New Delhi, would have been a likely place for the location of such a document. But all we have is Kabir's word, and no serious contradiction of it. It is surprising that a man who spoke fearlessly on the most sensitive issues right from the age of fifteen, should have become so diffident about expressing his views about his colleagues that he would want those parts withheld. Moreover, the thirty pages contain nothing sensational or controversial. A copy each of the complete text was deposited at the National Archives, New Delhi and the National Library, Calcutta. A third copy must have remained in Kabir's possession which he handed to Asia Publishing House.

According to Kabir, Azad was unable to find time to work on the book. This was a fairly typical trait, judging from the experience of Fazluddin Ahmed and of Abdul Razzaq Malihabadi, both of whom had to draw blood from stone to make Azad write about himself.[1] The plan of *India Wins Freedom* was as follows: Volume One was to be about his personal life, from birth to 1937, Volume Two was conceived to be what *India Wins Freedom* is in its present form, and Volume Three was to contain the events following the partition. There are frequent references in the book to certain events being explained in 'another volume'.

The difficulty of translating Azad's fluent and flawless Urdu into English is expressed by Kabir in his Preface.

> The difference in the genius of Urdu and English makes the task of interpreting Maulana Azad's thoughts still more difficult. Urdu, like all other Indian languages is rich, colourful and vigorous. English, on the other hand, is essentially the language of understatement and when the speaker is a master of Urdu like Maulana Azad, the plight of the writer who seeks to express his thoughts in English can easily be imagined.

What Kabir does not mention is his own unfamiliarity with Urdu which was compounded by the fact that his narrator was the undisputed master of not only Urdu but also of Persian and Arabic, and one who freely used words from these languages even in his everyday speech. Neither does he draw the reader's attention to Azad's preference not to publish anything in English in his name unless it was essential for official business. Two important examples of the exceptions he made are his Introduction to *A History of Philosophy: Eastern and Western* by Dr S. Radhakrishnan and the addresses he delivered as Minister of Education. Unfortunately their original Urdu versions were not preserved. It is important to note here that some of these even in their translation retain the flavour of Azad's language, leading to the possible conclusion that they were done by Urdu scholars like Saiyidain or Ashfaq Husain.[2]

It is, therefore, difficult to accept that Azad, who was so particular about vocabulary and expression, so hesitant to write about himself, so reluctant to allow anyone access to anything personal, gave unconditional approval to Kabir to publish his autobiography. Why was the same compliance not shown to Fazluddin or Malihabadi, both of whom, unlike Kabir, were his lifelong friends? This remains somewhat a mystery which may partially be answered by the timing of the event, i.e. the draft being presented to him at the stage of his life when his health was declining[3] and he was not in a position to make substantive changes. In any case, as said earlier, there is no written record of his permission to Kabir. However one looks at it, there is little doubt that had he lived he would never have permitted Kabir's draft to go to press as his autobiography. Had he read it he would have been appalled at its utter incapacity to reflect any one of the distinguishing features of his style.

The reader's difficulty is compounded when he views *India Wins Freedom* as an autobiography along with *Tazkirah* and *Ghubar-i-Khatir*. When a certain thought is expressed in Kabir's language it has no resemblance to an identical thought expressed by Azad in Urdu. A few examples of the two styles may illustrate the point. This is Azad's account of his birth in *India Wins Freedom*:

I was born in Mecca in 1888. In 1890, my father came to Calcutta with the entire family.

Aside from the fact that the above date of arrival to India has been invalidated by several accounts,[4] the staccato in the above is in stark contrast with his lyrical account of the same event in *Tazkirah*:

I, who am a homeless wanderer, a stranger to my times and myself, nourished on wounded sentiments, imbued with the fullness of longing, a wreck of unfulfilled desires, named Ahmed, and called Abul Kalam, was born in 1888 (1305 AH) coming into a world whose existence is a presumption, from a nonexistence that has the semblance of reality, and became exposed to the allegation of being alive.[5]

In the expression of similar sentiments, *India Wins Freedom* is as different from *Ghubar-i-Khatir* and *Tazkirah* as if it were an outflow of an entirely different impulse. Expressed in Kabir's language, the ideas are barely recognizable as Azad's. Companion passages about the death of his wife further substantiate the point. In *India Wins Freedom*, he writes,

I was now returning after three years but she was in her grave and my home was empty. I remembered the lines of Wordsworth:
But she is in her grave, and Oh!
The difference to me. I told my companions to turn the car, for I wished to visit her grave before I went home. My car was full of garlands; I took one and placed it on her grave and silently read the Fatiha.

In *Ghubar-i-Khatir* the same sentiment is expressed but the language even in translation has the stamp that qualifies him as a master in the art:

Thus ended twenty-six years of our married life. Death stood like a wall between us. We could still see each other but from either side of this wall. During these few days, I have had to walk the path that usually takes years to cross. My forbearance is still there but the strain of the journey has drained all sensation from my feet.

Ghafil niyam ze-raah wale aah chaara neesl
Zeen rehzanan ke bar dil-e-agaah me zanand.

(I am not unaware of the path but there is no other way
Knowingly I have allowed the thieves to pillage my heart)

Although *India Wins Freedom* narrates the events of a critical
period of Azad's life, the question is how much of it is autobiography and how much Kabir's recounting of the facts? Statements
occur which contradict Azad's own views. One sentence in the
very first paragraph is unlike anything Azad ever wrote about
his ancestors.

After him (Jamaluddin), the family became more inclined to worldly
affairs and several members occupied important positions.

Neither in *Tazkirah* nor in *Ghubar-i-Khatir*, both works of
his own hand, is there any indication that his ancestors became
'inclined to worldly affairs'. Infact he takes great pride in the fact
that his ancestors always rejected worldly riches.[6] This may be
a case of Kabir misinterpreting the dictation, which is possible
given his unfamiliarity with Azad's idiom. What is incredible is
that Kabir asserts in the preface that, 'He (Azad) was satisfied
with the manuscript and it could be sent to the printers'.

As stated above, Azad's interaction with Kabir on the publication of *India Wins Freedom* is entirely inconsistent with his
treatment of most of his other publishers and amanuenses. Kabir
claims that Azad had thoroughly examined the manuscript. After
the first draft was completed, Kabir says, he read it first by himself and then with Kabir. He then read the book for the third time
and decided to withhold thirty pages. He read it a fourth time
when Kabir was in Australia in November 1957. Upon Kabir's
return he read it chapter by chapter, indeed sentence by sentence
with Kabir. He gave his final approval on 26 January 1958, about
one month before his death on 22 February 1958. The time and
care Azad seems to have lavished upon this work, if one was to
believe Kabir, is unmatched by the time and care which went into
any other work except perhaps *Tarjuman-ul-Quran*.

The fact is that Azad rarely needed to revise his writing. This
is evident in his draft of the first edition of *Tarjuman-ul-Quran*,

preserved in the archival collection of the Indian Council For Cultural Relations Library. His Urdu translation of the Word of Allah, along with its *tafsir* (commentary), the most momentous task 'a Muslim can ever dare to undertake, written in his fine handwriting is as good as the printed word. What creates doubt about *India Wins Freedom* as being Azad's work is not only that Kabir's prose was an inadequate vehicle for his literary style or the intricacy of his mind, but the errors and the virtual absence of style. Kabir's insistence that Azad's approval of the work was blanket and unconditional confirms the hypothesis. Azad never gave such hearty approvals.

Another unusual fact is Kabir's revelation that Azad wanted the book to appear on his seventieth birthday. In no more than two places in his entire corpus does Azad ever refer to his birthday. Birthdays were not his favourite subject and we never read any account of a birthday celebration. The anxiousness to mark a birthday by the release of his autobiography, therefore, appears odd.

The account of his early life is contained in a total of fourteen pages, which Kabir writes is a synopsis of volume one in which Azad intended to cover the first part of his life. Kabir further states that he had Azad's permission to use the synopsis as an introductory chapter. None of the events described in these fourteen pages have the poignancy of the same events when they are inscribed in Azad's own hand. The part about Begum Zuleikha's death has been described above. The great spiritual conflict which accompanied his struggle against the *taqlid* (imitation) of his ancestors, described in such powerful language of revealing and concealing feelings in *Ghubar-i-Khatir*, is mentioned briefly here in the same breath as the other events of his early life. This passage, for example, is the only expression in *India Wins Freedom* of his discontent with the fissures within Islam and of his anguish when he broke the bonds of *taqlid*:

Neither could I reconcile myself with the dogmatic assurance with which each sect branded the others as mistaken and heretical. If religion expresses a universal truth, why should there be such differences and conflicts among men professing different religions? Why should each religion claim to be the sole representative of truth and condemn all others as false? For two or three years this unrest continued and I longed to find a solution of my doubts. I passed from one phase to another and a stage came when all the old bonds imposed on my mind by family and upbringing were completely shattered.

The descriptions of this traumatic experience in *Tazkirah*, *Ghubar-i-Khatir*, and even *Kahani*, which are detailed in previous chapters,[6] are such that stun the reader into silent deference for the young man who is on the verge of heresy. In the above quoted passage, it is a bloodless narration.

To conclude the trajectory of Azad's leadership, however, the events recorded in *India Wins Freedom* have to be taken into account. *Ghubar-i-Khatir* ends with his release from Ahmednagar Fort. In *India Wins Freedom* Azad writes that his health was seriously affected during this prison term. When he was released on 15 June 1945 he had lost forty pounds. Just prior to his release he learnt that Wavell, who was now Viceroy, had gone to London to discuss the future of India with the Secretary of State for India. He had also heard that on his return Wavell had announced that a conference would be called in Simla to which leaders of the Congress, the Muslim League and other political parties would be invited. Its purpose would be to discuss the future of the Indian dominion.

The day after his release from prison, Azad writes that he received an invitation to the Simla Round Table. He convened a Working Committee meeting on 21 June at which he was authorized to represent the Congress at Simla. Azad writes that he had found Wavell very 'reasonable, sincere and frank'. His approach was different from that of Cripps who had 'highlighted the strong points and tried to slur over the difficulties'. Interestingly, he had found Wavell playing the politician, when he had approached him earlier in his capacity as Commander-in-Chief, and now that he was the Viceroy, he spoke more as a soldier than as a politician!

The gist of Wavell's proposals was that no far reaching constitutional changes could be carried out for the duration of the War but the Viceroy's Executive Council would be completely Indian and he would endeavour to set up a convention that the Viceroy would always act upon the advice of the Council. Azad writes that he felt this proposal was substantially the same as Cripps' but the difference was that now the atmosphere had changed. Cripps made his proposal at a time when the British were in dire need of Indian cooperation. Now the war was over and the Allies had triumphed over Hitler. Azad, therefore, recommended acceptance, for which he was able to secure the consent of his colleagues contingent upon a few clarifications to be sought from Government.

There was perceptible tension when the leaders of various political parties arrived on the lawns of Viceregal Lodge on the morning of 25 July 1945. Wavell records that when Azad stretched out his hand, Jinnah refused to shake it.[7] The question before the delegates was: how should the Executive Council be formed? Jinnah declared that since Muslim League was the only party which represented the Muslims, all Muslim members of the Executive Council had to be nominees of the League. This view violated the principle to which Azad along with some Congressmen had adhered to all their lives. He argued that Congress was a national and not a communal party, therefore it had every right to nominate Muslims or for that matter Christians, Parsees or Sikhs along with Hindus:

> I asked the Conference what right Mr Jinnah or the Muslim League had to dictate who the Congress should nominate. If the Congress put forth the names of Muslims, Parsees, Sikhs or Christians this would reduce the number of Hindu representatives, but how did it concern the Muslim League?

Jinnah had his own reasons for refusing to concede to Azad's view which are outside the scope of this discussion. But Azad had advanced this view because he believed that if Congress made any move which had the slightest whiff of communalism, it would devastate its guiding principle. He was willing to agree that provided the League conceded the principle that Congress would nominate Muslims if it wished, he would not insist on the practice. He was prepared to stake his position in Congress and make his colleagues agree not to actually nominate Muslims so long as the League conceded that the Congress had the right to chose whomsoever.

The newly elected Labour party, headed by Attlee, called the General Elections in 1945. Congress won over 91.3% of the general vote and Muslim League won nearly 75% of the Muslim vote. Congress was victorious in all the provinces except Bengal, Punjab and Sindh. In Bengal, the League was the largest single party. In Punjab, the Unionists and the League were equally balanced. In Sindh, the Muslim League won a large number of seats but could not secure a clear majority.[8] In terms of the net gain, the League percentage jumped from 4.4% Muslim vote in 1937 to 75% Muslim vote in 1945. This outcome reinforced Jinnah's confidence that only he could represent the Muslims.

Azad's role in the formation of the Ministries as described by him in *India Wins Freedom* is, once again, uncharacteristic. The wheeling-dealing role which he assumed, according to his own account in *India Wins Freedom*, bears no resemblance to the role that a boy of fifteen years had outlined for himself in 1903. He had vowed to live upto the name that he had given to his first journal, *Lisan-us-Sidq*, meaning 'The Voice of Truth'. If one were to believe Kabir's word as Azad's, it follows that Azad manipulated Punjab politics in a manner that the Unionist party without a clear majority was able to form the government with Congress support. He records Nehru's anguish at this (machiavellian) move as well as his own disappointment that Nehru was not supportive of what can only be described as highly unscrupulous politics:

> Jawaharlal took the line that the policy I had adopted in Punjab was not correct. He even said I had brought down the prestige of the Congress... Through my endeavours, the Muslim League had been isolated and Congress, though it was a minority, had become a decisive factor in Punjab affairs.

A comparison of this with an incident recorded by Aruna Asaf Ali reflects the absurdity of giving credibility to Kabir's misinterpretation of what were Azad's unshakable beliefs. No matter how little Kabir understood Azad's spoken Urdu, he could not have entirely missed the point of his lifelong creed of respecting the majority view. When the Communists won the Assembly elections in Kerala, Aruna Asaf Ali recalls that Azad was completely unruffled:

> He said without a moment's hesitation, '*Agar ek vote sey bhi un ki aksariyat ho to hukumat un hi ki honi chahiye*' ('Even if they have a one vote majority the government should be theirs'.)[9]

This is the exact opposite of what Kabir would have us believe. What he ascribes to Azad seems incredible to anyone who has read his original writings in Urdu. If taken seriously, they would negate everything Azad ever stood for. Nehru, Kabir writes, took exception to the fact that Congress wanted to participate in the government without being the majority party. He said that this move would force it to make compromises and deviate from its principles. Once again, for scholars of Azad there is no doubt that Azad would himself have strongly held and propagated the view that has been attributed to Nehru. What made Kabir write this in Azad's name and, above all, why Azad allowed it to be published, will ever remain a mystery.

The new labour government, Azad writes, 'was studying the Indian situation in the right spirit'. That Indian freedom was imminent, was attested by a Parliamentary delegation which visited the country in 1945–6. On 17 February 1946, a Cabinet Mission for India was announced, consisting of three members. Secretary of State for India, Lord Pethick-Lawrence, President of Board of Trade, Sir Stafford Cripps and First Lord of the Admiralty, A.V. Alexander. The objective before the Mission was to 'provide a full self government for India'.[10]

The communal problem remained at the core of the Indian question. Azad writes that there was only one way to eliminate from the mind of the Muslims the fear of domination by a Hindu majority; to frame a constitution which would ensure autonomy to the provinces in as many areas as possible. He felt that the claims of provincial autonomy had to be reconciled with national unity. A formula had to be devised whereby a minimum number of subjects would be declared as the essential responsibility of the central government, a larger number the provincial responsibility, and a third optional list would be of subjects which could be dealt with by the centre if the provinces so wished. This arrangement, he felt, suited a country like India, given the constitutional framework that was starting to evolve and the conditions which were likely to govern her administration.

He met the Cabinet Mission on 6 April 1946 and apprised them of his formula for resolving the communal problem. Having first secured their approval, he then apprised the members of the Congress Working Committee. Why Azad reversed the process of consultation is difficult to explain. One reason may have been his conviction that this was the only way of reconciling the Muslims to the Congress and if he could convince the British he could then offer it as a package to his colleagues with lesser likelihood of their turning it down. Patel raised the question that restricting the centre to three subjects (Defence, Foreign Affairs, Communications) was not advisable. Currency and finance 'from the nature of the case' also belonged to the centre. But Gandhi's favourable response to Azad's proposal evoked a positive reaction from the members.

On 15 April 1946, Azad issued a statement which is the landmark document on the Muslim question. He stated that he wanted to place the case before the Muslims because since passing the Lahore Resolution (later called Pakistan Resolution) in 1939, the League had moved further along the path of separatism. He repeated his formula for what he always maintained was the best interest of the Muslims. Having examined the Pakistan scheme from the point of view of India as a whole as well as for the Muslims of India, he wrote, that he considered it harmful for both because it created more problems than it solved. First, the idea of *Paki*stan, he contended, was against the spirit of Islam, since it implied that some areas are *pak* (pure), some are not. Islam recognizes no such division. The Prophet has said, 'God has made the whole world a mosque for me'.

In terms of numbers, he said, there are enough Muslims to count as a substantive factor and declared that as a Muslim he could not for a moment give up his right to treat the whole of India as his domain or his share in shaping its political and economic life, 'To me it seems a sure sign of cowardice to give up what is my patrimony and content myself with a mere fragment of it'. He then refuted the logic of Jinnah's two-nation theory by saying that if Hindus and Muslims are 'two nations' then the two confront one another in every hamlet, village and town, and consequently should be separated in each one of the units.

He advances, once again, his argument about the harm to Muslim interest caused by the separatists. If India is divided into two states, he writes, one Hindu and one Muslim, in the Hindu part, Muslims will be scattered in small minorities all over the entire region. They will wake up one day to discover that they have become aliens and foreigners and 'left to the mercies of an unadulterated Hindu Raj'. Their position in Pakistan too, he writes, will be vulnerable and weak and whatever little majority they enjoy will be offset by the economic, educational and political lead enjoyed by the non-Muslims of those areas. Despite all this, however, even if Pakistan were to become overwhelmingly Muslim, it would still not solve the problem of the Muslims of India.

> Two states confronting one another offer no solution of the problem of one another's minorities, but only lead to retribution and reprisals by introducing a system of mutual hostages. The scheme of Pakistan, therefore, solves no problem for the Muslims.

The question then arises, he says, is that why despite this potential harm, are so many Muslims supporting separation? For this hardening attitude of the Muslims, Azad puts the blame partly on the paranoia of the communal Hindus. They read into the formation of the League, a Pan Islamic conspiracy which they opposed out of fear. This became an incentive to the followers of the League who acted upon the simple logic that if Hindus were opposed to something, it must be of benefit to the Muslims. An emotional frenzy was thus created, which made persons immune to reason. Azad then outlines his formula (which he refers to as the Congress formula), stated above, that the only viable solution to India's problem is to allow devolution of power to the provinces which will enable the country to flourish as a whole.

The Cabinet Mission, Azad writes, was favourably disposed towards his solution. Meanwhile the League's demand for a separate homeland for Muslims was also crystallizing. However, the Mission was not prepared to concede this demand. On 16 May 1946, Attlee announced the Cabinet Mission Scheme in the House of Commons which, Azad writes, was basically the same as his 15 April statement. The only addition made was to divide the country into three zones, A, B, and C, the purpose being to give greater assurance to the Muslim minority and to assuage the legitimate fears of the League.

The League was completely opposed to the scheme at the beginning. But it had to ultimately concede the point that there was no fairer solution of the minority problem. Jinnah recommended that the League Council should accept the plan and the Council voted unanimously in its favour. Azad also got the Working Committee to give its unanimous approval. The matter seemed to have been resolved, Azad writes, with negotiation and agreement and not by violence. 'We rejoiced but we did not then know that our joy was premature, and bitter disappointment awaited us.'

The by now famous statement of Nehru which altered the 'course of history'[11] and undid all that Azad had managed to accomplish by way of negotiation, is given a detailed analysis in *India Wins Freedom*.

Having reached the end of his term, Azad did not seek re-election as Congress President. Nehru's first task as the new President was to call a press conference in Bombay on 10 July 1946. At the meeting, responding to questions of journalists, he said that Congress had agreed only to participation in the Constituent Assembly and considered itself free to change or to modify the Cabinet Mission Plan:

> Congress would enter the Constituent Assembly completely unfettered by agreements and free to meet all situations as they arise.[12]

Jinnah viewed Nehru's statement as Congress' rejection of the Cabinet Mission plan. He felt that the Congress President's declaration that the scheme could be changed through a majority vote in the Constituent Assembly, would mean in effect that the minorites would be placed at the mercy of the majority. In its meeting on 27 July 1946, the League Council declared that the demand for Pakistan was the only course left open for the Muslim League.

This development was a stunning blow to Azad. In a last ditch effort, he persuaded the All India Congress Committee to pass a resolution reaffirming its acceptance of the Cabinet Mission Plan in its entirety. But Jinnah, Azad writes, had lost faith in the integrity of the Congress:

> He argued that if the Congress could change so many times while the British were still in the country and power had not come into its hand, what assurance could the minorities have that once the British left, Congress would not go back to the position taken up in Jawaharlal's statement?[13]

16 August 1946, was declared by Jinnah as Direct Action day, which in Azad's words 'was a black day in the history of India'. Calcutta, Azad writes, was plunged in an orgy of bloodshed, murder and terror. The same pattern was repeated throughout India. In the shadow of these disturbances, the parliamentary sub-committee of Congress met to discuss a proposal to be submitted to the Viceroy for the formation of the interim government. This was done in response to the Viceroy's invitation of 12 August to the Congress President Jawaharlal Nehru to form the interim government at the centre.

The interim government was formed in September 1946. After several rounds of negotiations with Wavell and reassurances by Congress, the League joined the Constituent Assembly on 15 October. Azad declined joining the interim government because he felt that he could render greater service by remaining outside. He also declined the offer to become President of the Constituent Assembly. Azad's statement that the interim government was born in an atmosphere of distrust and suspicion between the Congress and the League, assumes great importance in the light of the subsequent events.

Too much calculation and agonizing went on inside the Congress regarding every decision, whether a major one such as what portfolios should be offered to the Muslim League, or a minor one such as what protocol should be followed in issuing invitations for the pre-cabinet informal meetings. Then there were the permanent impasses. Azad cites the case of Liaqat Ali, the Finance member, 'whose persistent interference made it difficult for any Congress member to function effectively'. On the interpretation of the clauses about groups 'A' 'B' and 'C' in the Cabinet Mission Plan, the Congress and League differences persisted. Prime Minister Attlee invited Nehru, Jinnah and Wavell to hold discussions in London in December 1946, about the grouping issue. The British Cabinet supported the League's interpretation of the grouping. But that too, Azad writes, 'did not heal the breach between the Congress and League.'

On 15 January 1947, Azad joined the interim government as the Education Member. A month later on 20 February 1947, 'His Majesty's government announced its intention of transferring the power of British India into Indian hands by June 1948'.[14] Wavell disagreed with setting a deadline for the transfer of power unless the two parties had reached an understanding. But not being successful in convincing Attlee, he offered his resignation. Meanwhile, Liaqat Ali presented a budget which sent shock waves through Congress circles. Azad writes that Liaqat Ali 'proposed taxation measures which would have impoverished all rich men and done permanent damage to commerce and industry'. Ostensibly this was in keeping with the declared policy of the Congress that inequalities must be removed and capitalist society must be replaced by one with a socialist bias. But some Congressmen, writes Azad, opposed it because they were secretly in sympathy with the industry. They called it a politically motivated budget which aimed at harrassing the business community since the majority of them were Hindus. The budget proposals, they declared, were communally motivated. Azad felt that since the budget was consistent with the declared Congress objectives, its proposals should have been examined on merit and supported.

Mountbatten was sworn in as Viceroy of India on 22 March 1947. He declared partition *fait accompli* and impressed on the Congress and Muslim League the inevitability of partition. The first person who came out in support was Patel; Azad calls him founder of the Indian partition. In describing Mounbatten's method of influencing Congressmen, Azad projects him as a master gamester watching his prey and striking at the right moment. He won Nehru through two 'baits', writes Kabir in the voice of Azad, Lady Mountbatten and Krishna Menon, both of whom enjoyed his complete confidence.

Despite Mountbatten's determination to affect partition, Azad used all the arguments he could muster to convince his colleagues that partition would not solve the communal problem, it could only make it a permanent feature of Indian polity. Creating two states based on communal hatred would create a self-fulfilling prophecy. It was Jinnah who had raised the slogan of two nations, and to allow the country to be partitioned would be to accept Jinnah's logic. But his appeal was unheeded by most Congressmen. Some were convinced that Hindus and Muslims were two separate nations, others regretfully admitted that there was no other alternative. Jinnah, Kabir ghostwrites, till perhaps the very end, used Pakistan as a bargaining counter but now 'the real flag bearer (of Pakistan) was Patel'.

Gandhi remained the only one opposed to partition. But despite having said that Congress would have to accept it over his dead body, he ultimately capitulated. Although not before he had made his last effort to maintain the integrity of India and suggested that Jinnah should be invited to form the government and choose the members of cabinet. Such a move would have averted the partition, but Nehru and Patel were vehemently opposed. Azad's analysis of the partition decision in *India Wins Freedom* tries to take a multi-linear view of the events. Congress, he says, was always wary of a weak centre but had agreed to it only to meet the objection of the League. The suggestion of Mounbatten that 'it would be better to give up a few small pieces in the north-west and north-east and then build up a strong and consolidated India' fell on responsive minds. 'Lord Mountbatten', Kabir writes, 'did not feel so strongly about the Cabinet Mission Plan since it was not the child of his brain. He wanted to be remembered in history as the man who solved the Indian problem'.

Azad made his last attempt to avert the partition by suggesting to Mountbatten in May 1947, at the Viceregal Lodge in Simla, that the transfer of power may be delayed for a year or two. He had made this suggestion earlier to Gandhi but the latter had shown no enthusiasm for it. Azad argued that if a decision were taken immediately, partition would become inevitable, whereas a better suggestion may emerge in a year or two. When he drew Mountbatten's attention to the riots in Calcutta, Noakhali, Bihar, Bombay and Punjab and talked of 'rivers of blood' if the country were divided in such a communally charged atmosphere, Mounbatten gave him 'complete assurance'. In retrospect Azad felt that Mountbatten had already made up his mind to persuade the British Cabinet to accept his plan of partition. His words of reassurance were not quite genuine.

The details of the Mountbatten plan were published in a White Paper released on 3 June 1947. The date designated for the transfer of power into Indian hands was 30 June 1948 and the price for freedom was partitioning India into two separate states. Azad describes the feelings of the Khudai Khidmatgars and their leaders, the Khan brothers, and says that this was a barefaced betrayal by Congress. He records the appeal of Khan Abdul Ghaffar Khan to the Working Committee at which he spoke the famous words that the Frontier would regard it as ultimate treachery if the Congress now threw the Khudai Khidmatgars to the wolves! Nothing, however, moved the leaders from their separatist stand.

The partition resolution was finally presented to the All India Congress Committee at its meeting held in Delhi on 14 June 1947. It was moved by Govind Vallabh Pant. Azad spoke against the motion and said that partition was a tragedy, that it must be accepted only if we demand freedom here and now, that it is an unfortunate indication of our political failure.

> We should accept our defeat but we should, at the sametime, try to ensure that our culture was (sic) not divided. If we put a stick in water it may appear that the water has been divided but the water remains the same and the moment the stick is removed, even the appearance of division disappears.[15]

At the end of the first day's debate there was a very strong feeling against the Working Committee's resolution. It was only after Gandhiji's intervention that the matter was put to vote. Still twenty-nine voted for and fifteen against the motion. The atmosphere was rife with insidious communal propaganda. It was implied that partition was being accepted on the basis that in India and Pakistan there would be hostages who would be responsible for the security of the minority community in the other state.

Despite remarking on Mountbatten's unseemly haste in carrying out his partition plan, Azad found in him an efficient and reasonable administrator. Once Mountbatten's partition plan was accepted, Azad writes that he went about its implementation in a business-like way. He appointed a Boundary Commission, with Radcliffe as the Chairman, and sent him to do a field survey in Punjab, despite the scorching heat of June. But even he could not prevent the division of the army or of the services on a communal basis. Azad found himself helpless in stopping the natural succession of events which ultimately communalized the army and the civil service. Initially, it appeared that he had an ally in

Mountbatten, but nothing which he did could have reduced the impact of the inevitable polarization which followed.

On 14 August 1947 Mounbatten went to Karachi to inaugurate the Dominion of Pakistan. At midnight the (Indian Dominion was born. For Azad it was the 'end of a dream'.[16] He had finally lost his fight. Still he found himself unable to leave the battleground. Forty million Muslims were left behind, hiding their fear and despair in what had essentially become Hindu India.

The last pages of *India Wins Freedom*, reflect Azad's apprehension which had been the unwritten warning in all his speeches and writings of this period. Finally reduced to a comment by Humayun Kabir, it says that the acceptance of partition was 'only in a resolution of the Working Committee of the Congress and on the register of the Muslim League. The people of India had not accepted partition'.[17] It says that the Hindus and Sikhs 'were to a man opposed to partition' plus there was a large section of the Muslim community which did not support it either. Even the Congress leaders had accepted it out of anger, resentment or a sense of despair. Driven to making a decision under the stress of passion, they were unable to foresee the implication of their action. That a national organization like Congress had taken a communal decision was unbounded tragedy.

The fact that the left-over Muslims declared that they had been deceived by the Muslim League, was due to their inability to comprehend, when they had reached the peak of their enthusiastic support, the implication of the creation of Pakistan:

> It is strange but the fact is that these Muslim Leaguers had been foolishly persuaded that once Pakistan was formed, Muslims whether they came from a majority or minority province would be regarded as a separate nation and would enjoy the right of determining their own future.[18]

Azad's worst fears had now become reality. The Muslim majority provinces had gone out of India, Punjab and Bengal had been divided, and the Quaid-i-Azam had gone to Karachi leaving the message that now that the country was divided, the Muslims who had remained behind should become loyal citizens of India. The truth of the matter was that the Leaguers who were left behind were literally on sufferance. Azad writes that it had now become clear to them that the only result of the partition was that their position as a minority had become much weaker than before. In addition to the vulnerability of their position, they were now the victims of the anger and resentment which had been created against them in the Hindu mind.

The last pages of *India Wins Freedom* are prophetic in their import. They challenge anyone to deny that the creation of Pakistan has solved the communal problem. 'The basis of the partition was enmity between the Hindus and Muslims. The creation of Pakistan gave it a permanent constitutional form'.[19] The fact that the subcontinent is divided into two states which look at each other with hatred and fear, Azad says, is the most regrettable outcome of this event. He then predicts the further fragmentation of Pakistan given the geographic anamoly of East Pakistan. Lastly, in a statement which finally upturns the youthful zest he once had for Pan Islamism, he declares that religion has never been a binding factor in the formation of nations:

It is one of the greatest frauds on the people to suggest that religious affinity can unite areas which are geographically, economically, linguistically and culturally different. It is true that Islam sought to establish a society which transcends racial, linguistic, economic and political frontiers. History has, however, proved that after the first few decades or at most after the first century, Islam was not able to unite all the Muslim countries on the basis of Islam alone.[20]

The very last comment in the book is about the internal incompatibility between the three provinces of West Pakistan: Punjab, Sindh and Frontier, which are 'working for separate aims and interests'. The stand of those who believed that partition was inevitable or of those who held that it was wrong and could have been avoided, Azad concludes, will be vindicated by the historical events of the future.

In his Introduction to the American edition of *India Wins Freedom*, Louis Fischer writes, 'The fight for freedom under moral leadership breeds giants, the task of governing through compromise cuts them to normal size'. Barring the cliché, the epithet appropriately describes the trajectory of Indian leadership. The question of partition, as discussed above, was opposed by the national leaders on political, moral and economic grounds. In the end, with a few exceptions, all of them including Gandhi and Nehru accepted the Mountbatten plan. Among the few who stuck to the original undertaking of the Indian National Congress to the people of India were Abul Kalam Azad, Khan Abdul Ghaffar Khan, Saifuddin Kitchlew and a few others.

At the end of the day, when the matter was being put to vote, Azad, almost alone, was guarding his stand. By nature he had always been a loner. He had recounted in his writings how he had to carve his path away from the beaten track and slake his thirst away from the public fountain. It was a lonely path he had chosen when as a fifteen year old he had placed his foot on the road to Independence. The century was then three years old, and none of the men who had sat around the table with him earlier in the day and voted 'Yes' to partition, were around. The path he had chosen was his *Sirat al Mustaqeem* (Straight Path). Forty-three years later, in 1946, he was still holding fast to his sacred ground while the winds of public opinion, especially the biting ones of his own *quom* lashed against him.

notes

1 Azad wrote so much about himself in *Ghubar-i-Khatir*, without any persistent reminders. This provides an important insight into his reluctance. This has been discussed in the chapter on *Ghubar-i-Khatir*.

2 Khwaja Ghulamus Saiyidain and Syed Ashfaq Husain were Joint and Additional Secretaries in the Ministry of Education during Azad's term as Minister.

3 Shorish Kashmiri, editor *Chattan*, records that Azad's health was failing. See Hameed, ed. *India's Maulana*. 'The Last Journey'.

4 The most authoritative source is *Ghubar-i-Khatir*. Others include *Kahani, Zikr-e-Azad*, and an article based on an interview of Azad's sister Fatima Begum by Khwaja Ahmed Faruqui.

5 This last portion of *Tazkirah* was translated by Prof. Mohd. Mujeeb, in *Maulana Abul Kalam Azad: A Centenary Volume* ed. Humayun Kabir.

6 See Chapter 11 for textual quotations from *Tazkirah* and *Ghubar-i-Khatir* on this subject.

7 Penderel Moon (ed.), *Wavell, The Viceroy's Journal*, quoted by V.N. Datta, p. 171.

8 Ayesha Jalal, *The Sole Spokesman* quoted by V.N. Datta.

9 Aruna Asaf Ali, 'Reminiscences' in *India's Maulana* Volume I, p. 109.

10 Words of Pethick-Lawrence quoted by Datta.

11 *India Wins Freedom*, p. 164.

12 Ibid.

13 Ibid., p. 167.

14 British statement of 3 June 1947. See *India Wins Freedom*, Appendix 5.

15 Ibid., pp. 214–15.

16 Title of Chapter 15 of *India Wins Freedom*.

17 Ibid., pp. 224–5.

18 *India Wins Freedom*, p. 227.

19 Ibid., p. 247.

20 Ibid., p. 248.

epilogue

ONE OF THE LAST POEMS WRITTEN by Dr Mohammad Iqbal, the renowned poet laureate who both India and Pakistan think of as their very own, was in the form of a *mathanavi* shortly before his death in 1938. It was entitled *Pas che bayad kard* (What shall we do now). Its first line was *Pas che bayad kard ai aqwaam-e-sharq*! (What shall we do now O people of the East!) This line sets the tone for the epilogue about the man Abul Kalam Azad.

Azad's struggle for the fulfilment of his two dreams which had begun forty-four years ago in 1903, had run its course by 1947. His first dream was to attain Independence, referred to in *Al Hilal* and *Al Balagh* as his *nasbul ain* (goal). It had been fulfilled but at a price which he had always refused to negotiate; freedom for a 'truncated and moth-eaten India', a phrase used by Jinnah for the Pakistan that he had won, which was equally applicable to India. The outcome was diametrically opposed to his declaration in 1923 that he would refuse to surrender the unity of India for the attainment of Swaraj even if an angel were to descend from heaven with the offer.

His second dream about leading his *quom* on the path to glory, the prime factor which motivated him to enter politics, had turned into a nightmare. Not only was the *quom* in disarray but its very existence, as far as the Muslims of Delhi, Uttar Pradesh and Punjab were concerned, was in jeopardy. The political compromise made in this regard by his Congress colleagues was tantamount to betrayal. Fresh on his mind was a similar betrayal of the Khudai Khidmatgars which had made their leader Khan Abdul Ghaffar Khan lash out that he and his people had been thrown to the wolves.[1]

Ansar Harvani, a veteran politician, who as a young man in 1945 was detained with Azad at the Bankura prison said, 'Following the partition Azad was a broken man, as if he had lost interest'.[2] Harvani's words spoken with the hindsight of fifty years are hardly surprising. Azad had witnessed the gruesome tragedy of the exchange of human beings across the borders of India and Pakistan. He may have heard of the anguished remark of Gandhiji, spoken in the context of Muslims being repatriated to Pakistan, which Qazi Jalil Abbassi still remembers:

Maulana Azad ko kis se badlen?
(With whom shall we exchange Maulana Azad?)[3]

Never a man to speak about his feelings especially at this juncture of his life when there was no '*sidiq-i-mukarram*' with whom he could share his *ghubar-i-khatir*[4] the extent of his personal anguish would have remained a matter of conjecture if not for what happened on 24 October 1947. On that Friday afternoon he addressed a large crowd of Muslims at Jama Masjid, the principal mosque of Delhi. There is no record that Azad or any other prominent leader of the Indian National Congress had been invited in a decade or so to deliver an address in this great historic mosque. It was a very special event as also were the circumstances in which the invitation had been extended to Azad.

The Muslims of Delhi had been huddled up in their homes with fear of the Hindu backlash. Thousands of them had been killed or forced to migrate to Pakistan in the wake of the massacres which had occurred on both sides of the new border. The leaders of the Muslim League had fled from India to their newly born country. In that desolate autumn of 1947, the Indian Muslims felt that they had been deserted and abandoned. From the gloom and despair of their streets and *mohallas*, they came out that day to the Jama Masjid to hear what the venerable leader of Congress, the great Maulana, who was also a member of the new Government of India as the Minister of Education, had to say about the situation in which they found themselves. They were also hoping to hear about the arrangements that the government had made to safeguard their lives and properties.

The *khutba*, (the sermon that constitutes an integral part of the Friday congregation of Muslims) that Azad gave that afternoon was extraordinary in several ways. First, it was a short *khutba*, perhaps the shortest he ever delivered in his life. Second, every important principle for which he had stood in the forty-four years, which was the sum total so far of his political life was replayed, with marked poignancy, for the last time. The analogy of pouring a *darya* (river) into a *kooza* (goblet) can be applied here. This was also the closest Azad ever came to achieving the high pathos of Greek tragedy at the end of which there was catharsis for the viewers. The high diction, elevated prose, masterly rhetoric, and the tonal quality of the *khitabat* of his *Al Hilal* days were all present. There was only one important departure. This was the only address of his life in which he allowed himself to ventilate his personal feelings. For once in his life he seemed to be exposing his innermost emotions, obliterating the distance, formality and aloofness he had always maintained between himself and his audience.

That afternoon Azad was not before the kind of audience which he usually addressed. The venue, however, was of great political significance, Jama Masjid being the most important mosque of India. The audience was his own battered *quom*. As he took his seat on the *mimber* (pulpit) it became evident that he was emotionally charged. He began his *khutba* by addressing his audience as *Azizo* (All you present that I hold dear). The first thing he said was that he was not in their midst just to avail himself of the honour of delivering a *khutba* at the historic mosque of Emperor Shahjehan. This was not the first time that such an honour had been bestowed upon him.

In the decades gone by, he says, he had addressed them in this very mosque. But what had brought him here today he asked? He was here for the very reason which has caused the alteration in the expressions on their faces. Their expressions today were very different from what their faces wore in the old days. 'Old days' he said refers to the period of Khilafat agitation. At that time he had seen their faces reflecting contentment and not anguish, and their hearts were filled with confidence not insecurity.

> Today seeing the anguish on your faces and a sense of desolation in your hearts, I cannot but recall the forgotten but painful chronicles of the past.[5]

In a minute after this start, whether it was the pathetic plight of his people, or the atmosphere of this great mosque, or the welling up of his own feelings, Azad plunged into the gathering his verbal dagger:

> Do you remember, when I called out to you, you cut off my tongue. I picked up my pen, you severed my hand. I wanted you to walk at my side but you sliced off my feet. I tried to turn my side, you broke my back. So much so that when the bitter politics of hatred of the last seven years [the period between the passing of the Pakistan Resolution by the Muslim League and the partition] which has left you bereft now, was at its peak, I tried to take you off the high road to danger. But you not only ignored me, you revived the well-established traditions of *ghaflat* and *inkar* (neglect and refusal to listen to saints and prophets). The result has become manifest. You are surrounded by those very dangers for the avoidance of which you had forsaken the *Sirat-al-Mustaqeem* (Straight Path).

The reprobatory rhetoric proved too much even for the deliverer of the *Khutba*. For a moment he broke down:

Such puchho to mein ek jumood hoon, ya ek dur uftaada sada jis ne watan mein reh kar bhi gharibul watani ki zindagi guzari hai.

This sentence is untranslatable, not only in its pathos but in its general implications. The key words are *jumood, dur uftadta sada* and *gharibul watani. Jumood* means a state of being which is inert or motionlessness personified. *Dur uftada sada* means an inaudible voice from some distant space that reaches no one. *Gharibul watani* is the status of an individual who nobody in the *watan* (native land) is prepared to help or own. Translated into English it would approximate the meaning that he felt that as an individual he was inert therefore incapable, a voice which was inaudible, and as a person he lived in his homeland, but lived the life of one who did not belong to the land.

Immediately recovering from this betrayal of his feeling, he elaborates, without naming names, that his complaint is not against the Hindus or the Congress. Using the analogy of a bird, his next sentence is:

I do not mean to say that my feathers and wings had been clipped at the base which I had chosen for myself from the very first day. And I do not say that there was no place left for me to make a nest for myself. What I want to say is that *mere daaman ko tumhari dast daraazion sey gila hat.*

The 'base' refers to the Congress, the 'place' to unified India. But the last sentence, again, is untranslatable. In it he gives expression to the hurt inflicted upon him by Muslims by using the subtle and sophisticated analogy of the 'garment' (*daman*) and the 'insinuating hands' (*dast daraazion*). The garment is Azad himself and the insinuating hands are the attacks on his person and politics by his *quom* and the Muslims' ultimate refusal to accept his leadership. He says, 'My feelings are wounded and my heart is in a state of shock'.

That Azad saw himself in the prophet-like role upbraiding his own *quom* because it has caused its own doom becomes evident in the images he invokes throughout the *khutba*. He refers to *mushrikeen-e-Makka* (residents of Mecca who indulged in *shirk*, i.e., polytheism). They too had similarly indulged in all the stages of *ghaflat* and *inkar* (denial and transgression). Like all earlier prophets, he too felt that he had been badgered by the callousness of an ungrateful *quom*. He reminds them of how blatantly they had neglected his warnings. He had warned them that for a worthy life their acceptance of the two-nation theory was like contracting a fatal disease. The pillars on which they had decided to lean were fast crumbling. But they had not stopped to think that the course of history could not be reversed according to individual whims.

There was a time, he reminds them that he had said that a political revolution had been written in the destiny of India. Her chains of slavery, he had said, were going to be smashed by the twentieth century's winds of freedom and if the Muslims hesitated to keep pace with the times, the future historian will write that seventy million members of a certain *quom* took a stand which is typical of a people who are bent upon being wiped off the slate of history. Referring to the teachings of the Prophet of Islam, he reminds the audience that thirteen hundred years ago, an Arab *ummi* (one not versed in reading or writing) had said:

> For those who have faith in Allah, and remain firm there is neither any fear nor any despair.

Urging the Muslims to overcome their slavish mentality, he says that there are still vacant pages in the chronicles of their nation in which they can feature with dignity, provided they can break out of their old ways of thinking. They should start by questioning this 'life of escape' which they have adopted in the name of Hijrat (migration to Pakistan). They must ask themselves where they are headed for and for what reason?

He exhorts them to become worthy of their glorious past and to make a promise to themselves that they will not run away from its mementoes. He then repeats the mantra that he had evolved and offers it as a pledge to the *quom:*

> Let us make a pledge that this land is ours. We belong to it and the basic decisions about its destiny will remain incomplete without our voice.

Having given them the first word of hope in this time of despair, he then uses the metaphors of light and darkness which are a characteristic and distinguishing feature of his prose, whether written or spoken:

> Stars have plummeted but the sun is still shining; ask to borrow its rays and unroll them in the dark alleys which desperately need to be brightened.

In his stern voice he tells the *quom* to eschew the life of *kasa lesi* (begging and sycophancy) which has become their norm before foreign rulers. The shame he had felt at seeing his *quom* prostrate itself before the *haakim* (ruler) was something he never wished to feel again. He warns them never to fawn before their new rulers, the Hindus. First, he reaffirms his original premise that Muslims, provided they are true believers, cannot allow themselves to be overcome with cowardice or *ishte'aal* (provocation). The fact that their false *rahbars* (leaders) have withdrawn support should not be a cause for desperation. This climate of despair will also pass off so long as their faith in Allah remains unshaken.

This outburst of his hurt and anger is quite uncharacteristic. But having ventilated his feelings, he changes the tenor of his *khutba*, saying that he does not want to rake their wounds but posit one question:

> What now?

Like the one lakh and twenty-four thousand prophets (as legend would have it), Azad too offers his prescription to the *quom*. Not surprisingly, it is exactly the same prescription that he had offered back in 1912, when he had begun to see himself in the contours of *amir-e-karvan* forty-four years ago. His words are a *baazgasht* (echo) of his *Al Hilal* days:

> Behold! The tall minarets of the *masjid* are accusing you. Where have you lost the pages of your history? It was only yesterday that with the waters of the Jumna, your caravans, arriving in triumph, had performed *wuzu* (ablution for saying *namaz*). The soil of Delhi has been nurtured with your blood and today you are afraid of even living here.

The bold adventurousness of their forefathers which was a hallmark of the Muslims has become a thing of the past:

> Today you fear the earth's tremors, once you were virtually the earthquake itself. Today you fear darkness, but don't you remember? Once your very existence was radiance. Clouds have rained some dirty waters and you have hitched up your trousers for fear of getting wet. Those were your forefathers who plunged headlong into the seas. They trampled the mountains, laughed at the bolts of lightning, turned away tornadoes and made the squall alter its course. It is a sure sign of the death of faith when those who played with the collars of emperors start clutching at their own throats. Of God's existence they become oblivious as if they never believed in him.

Having reminded them of their past, he then makes the final offer to his *quom*. What he tells them now is the same as what he had told them in 1912. It was said in the epigraph of the first issue of *Al Hilal*. One line from *Sura al Imran* which holds out the promise of hope for the Muslims provided they are *momins*.

Wa la tehnu wa la tehzinu wa antum ala alona in kuntum mominin.

So lose not heart, nor fall into despair; for you will gain mastery if you are true in faith. (3:139)

On this note the *khutba* ends.

And now we come to the final word. In the name of religion, Azad had tried to mobilize the Muslims to throw off the imperial yoke. From the beginning he had felt that the ulema had misled the *quom* by misinterpreting religion and thereby sinking the Muslims into a morass of blind *taqlid* (imitation) and false rituals. Therefore the only way out for him was to give his *quom* his own interpretation of the Koran which would ultimately become their sole guide in all matters. Thus *Tarjuman-ul-Quran* came to be written.

The *quom*, however, would not heed or hear Azad. Why? Was it blindness on its part or a stubborn refusal on Azad's part to accept a recurring historical pattern in the political behaviour of the Muslims? What Azad could not accept was the fact that throughout history, Muslims have never been able to launch a successful political revolution in the name of religion. Was he wrong in assuming that the Muslims had given him a rousing reception in the *Al Hilal* and *Al Balagh* days because of the new interpretation of religion which, prophet-like, he had offered them as the only way of elevating them from their abject state? Doubtless, they had given him a rousing reception but they had welcomed him as a political and not as a religious saviour. It was when they discovered that he was not prepared to budge from his stand which was firmly anchored in religion, that they rejected him like they had always rejected the imams and *auliyas* in the days of yore. The words he spoke to Malihabadi in 1921[6] prophesy this rejection, regardless of the fact that in his own way, he was to fight it all his life:

I was born in an enslaved country. This country, in addition to slavery, is encumbered by *qadamat parasti* (archaism), *taqlid* (imitation), and *jumood* (inertness). My path has not been straightforward. Unlike Napoleon I do not have a single compartment in my brain. At any one time I have had to open many compartments. But the result? There is no one to understand. I am *mazloom* (wronged). Probably history's single most *mazloom* human being. I should have been born centuries later. But it was the unfortunate sport of nature that I was dropped into the lap of these times. People use the expression 'forgetfulness of nature'. I am an *ibrat angez* (serving as a warning) example of nature's forgetfulness.

All prophets are born in advance of their times. They endure hardships and hostilities but remain immersed in their work. This, however, should not imply that they are unaffected by their environment. The Prophet of Islam is known to have endured a basket of filth thrown on his revered head each day he passed underneath the house of an old woman. We are not privy to his feelings but we can surmise the difficulty with which a man as fastidious and aesthetic as Azad endured the garland of shoes flung at him by students at the Aligarh station in 1947, to express their anger at his stand against demanding a separate homeland for the Muslims. This, as the seventeenth century English playwright Congreve said, is the way of the world.

Had Azad capitulated before the rising tide of separatism, his personal tragedy would have turned to triumph. Some call this stubbornness the 'fatal flaw' which culminated in the tragedy of Azad. The verdict of history, however, appears to be different.

notes

1 See *India Wins Freedom*, p. 226.

2 Related to the author in a personal interview, March 1992.

3 Narrated to the author by the veteran Congress leader in April 1992.

4 See Chapter 11, *Ghubar-i-Khatir*.

5 All references to this *Khutba* are from *Khutbat-e-Azad* edited by Malik Ram.

6 *Zikr-e-Azad*, pp. 117–18.

select bibliography

THE ITEMS LISTED IN THIS BIBLIOGRAPHY have direct relevance to the study undertaken for this volume. For a complete bibliography of Azad (until 1989) refer to *India's Maulana* Volume II edited by Syeda Saiyidain Hameed, published by the Indian Council for Cultural Relations and Vikas in 1990.

This bibliography has been arranged under the following headings:
1. Works by Maulana Abul Kalam Azad.
2. Works on Maulana Azad or relating to this study.
   a. In Urdu
   b. In English

works by maulana azad

With the commemoration of Maulana Abul Kalam Azad's centenary year in 1988, an important change occurred in the preparation of bibliographies on Azad. In the past, Azad's writings, most of which were contained in his journals *Al Hilal* and *Al Balagh*, had been available to readers, piecemeal, in various selections or in individual editions. The journals themselves were placed in the rare book sections of libraries and were consequently rendered inaccessible. The centenary year reproduced in a photocopy edition all the issues of the weekly *Al Hilal* from 1912 to 1914. Therefore what had been reflected in scores of entries in previous bibliographies (for example the bibliography in Ian Henderson Douglas, Abul Kalam Azad: An Intellectual and Religious Biography, Oxford, 1988) is contained in a single entry in this bibliography. Secondly, during the last decade, particularly at the end of the eighties, Malik Ram, a meticulous Azad scholar, produced carefully edited collections of Azad's addresses and correspondence which were commissioned by the Sahitya Akademi. The net effect of his work on the bibliographies of Azad was the same as that of the *Aksi* (photo) edition of *Al Hilal.* Thirdly, the centenary year became the occasion for collecting and producing Azad's works in various editions which often contained nothing either of textual or editorial value. Such redundant materials have been excluded from this bibliography.

Abul Kalam ki Kahani khud unki Zubani, compiled by Abdul Razzaq Malihabadi, Lahore, Chattan Publications, 1960.

Al Hilal (3 Volumes), Lucknow, Uttar Pradesh Urdu Academy, 1988.

Al Balagh, Calcutta, 1915–1916, Original file, Gosha-e-Azad, Indian Council for Cultural Relations Library, New Delhi.

Baikaat (Boycott), Meerut, Quomi Darul Asha'at, 1921.

Ghubar-i-Khatir, (Inscribed by the author), Maktaba-e-Ahrar, Azad Hind Publications, Lahore, No date.

Ghubar-i-Khatir, edited by Malik Ram, New Delhi, Sahitya Akademi, 1967.

India Wins Freedom, Madras, Orient Longman, 1988.

Intikhabaat-e-Khutbaat-e-Jamiatul Ulema-e-Hind, Lucknow, U.P. Urdu Academy, 1989.

Islam aur Nationalism, Lahore, Al Balagh Book Agency, 1929.

Intikhabaat-e-Madina Bijnor, Lucknow, U.P. Urdu Academy, 1988.

Jamiash al-Shavahid fi Dukhul-e-Ghairul Muslim fi'l Masajid (Collection of evidences of entry of non-Muslims in mosques), Delhi, Maktaba-e-Mahaul, 1960.

Karvan-e-Khayal, edited by Mohammad Abdul Shahid Khan Sherwani, Bijnor, Madina Press, 1946.

Khutbat-e-Azad, edited by Malik Ram, New Delhi, Sahitya Akademi, 1974.

Lisan-us-Sidq, compiled by Abdul Qavi Dasnavi, New Delhi, Maktaba Jamia, 1988.

Mazamin-e-Al Balagh, edited by Mahmudul Hasan Siddiqui, Delhi, Hindustan Publishing House, 1944.

Musalman Aurat, translation of Farid Wajdi's *Al Mar'at al Muslims*, Delhi, Firdaus Publications, 1985.

National Tehrik, Manuscript (unpublished) Indian Council for Cultural Relations Library, New Delhi.

Parliamentary Debates, Lok Sabha, 1954.

Paigham, Calcutta, 1921, Patna, Khuda Bakhsh Library, 1988.

'Preface' to *History of Philosophy: Eastern and Western*, edited by S. Radhakrishnan, London, Allen and Unwin, 1953.

Quol-e-Faisal, Calcutta, Al Balagh Press, 1922.

Sarmad Shaheed, Lahore, Malik Mohammad Din, no date.

'Sarmad Shaheed' in *The Rubaiyat of Sarmad*, edited and translated by Syeda Saiyidain Hameed, New Delhi, Indian Council for Cultural Relations, 1991.

Speeches by Maulana Azad: 1947–1955, New Delhi, Publications Division, 1956.

'Speeches at Mirzapur Square, 1 and 15 July 1921', unpublished manuscript. Gosha-e-Azad, Indian Council for Cultural Relations Library, New Delhi.

Tarjumanul Quran, (3 volumes), Maktaba-e-Saeed Nazimabad, Karachi, no date.

Tarjuman-ul-Quran, edited and translated by Syed Abdul Latif in two volumes, Bombay, Asia Publishing House, 1967.

Tazkirah, edited by Malik Ram, New Delhi, Sahitya Akademi, 1985.

works on maulana azad

english

Abduh, Ghulam Rasul, *Educational Ideas of Abul Kalam Azad*, New Delhi, Sterling Publishers, 1973.

Ali, Syed Amir, *Spirit of Islam*, London, Methuen, 1967.

Aziz, K.K., *The Pakistani Historian*, Lahore, Vanguard, 1993.

Malsiani, Arsh, *Abul Kalam Azad*, New Delhi, Publications Division, 1976.

Chopra, P.N. *Maulana Abul Kalam Azad: Unfulfilled Dreams*, New Delhi, Interprint, 1990.

Datta, V.N., *Maulana Azad*, New Delhi, Manohar, 1990.

Desai, Mahadev, *Maulana Abul Kalam Azad: A Biographical Memoir*, Agra, Shiv Lal Agarwal, 1946.

Douglas, Ian Henderson, *Abul Kalam Azad: An Intellectual and Religious Biography*, edited by Gail Minnault and Christian Troll, New Delhi, Oxford University Press, 1988. Records of the Foreign and Political Department 1914–22, India Office Library, Blackfriars Street, London.

Faruqui, I.H. Azad, *The Tarjuman-ul-Quran*, New Delhi, Vikas, 1982.

Gandhi, Rajmohan, *Eight Lives: A Study of the Hindu-Muslim Encounter*, New Delhi, Roli Books International, 1986.

Gopal, S., *Selected Works of Jawaharlal Nehru*, New Delhi, 1975.

Hameed, Syeda Saiyidain, *India's Maulana* (4 Volumes), Volume I *Tributes and Appraisals*, Volume II *Selected Works*. Volume III *Pramukh Kritiyan*, Volume IV *Intikhabaat-e-Mazamin*, New Delhi, Indian Council for Cultural Relations and Vikas, 1990.

Haq, Mushirul, *Muslim Politics in Modern India, 1857–1947*, Meerut, Meenakshi Prakashan, 1970.

Hasan, Mushirul, (ed.), *Islam and Indian Nationalism: Reflections on Azad*, New Delhi, Manohar, 1992.

Home, Political Department 1914–22, *Unpublished Records*, India Office Library, Blackfriars Street, London.

Husain, Syed Abid, *Destiny of Indian Muslims*. Asia Publishing House, 1965.

Kabir, Humayun, *Maulana Abul Kalam Azad: A Memorial Volume*, Bombay, Asia Publishing House, 1959.

Mujeeb, Mohammad, *The Indian Muslims*, London, Allen and Unwin, 1967.

Nizami, Khaliq Ahmed, *Maulana Azad*, Delhi, Idara-e-Adabiyat, 1990.

Kumar, Ravindra, *Selected Works of Maulana Abul Kalam Azad*, (1936–1958) 11 Volumes, Atlantic Publishers, 1991–1992.

Saiyidain, K.G., *Maulana Azad's Contribution to Education*, Baroda, Maharaja Sayajirao University, 1961.

Tirmizi, S.A.I., *Maulana Abul Kalam Azad: A Pragmatic Statesman 1923–1942*. New Delhi, Commonwealth Publishers, 1991.

Venkataraman, R., *Maulana Azad and the Unity of India*, Speech, Indian Council for Cultural Relations, 1992.

Select Bibliography

Urdu

Azmi, Abdul Lateef, *Mautarzeen-e-Abul Kalam Azad*, New Delhi, Maktaba Jamia, 1990.

Mughni, Abdul, *Maulana Abul Kalam Azad: Zehn-o-Kirdaar*, New Delhi, Anjuman Tarraqqi Urdu, 1991.

Mughni, Abdul, *Abul Kalam Azad ka Asloob-e-Nigaarish*, Aligarh, Education Book House, 1991.

Dasnavi, Abdul Qavi, *Talaash-e-Azad*, published by the author, 1990.

Dasnavi, Abdul Qavi. *Taadgaar-e-Azad*. Lucknow, U.P. Urdu Academy, 1988.

Malihabadi, Abdul Razza, *Zikr-e-Azad: Maulana Azad ki Rifaqat mein artis saal*, Calcutta, Daftar Azad Hind, 1960.

Shajehanpuri, Abu Salman, *Maulana Abul Kalam ki Sahafat*, Karachi, Idara-e-Afkar-o-Tehqiq, 1989.

Ansari, M. Ziauddin, *Maulana, Sir Syed aur Aligarh*, New Delhi, Anjuman Tarraqqi Urdu, 1992.

Ansari, Z., *Abul Kalam Azad ka Zehni Safar*, New Delhi, Maktaba Jamia, 1990.

Bedar, Abid Raza, *Maulana Abul Kalam Azad*, Rampur, Institute of Oriental Research, 1968.

Faruqui, Ziaul Hasan, *Maulana Abul Kalam Azad-Fikr-o-Nazar ki chand Jehtain*, New Delhi, Maktaba Jamia, 1994.

Hasnain, Syed Mohammad, *Khutut-e-Shibli ba Naam-e-Azad ba Qalam-e-Shibli*, Patna, Bihar Urdu Academy, 1988.

Hali, Maulana Altaf Husain, *Mussaddas-e-Hali* or *Madd-o-Jazr-e-Islam*, *Sadi* edition, Delhi, Hali Publishing House, 1935.

Hali, Maulana Altaf Husain, *Hayat-e-Javaid*, Lahore, Akademi Punjab, 1957.

Anjum, Khaliq, *Maulana, Abul Kalam Azad: Shakhsiyat aur Karname*, Delhi Urdu Academy, 1985.

Ram, Malik, *Kuchh Abul Kalam Azad ke baare mein*, New Delhi, Maktaba Jamia, 1989.

Noorani, A.G., *Indian Political Trials*, New Delhi, 1976.

Parti, Rajesh Kumar, (Compilation) *Aasaar-i-Azad*, New Delhi, National Archives, 1990.

Qutubullah, (Compilation) *Maulana Azad ka Nazariya-e-Sahafat*, Lucknow, U.P. Urdu Academy, 1988.

Khan, Rasheeduddin, (edited) *Maulana Abul Kalam Azad: Ek Hamageer Shakhsiyat*, New Delhi, Taraqqi Urdu Board, 1989.

Siddiqui, Atiq, (edited) *Aieena-e-Abul Kalam: Majmua-e-Maqalat*, New Delhi, Anjuman Taraqqi-e-Urdu, 1976.

Saiyidain, Khwaja Ghulamus, *Aandhi mein Chiragh*, New Delhi, Taraqqi Urdu Bureau, 1982.

Sherwani, Riazur Rahman Khan, *Mir-e-Karavan Maulana Abul Kalam Azad*, Karachi, Idara-e-Tehqiq-o-Afkar, 1988.

Naqvi, Shariful Hasan, (edited) *Aiwan-e-Urdu: Azad Number*, Delhi Urdu Academy, 1988.

Tirmizi, S.A.I., *Maulana Abul Kalam Azad aur Jadeed Hindustan*, Delhi Educational Publishing House.

Zaidi, Ali Jawwad, (Compilation) *Anwar-e-Abul Kalam*, Srinagar, Saqafati Sub-Committee, 1959.

index

about the author

SYEDA SAIYIDAIN HAMEED was born in Kashmir and currently resides in New Delhi, India. She holds a BA from Delhi
University, an MA from the University of Hawaii, and a PhD
from the University of Alberta. Since 1986, she has authored
more than 20 books and articles pertaining to women's, religious
and minority rights in South Asia. She currently serves on the
Planning Commission of the Indian government with responsibilities including health, women and children, and minority
rights. She is also the Chancellor of Maulana Azad National Urdu
University in Hyderabad—a university committed to providing higher, technical and vocational education to women in the
Urdu language.

Hameed has translated and edited books on gender and development, Sufism, Allama Iqbal, and Maulana Abul Kalam Azad.
In addition to these, she has selected, introduced and translated an anthology of Ismat Chughtai's short stories entitled
The Quilt and Other Stories and a selection of short stories by
women writers in Urdu called *Parwaaz*.